Blacks in Topeka, Kansas
1865–1915

Blacks in Topeka, Kansas 1865–1915

A Social History

Thomas C. Cox

Louisiana State University Press
Baton Rouge and London

For my family

Copyright © 1982 by Louisiana State University Press
All rights reserved
Manufactured in the United States of America

Designer: Patricia Douglas Crowder
Typeface: Linotron 202 Baskerville
Typesetter: Graphic Composition, Inc.
Printer: Thomson-Shore, Inc.
Binder: John Dekker & Sons

Library of Congress Cataloging in Publication Data

Cox, Thomas C.
   Blacks in Topeka, Kansas, 1865–1915.

   Bibliography: p.
   Includes index.
   1. Afro-Americans—Kansas—Topeka—History.
2. Topeka (Kan.)—History. I. Title.
F689.T6C69   978.1′6300496073   81–14310
ISBN 0–8071–0975–4   AACR2
ISBN 0–8071–2422–2 (pbk.)

Contents

	Preface	vii
Chapter 1	Background and Initial Settlement, 1854–1865	1
Chapter 2	Reconstruction, the Frontier, and Community Development, 1865–1880	21
Chapter 3	The Exodus	46
Chapter 4	Social Order and Social Structure, 1880–1896	82
Chapter 5	Protest Organization and Political Action, 1880–1896	111
Chapter 6	Social Order and Social Structure, 1896–1915	136
Chapter 7	Protest Organization and Political Action, 1896–1915	166
	Epilogue	197
	Appendix: Tables and Maps	199
	Bibliography	217
	Index	231

Preface

*I*n this study of blacks in Topeka, Kansas, the year 1865 signifies the first reference to Negroes residing in that city, according to the census. By 1915, demographic patterns had stabilized and social, economic, political, and institutional structures were firmly established. The collateral development of the local black press and of organized protest provided important media for communication at home and facilitated contacts with Negro communities throughout the country. Interracial relations in Topeka during this fifty-year period reflected events and issues endemic to that locale and were shaped by factors which defined the nature and the quality of race relations throughout the nation.

Selective comparisons are made between black Topeka and Negro communities in other cities. In cumulative effect, the institutional, social, economic, and political development of black Topeka provided its citizens with more effective means of exercising control over their destiny than was evident in other black urban communities. By focusing on Topeka, I hope to enhance our knowledge of Negro life in the urban environment. Understanding that experience, moreover, can help to explain the significance of many of the social, economic, and political forces current in the nation at large.

I will examine the internal and the external factors which determined growth and change over time in black Topeka. Central to my concerns are economic and political development, associational behavior, social stratification, and patterns of culture, as discrete phenomena and as elements in a configuration which defined the community. The census manuscript schedules, 1865 through 1895, provided an important data source for compiling descriptive statistics on the Negro population, thereby permitting some precision in the analysis of community growth and change. Local black newspapers illuminated individuals and revealed the quality and texture of their lives. The voices of black Topekans and their perceptions of themselves are important parts of the narrative. I make no pretense of writing history from the bottom up. Yet, where the sources and reliable impressionistic evidence permit, I have made a deliberate effort to explore the Negro community at all class levels.

Within two years of its inception, the Negro community established protest organizations through which black Topekans evaluated alternative strategies for combating race oppression. Organized protest became increasingly sophisticated and matured into a major community institution. The debate in those forums, notable for both substance and rigor, provides compelling evidence that Negroes subjected most aspects of their condition as a race and as citizens to thorough, reasoned scrutiny. That quest for full civil liberty and equality, moreover, was a practical matter affecting many areas of public life.

Discrimination created the precondition for organized protest, which, in turn, fostered intellectual growth and the development of doctrines of race progress. Although subject to varying definitions, race advancement emerged as the overriding metaphor for black values and aspirations in Topeka through the end of the nineteenth century. I will evaluate the social significance of philosophies of race progress and ascertain how those concepts reflected or influenced other historical processes. The extent to which Topeka Negroes responded to the ideas, the indulgences, and the inspirations which defined American intellectual development in general will also receive careful attention. In sum, my task is to examine black Topeka in intimate detail and in interdisciplinary perspective. Therein revealed will be that community's niche in the social history of black America and of the nation.

I owe a great debt of thanks to the University of Kansas history department. The late George Anderson, Dionysios Kounas, David Katzman, Phillip Paludan, William Tuttle, Donald McCoy, Clifford Griffin, and

John Clark were especially helpful. They and the rest of that faculty exemplify the best in the historian's craft and in the art of teaching. Likewise, the Princeton University history department provided examples of discriminating scholarship and a stimulating environment for intellectual growth. My work with James McPherson, Arthur Link, James Banner, and Theodore Rabb refined my research skills and added acuity to my judgment as a historian.

Three persons in particular contributed immeasurably to this undertaking. David Katzman first quickened my interest in social history and in the potentialities of an interdisciplinary approach. James McPherson gave inspiration, encouragement, and guidance at all stages in the development of this study. Nell Irvin Painter, through her own scholarship and solid criticism of my work, set a definitive example for quality and sensitivity in the analysis of black American history.

The Kansas State Historical Society provided the major sources for my study. It is a first-rate research institution. Their care and preservation of primary materials on Kansas and on the trans-Mississippi West reflect a fine sense of history. Jean Roberson, Ruth Gleason, and Vera Bridwell, in particular, gave meaningful direction through the sources as well as friendship and abundant good humor. Firestone Library at Princeton University provided many important primary materials on Kansas in regional and in national perspective. That Firestone covered my small portion of American history with such thoroughness bespeaks the quality of that institution. Additional thanks go to the Kansas History Teachers' Association, which encouraged my initial investigation of the state's history. The Faculty Research Fund at Middlebury College helped defray the cost of revising the manuscript. The staff at the Louisiana State University Press, especially my editor, Barbara Phillips, have been very helpful in the final preparation of the manuscript for publication.

There have been many friends and colleagues who contributed to my bringing this project to fruition. Michael and Judy Olinick, John M. McCardell, Nicholas Clifford, Nancy Weiss, and Mamie Williams merit special mention for reading parts of the text and for offering valuable criticisms. I cannot calculate the debt I owe my family, to whom this book is dedicated. The intellectual rigor of their lives as well as their love and faith continue to guide me. Lastly and most profoundly, I want to thank my wife Gerry. Her qualities of mind and constructive criticism were invaluable. I am all the more grateful for her love, friendship, and endurance.

Blacks in Topeka, Kansas
1865–1915

Chapter 1
Background and
Initial Settlement
1854–1865

*C*laymore Chattilon, alias Clement Shattio, of French descent and born in St. Louis, Missouri, purchased a farm in 1852 located one mile west of the region that became Topeka, Kansas Territory. He is reputed to have been Topeka's first white settler. Shattio's wife and the mother of his children was Ann Davis Shattio, a full-blooded Negro of free parentage born in Palestine, Illinois, in 1817. At the age of ten she was stolen from her family and taken to Missouri as a slave, where she served several masters. When, where, and under what circumstances Ann Davis met Shattio are unclear. In one account, Ann Davis acquired a witnessed certificate of freedom for herself and two children in 1849 from one Samuel Lewis while still in Missouri, before her association with Clement Shattio. According to another, she bought her freedom from an unidentified party in 1859. If the latter account is accepted, Davis did not obtain manumission until nine years after her marriage to Shattio in 1850. This suggests that freedom was not a part of her dowry.

Responding to the itch for farm sites that infected many Missourians, Shattio emigrated at some undetermined time after 1845. The first record of Shattio's residence in Kansas located him in Uniontown in 1848. At an unknown date and for unknown reasons, he moved to Topeka, probably before the territory became a battleground in 1854. If the two children, Elizabeth, fourteen years old, and William, age twelve in 1860, both of whom were born in Kansas, were the issue of the Shattio-Davis association, theirs was a relationship of some tenure. By these terms,

Shattio must have come to Kansas at least two years before he arrived in Uniontown in 1848, with Ann Davis pregnant and Elizabeth in tow.

One is at a loss to define Shattio's convictions about slavery and thus to determine the status of Ann Davis and the two children in this scheme. Doubtless Shattio's options in Kansas were few. The distinct anti-Negro strain in the Free-State movement and the more obvious dangers from incumbent proslavery forces, particularly rabid about fugitive slaves, would have mitigated against acknowledging Ann Davis as spouse until 1859. That date, a turning point in the history of territorial Kansas, provides a basis for two hypotheses regarding Davis' status. In the relatively clearer air when the era of Bleeding Kansas was over and the antislavery verdict was assured, Ann Davis stepped forth free and as wife. Another possible explanation is that Clement Shattio was forced to remove the shackles from his slave in conformity with Kansas constitutional law in 1859.[1]

The issues and events which dictated the status of Ann Davis Shattio were part of a larger question of slavery extension in the trans-Mississippi Valley. This was a reigning issue in national affairs, from 1854 to 1861, which culminated in the Civil War. In that period, the proponents of the Free-State movement debated the question of black laws and Negro exclusion in a series of constitutional conventions, the most important of which took place at Wyandotte, Kansas, in 1859. Both the debate and the provisions of law set forth at the Wyandotte Constitutional Convention revealed a full spectrum of attitudes toward race and established the terms for the presence and status of Negroes in Kansas after statehood. Important political, legal, and constitutional developments in territorial Kansas and in Washington prior to the Wyandotte convention also dictated the nation's course; they are essential reference points in the earliest history of black Topeka.

The 1850s was a decade of contrasts in America; it began with optimism and sectional détente but concluded with financial collapse and an impending civil war. In the intervening time, the nation brought to frui-

---

1. Eighth Census of the United States, 1860, in National Archives, Microfilm 653, Kansas, Reel II, 352, Shawnee County; James L. King (ed.), *History of Shawnee County, Kansas, and Representative Citizens* (Chicago, 1905), 60; Noble Prentis, "Aunt Ann's Story," (white) Topeka *Commonwealth*, May 12, 1878, reprinted in *Kansas Historical Quarterly*, XXXV (1969), 89–92.

Background and Initial Settlement, 1854–1865

tion the economic revolution begun after the War of 1812. Industrialization became rooted firmly on the northeastern seaboard. Railroads and settlement began to knit America's new frontiers. The prices for cotton, sugar, and slaves in the South were on the rise. Prosperity abounded. The Compromise of 1850 seemed to hold the slavery extension controversy in abeyance, although southerners viewed the concession of the stiffened Fugitive Slave Law as the merest sop to their ultimate interests.

National growth and population expansion in the 1850s dictated the need for legislation giving political definition to the Nebraska Territory as a means of harnessing its economic potential and as a prelude to opening it up for settlement. In the process, however, the never-quiescent issues of slavery extension and sectional rivalry emerged as definitive components in determining means and ends in westward expansion.[2]

The Kansas-Nebraska Act, signed by President Franklin Pierce on May 30, 1854, provided for the organization of the Nebraska country north of the thirty-seventh parallel into two territories, Kansas and Nebraska. The act declared the Missouri Compromise "inoperative and void [and] . . . inconsistent with the principle of non-intervention by Congress with slavery in the states and territories." Popular sovereignty, moreover, would determine the disposition of the slavery extension controversy. The revocation of the Missouri Compromise broke a solid bargain between the North and the South to exclude slavery from the Louisiana Territory north of 36°30', the latitude of Missouri's southern border.

By any terms, the act presaged continuing sectional rancor. Between 1854 and 1856, the era of Bleeding Kansas, the odds weighed heavily on the side of proslavery. Popular sovereignty, the bane of northern

2. Raymond G. Gaeddert, *The Birth of Kansas*, Social Science Studies (Lawrence, 1940), 20, 21; Roy F. Nichols, "The Kansas-Nebraska Act: A Century of Historiography," *Mississippi Valley Historical Review*, XLVIII (1956), 197–99, 203–204; Allan Nevins, *Ordeal of the Union* (8 vols.; New York, 1947), II, 27–28, 92–93, 103; James C. Malin, *The Nebraska Question, 1852–1854* (Lawrence, 1953), 567; Frederick Merk, *Manifest Destiny and Mission in American History: A Reinterpretation* (New York, 1963), 211; David Donald, *Charles Sumner and the Coming of the Civil War* (New York, 1960), 278–83; Charles Sumner, *Speech of Hon. Charles Sumner in the Senate of the United States, May 19–20, 1856* (Boston, 1856), 13–19, 31–32, 50–54; Fawn Brodie, "Who Defends the Abolitionists," in Martin Duberman (ed.), *The Antislavery Vanguard: New Essays on the Abolitionists* (Princeton, 1965), 53.

radicals, seemed to provide a legislative fiat for Missouri's declared intent to make Kansas an outpost of slavery on its western flank.

Before the organization of the territory, many Missourians came across that state's western border to settle the Kansas hinterland. Those early Missourians in Kansas had no stated predisposition on the slavery issue. They were "sooners" who were interested primarily in getting a head start on the expected rush for land. Immediately after the passage of the Kansas-Nebraska Act, however, the Missouri border sprang alive. Organized plans for settling the new territory were set in motion. Geographical proximity, economic opportunity, and the rising clamor for the extension of slavery dictated that Missouri would figure prominently in the affairs of Kansas.[3] In order to put their interests on a solid foundation, Missourians established towns as a means of making firm their preemptory claim over the territory. They also formed a territorial legislature whose prime directive was to preserve the interests of slavery.[4] The imminent prospect of a migration of antislavery New Englanders, moreover, spurred Missourians to turn their initial advantage into firm political control. In the election of the first territorial legislature in 1855, legal residents were joined by Missourians who deluged Kansas and cast illegal ballots, thereby securing a resounding victory for proslavery. However flagrant that illegality, there were enough bona fide proslavery settlers in Kansas to make that intervention unnecessary.[5]

Northeastern proponents of the free-state cause, no less doctrinaire

3. For a review of the activity of Stephen Douglas and popular sovereignty, see: Malin, *The Nebraska Question*, 12–16; Nevins, *Ordeal of the Union*, II, 106; Robert W. Johannsen, "The Kansas-Nebraska Act and Territorial Government in the United States," *Territorial Kansas: Studies Commemorating the Centennial*, Social Science Studies (Lawrence, 1954), 18; Kenneth Stampp, "Stephen A. Douglas: A Statesman of Compromise," in Kenneth Stampp (ed.), *The Causes of the Civil War* (Englewood Cliffs, 1965), 99–103. Edward Everett Hale, *Kansas and Nebraska* (Boston, 1854), 195–213; Eric Foner, *Free Soil, Free Labor, Free Men* (New York, 1970), 226; Nichols, "The Kansas-Nebraska Act," 209.

4. William Frank Zornow, *Kansas: A History of the Jayhawk State* (Norman, Okla., 1957), 68–69; Malin, *The Nebraska Question*, 364–71; Walter Prescott Webb, *The Great Plains* (Boston, 1931), 184–85; James A. Rawley, *Race and Politics: Bleeding Kansas and the Coming of the Civil War* (Philadelphia, 1969), 80.

5. James C. Malin, *John Brown and the Legend of Fifty-Six* (Philadelphia, 1942), 515, provides aggregate data from the 1855 territorial census: of the 2,905 eligible voters in Kansas, 1,383 (47.6 percent) came from Missouri; Zornow, *Kansas*, 70; William E. Connelley, *History of Kansas, State and People* (5 vols.; Chicago, 1928), II, 344; U.S. Congress, House, *Report of the Special Committee Appointed to Investigate the Troubles in Kansas*, 34th Cong., 1st Sess., No. 200, pp. 3, 69–72, hereinafter cited as *Howard Report*.

than their proslavery antagonists from Missouri, organized the New England Emigrant Aid Company in Massachusetts in 1854. They came to Kansas with the avowed intention of rescuing the territory from the clutches of slavery. Horace Greeley, an opponent of the hated institution, found "no advantage left for liberty" if Kansas was lost to slavery. Speaking for free-state advocates in the United States Senate, William Seward declared: "We will engage in competition for the virgin soil of Kansas, and God give the victory to the side which is stronger in numbers as it is in the right."

Economic interests, however, counterbalanced antislavery attitudes in the Emigrant Aid Company. Eli Thayer, a founder of that organization, conceded as much: "The enterprise was intended to be a money-making affair as well as a philanthropic undertaking." In addition, the rejection of slavery did not indicate egalitarian attitudes toward Negroes. John Everett, an emigrant from the East with abolitionist leanings, asserted in a letter from Kansas to his father in Massachusetts: "They [free staters] have a strong instinct against slavery, do not want it about them, but they lack the strong moral sense which we feel ... the majority would dislike and resent being called abolitionists."[6]

As was the case with the proponents of slavery, an immediate priority of the Emigrant Aid Company after arrival in Kansas was to form towns as a permanent base for settlement as well as for the dissemination of political propaganda and influence. Frye W. Giles, one of the company's leaders, however, contended that "the animated idea of really forming a town was not generally entertained." Nonetheless, in addition to vested interests in the free-state cause, business provided incentives for town building. Typically, the members of that antislavery cohort were imbued with the entrepreneurial spirit which Robert Dykstra believes sustained the urban impulse in nineteenth-century America. In keeping with that projection of goals and incentives, the Emigrant Aid Company founded Topeka on December 5, 1854.[7]

6. Eli Thayer, *The Kansas Crusade* (New York, 1889), 14; Samuel A. Johnson, *The Battle Cry of Freedom* (Lawrence, 1954), 4–7, 10, 43; "Everett Papers," *Kansas Historical Quarterly*, VIII (1939), also quoted in Malin, *John Brown*, 516.
7. Malin, *John Brown*, 456; Johnson, *The Battle Cry of Freedom*, 81–82; Zornow, *Kansas*, 69; Frye W. Giles, *Thirty Years in Topeka: A Historical Sketch* (Topeka, 1886), 23; J. L. King (ed.), *History of Shawnee County*, 117; Robert Dykstra, *The Cattle Towns* (New York, 1972), 4.

Through boosterism, successful bond issue campaigns, and political influence, in 1859 Topeka won a popular vote for selection as the permanent site of the county seat. In that year Topeka employed similar techniques and a victory at the polls to secure designation as the capital of the territory, one indicator of power and prestige. The formula of ardent public and private support for city development, moreover, was effective in transforming Topeka into a leading railroad center by the end of the decade.[8]

The conquest of Kansas, of course, required more than ideals, enterprise, and town building; the free-state cause urgently needed settlers whose ballots and bullets would help wrest control of the territory from entrenched proslavery forces. Amos A. Lawrence, an eastern supporter of the Emigrant Aid Company, believed that distance precluded a heavy influx of emigrants from the Northeast: "We can pay some money, and we can hurrah; but we cannot send you men. The Western states will send them if you have them at all." The territorial census of 1855 revealed that Lawrence was correct; only 6 percent of the eligible voters in Kansas came from New England. Missouri contributed the largest increment, 48 percent. Settlers from the Old Northwest constituted only 20 percent. There were 151 free Negroes and 192 slaves in Kansas as a whole. The number of blacks in Topeka proper is unknown. In Shawnee County, however, there were 48 free Negroes and 33 slaves.[9] The number of Negroes in territorial Kansas was far smaller than the impending debate on slavery and Negro exclusion in a free-state caucus would suggest.

The federal census of 1860 indicated a decrease in the number from New England in Kansas. That decline was not as small or as historically significant as was the sharp drop in the percentage from Missouri and the proportional increase of 30 percent from the Old Northwest.[10] The contours of political change reflected demographic trends in evidence

8. Giles, *Thirty Years in Topeka*, 111, 247–53, 279–83; J. L. King (ed.), *History of Shawnee County*, 31, 59–60, 174–75; on Topeka and railroads, see G. W. Glick, "The Rehabilitation of the Santa Fe Railway System," *Kansas Historical Collections*, XIII (1915), 145; Zornow, *Kansas*, 141–46.
9. Malin, *John Brown*, 514–15; Carroll D. Clark and Roy L. Roberts, *People of Kansas: A Demographic and Social Study* (Topeka, 1936), 50, 58; Wallace E. Miller, *The Peopling of Kansas* (Columbus, 1939), 67; Zornow, *Kansas*, 186.
10. U.S. 1860 census.

between 1855 and 1859. Substantial migration from the Old Northwest, moreover, was a fulcrum for political developments. Indeed, the thrust of Emigrant Aid Company politicking in the intervening four years was to recruit that enlarging minority into the Free-State movement. Emigrants from the Old Northwest readily subscribed to the goals of the company. The development of constitutional and statutory law in the states which comprised that region indicated strong opposition to slavery and, collaterally, an antipathy toward free Negroes.[11]

The formation of a free-state party, the creation of a constitution, and the election of a free-state territorial legislature were the means by which the coalescing antislavery forces intended to drive slavery and its proponents from Kansas. The political stakes at Big Springs and at Topeka were part of Bleeding Kansas, 1854 to 1856, well-known events which propelled the nation toward war.[12] The emergence of Republicanism and the discussion of the Negro question at Big Springs and at Topeka, however, have particular relevance as a prelude to Wyandotte and statehood.

The Republican party accurately reflected the interests of the Emigrant Aid Company and of the antislavery cause. The Republicans advocated a migration of free farmers from the East to provide a bulwark against slavery. A majority of settlers and voters in the territory in such free-state enclaves as the one established in Topeka would break the conspiracy of slave power after fulfilling the prerequisites for statehood. Republicans also believed that free labor would make its superiority self-evident, thereby "awakening latent antislavery sentiment in the South and creating internal pressures for its downfall." Homestead land, made readily available to settlers, provided the practical basis for the free-soil

---

11. Eugene Berwanger, *The Frontier Against Slavery: Western Anti-Negro Prejudice and the Slavery Extension Controversy* (Urbana, 1971), 22–23, 98, 100, 107–108, 112, 114–15; Leon Litwack, *North of Slavery: The Negro in the Free States, 1790–1860* (Chicago, 1961), 68–72; Malin, *John Brown*, 211, 513; Rawley, *Race and Politics*, 150–51.

12. Charles Robinson, *The Kansas Conflict* (Lawrence, 1898); James C. Malin, "The Topeka Statehood Movement Reconsidered: Origins," *Territorial Kansas: Studies Commemorating the Centennial*, Social Science Studies (Lawrence, 1954), 39, 47, 59, 202, 235, 237, 735; Malin, *John Brown*, 68, 211, Chapters 3, 4, 7–9; Avery Craven, *The Coming of the Civil War* (Chicago, 1957), 344–45; Zornow, *Kansas*, 73; Stephen Oates, *To Purge This Land with Blood: A Biography of John Brown* (New York, 1970), 171; Osborn Perry Anderson, "A Voice from Harper's Ferry," in Benjamin Quarles (ed.), *Blacks on John Brown* (Urbana, 1972), 41–42.

ideology and supported the goal of economic development of the trans-Mississippi West.¹³

Republicanism, however, encompassed more than politics, ideology, and moral principle suited to material interests; it could not be reduced to Beardian simplicity. In Eric Foner's opinion, in that macrocosm of "values, fears, prejudices ... and commitments," economic concerns and the antislavery ideology coexisted with other strains of belief. Enlightened social conscience and the Protestant ethic also were important parts of the Republican ideology. It is clear, however, that Republicanism in Kansas, and in the nation at large, did not derive its motive or sustaining force from the espousal of civil liberty for Negroes. By these terms, Republicans were ill prepared to limit the rampant hostility toward abolitionists and Negroes which prevailed in the North and in the Midwest. Such mixed motives and contradictions were evident in the Republican alliance with the Free-State movement in Kansas. Practical politics, rather than ideology, provided the bond between Republicans and the diverse strands of antislavery opinion in the new territory. A tribute to the growing success of that partnership came from an enemy of the free-state cause.

In July, 1856, long before the antislavery victory was assured, David R. Atchison, a proslavery Democrat from Missouri, identified the resolve of the free staters and their Republican allies, as well as the increasingly trenchant antislavery opinion in the North as a whole: "With them it is no mere local question of whether slavery shall exist in Kansas or not, but one of far wider significance; a question of whether it shall exist anywhere in the Union."¹⁴ Increasing migration from the Old Northwest in the spring of 1857, moreover, enhanced the numerical superiority of the free-state forces. The tide of events through 1857 made proslavery partisans aware that a verdict for freedom was inevitable. The Dred Scott decision in 1857 also helped galvanize resistance to proslavery authority in Kansas and in Washington, thereby giving cohesion to the increasingly potent Free-State movement. The Republican party emerged from the imbroglio of Bleeding Kansas and attendant events in Washington as the guiding force in the political develop-

13. E. Foner, *Free Soil*, 26–29, 9; Litwack, *North of Slavery*, 116; Rawley, *Race and Politics*, vii.
14. Malin, *John Brown*, 120.

ment of the territory.[15] The implementation of Republican control and initial discussion of the disposition of the Negro question, however, were set forth at the free-state conventions at Big Springs and at Topeka in 1855.

In 1855 the free staters initiated organized efforts to break proslavery's hold on territorial government and to establish political order in their own ranks. Two correlative options were acted upon. The formation of a free-state political party was the main item of business at the meeting held in Big Springs in September, 1855. The creation of a constitution, the election of a free-state territorial legislature, and a planned bid for statehood dominated the agenda at the Topeka meeting in October and November of that year. The example of the American Revolution, as well as references to natural law and the social contract, provided ideological support for the deliberations at both conventions. In a literal and in a figurative sense the conferees spoke of "disenthralling ourselves from the slavery which is now fettering [us]" and of securing liberty and self-determination consonant with their rights as free men. An editorial in the *Kansas Free State* concluded: "It is not only our right but our duty to violate some unjust laws and to prevent the execution of all of them." The Lawrence *Herald of Freedom* also advocated revolution, rather than reliance on the courts and other government agencies "imposed upon us by armed men from a foreign state."[16] In addition, there were more prosaic concerns. Expediency, personal ambition, and hastily contrived gambits to counteract proslavery activity also dictated the political choices of antislavery proponents.

The Negro question, while not a dominant motif at Big Springs and at Topeka, received considerable attention. The discussion of the issue of free blacks and slaves in the territory in 1855 clearly reflected attitudes toward race and was an important prelude to the more extensive consideration of the Negro question at the Wyandotte Constitutional Convention in 1859 on the eve of statehood.

The free-state platform constructed at Big Springs resolutely denounced slavery in Kansas but skirted the issue of interference with that

15. Malin, *The Nebraska Question*, 12–16, 367–68; Craven, *The Coming of the Civil War*, 386–87; Malin, "The Topeka Statehood Movement," 135–36; Arthur T. Andreas, *History of the State of Kansas* (Chicago, 1883), 116.
16. Malin, "The Topeka Statehood Movement," 178–79; Malin, *John Brown*, 65.

institution in states where it already existed. Political necessity and the fear of rending the newly derived free-state coalition dictated that the easterners accede to the majority from the Old Northwest in opposing the admission of free Negroes into the territory. Accordingly, they resolved: "The best interests of Kansas require a population of free white men, and that in our state organization we are in favor of stringent laws excluding all Negroes, bond or free, from the territory." In addition to race prejudice, those advocates of the antislavery cause feared economic competition with Negroes as free laborers. The majority of free staters, moreover, did not want to meet the Negro "socially or politically as a free man."[17]

The disposition of the Negro question received relatively more detailed attention at the Topeka convention. Suffrage and office holding were limited to "all white male inhabitants" and to Indian males. The militia was to be constituted solely from the white population. The Topeka convention, however, avoided instituting black laws by submitting the question to a popular referendum: no black laws appear in the Topeka Constitution. The passage of the referendum on Negro exclusion, three to one, indicated widely pervasive anti-Negro sentiment. Throughout the territorial period the free staters used referenda to handle the Negro question. Thus public attitudes regarding the status of Negroes exercised some influence over legislative action and policy making. The official mind was no less clear in a proclamation signed by the executive committee of the Topeka convention: "The qualified electors of the territory . . . express their approval of the passage of laws . . . providing for the exclusion of free Negroes from Kansas." That prohibition also included mulattoes.[18]

The significance of the Wyandotte Constitutional Convention does not lie in its novelty. The issues brought forth there were similar to those considered at the Topeka convention in 1855. To a greater degree than at Topeka, however, the conferees at Wyandotte entertained serious, realizable plans for statehood. All facets of the territory's governmental

17. Arthur T. Andreas and W. G. Cutler (eds.), "The Minutes of the Big Springs Meeting," in Andreas, *History of the State of Kansas*, 95–97; for a comprehensive breakdown of the vote on black exclusion and other aspects of the Negro question, see Connelley, *History of Kansas*, I, 350–51, and Malin, "The Topeka Statehood Movement," 43; Malin, *John Brown*, 513.

18. Malin, "The Topeka Statehood Movement," 78, 145, 187, 197, 57.

and bureaucratic structure were acted upon. The full range of political and ideological opinion evident during the previous four years appeared in review. The conclave, moreover, represented the territory's variegated demographic and cultural makeup.

The Wyandotte convention provides an important reference point for the development of the legal structure of race and race relations in Kansas prior to statehood and the Civil War. Perceptions of race and the germ of racial prejudice, however, are more evident in the constitutional debate than in the document itself. Slavery and fugitive slaves, "the privilege of settlement" under which the delegates debated Negro exclusion, suffrage, and access to public institutions, were central categories for the discussion of the Negro question.

The slavery controversy in Kansas was put to rest as public policy in the Wyandotte Constitution. Section 6 of the Bill of Rights prohibited slavery and involuntary servitude except for "crimes" of an unspecified nature.[19] The debate, however, indicated that the delegates were not as unequivocal on slavery and fugitive slaves as that point of law suggests.

The delegates rejected a resolution allowing a twelve-month period of grace for slaveholders to remove their property from the territory. Nonetheless, they did not use this occasion to level any invective at the proslavery minority. It is plausible that the convention placed a greater premium on cooperation between erstwhile antagonists, among other compromises prerequisite to constitution making, than on a doctrinaire antislavery stance. The convention endorsed the "Peace Act," which purported to cancel old debts between proslavery and antislavery as well as "all criminal actions now commenced, growing out of political differences of opinion."[20] Rancor was evident, however, in the discussion of the Negro question in all of its dimensions. This reflected the late ascendancy of Republicans and the defensive posture assumed by their Democratic enemies, now colleagues.

If Negroes in Kansas were not to be slaves, contended proslavery Democrat William McDowell, they should be excluded from the state. Such resolutions favoring exclusion were either rejected or tabled by

---

19. *Kansas Constitutional Convention: A Reprint of the Proceedings and Debates of the Convention Which Framed the Constitution of Kansas at Wyandotte in July, 1859* [and] *The Constitution Annotated to Date, Historical Sketches, Etc.*, by the Authority of the State Legislature (Topeka, 1920), 491, hereinafter cited as *Wyandotte Convention*.

20. *Ibid.*, 492, 7.

the convention. Undaunted, McDowell continued to press for Negro exclusion and moved that a special committee on Negroes and mulattoes be appointed to inquire into the expediency of excluding them from settling in Kansas after the adoption of the constitution. A second proviso of the McDowell resolution was that all labor contracts made with Negroes were void. Whites concluding such contracts would be subject to fines, the monies from which "shall be used for the colonization of such Negroes and mulattoes and their descendants as may be in the state . . . and may be willing to emigrate." The majority voted to table that resolution.[21]

The issue of suffrage, noted William Hutchinson, a Republican with abolitionist leanings, "is not altogether a matter of policy . . . it is one of right." Hutchinson hoped that the word *white* would not be inserted in the suffrage section of the constitution. That limitation of civil liberty for Negroes "might have been justifiable a generation ago" but hardly befitted "the spirit of liberty which is now advancing before the world." Such action, moreover, would be inappropriate for Kansas, "the place to exercise these modern ideas."[22] Hutchinson's unvarnished idealism was no more in keeping with the temper of the convention than was the blatant prejudice of the Democratic representatives.

No less adamant on suffrage than on exclusion, McDowell proposed an amendment to the suffrage section requiring that no Negro or mulatto be entitled to vote in any election. "I came here," he said, "instructed to oppose Negro suffrage and equality." Proceeding from that mandate and "my own feelings," McDowell also advocated measures to prohibit Negro immigration and "to discourage the free Negro from here remaining." Both McDowell's proposed amendment and substitute proposals favoring restricted suffrage for Negroes were tabled by majorities of two to one. Nonetheless, Article V, Section 1, in the Wyandotte Constitution limited suffrage to "every white male person of twenty-one years and upwards."[23]

The access of Negroes to services in public institutions, the educational system in particular, provoked extensive controversy. The nomenclature of Negro exclusion, "white" or "white only," and references de-

21. *Ibid.*, 56, 121.
22. *Ibid.*, 300.
23. *Ibid.*, 302, 582.

noting complexion, "copper colored" and "sooty," punctuated the debate. The bane of race mixing in the common schools, suggesting social equality, emerged as a substantive issue and provided a basis for proposals of Negro exclusion from the common schools. John Greer, a Republican from Topeka, said that Negro exclusion from the schools would prevent the "extravagant mistake" of subjecting white children to "the consequences growing out of a mixture of races." Thus, he concluded, because "association governs conduct . . . I am opposed to giving the Negro and Mulatto either the political privilege . . . or the social privileges . . . which we claim for ourselves."[24]

Solomon Thatcher, a Republican, rejected an accusation that his party endorsed "amalgamation and racial equality." Thatcher, nonetheless, remained steadfast in rejecting discrimination. He identified exclusion of blacks from the common schools and public institutions as "a dark and forbidding feature repugnant to true Republicanism." John Burris, also a member of that party, injected an additional egalitarian note: "We must proceed upon the assumption that blacks are to live in common with whites." Accordingly, "they should be made as intelligent and as moral as education can make them." John Slough, a Democrat, said in rejoinder, "I shall never consent, by my vote, or by any action of mine that those upon whose natures God has stamped inferiority shall ever associate with my children in our common schools."[25]

At the conclusion of the debate, a majority of the conferees were in accord with the admonition of Republican delegate William Griffith to avoid the possible accusation of discrimination "between persons." "The time may not be far distant," Griffith continued, "when we may wish we had not done so." It would be far safer, he concluded, "to leave it to public sentiment" expressed through the legislature so that "the people can govern in this matter."[26]

Articles VI and VII of the Wyandotte Constitution, dealing with education and public institutions respectively, do not contain anti-Negro sanctions and, therefore, do not reveal the race prejudice evident in the debate.[27] Conceivably it was politically inexpedient for the convention

24. *Ibid.*, 178, 273.
25. *Ibid.*, 179–80, 176.
26. *Ibid.*, 175.
27. *Ibid.*, 583–94.

to incorporate that dimension of Negro exclusion in the constitution. The delegates feared that the document might be rejected by increasingly trenchant and powerful antislavery partisans in Washington. Kansans were well aware of Republican opposition to similar exclusion provisions in the Oregon Constitution which, in turn, endangered its passage in Congress.[28] In addition, such a breach of antislavery's vested interests might have incurred the wrath of the eastern press. Clearly, the interplay of political exigency and race prejudice existed in delicate balance at Wyandotte, governed in part by the shifting axis of national politics. In 1861, however, the state legislature enacted statutes which gave district superintendents of education the right to establish separate schools. The proviso that "equal educational advantages" be maintained for Negroes and for whites was left to the discretion of the district superintendents.[29]

The debate clearly indicated that civil liberty for Negroes was not a predominant concern of the convention at large. It seems to follow, however, that the sizable Republican plurality at Wyandotte, as a matter of course, would doom Democrat-sponsored anti-Negro measures to failure. Those political stakes notwithstanding, the final resolution on black exclusion from public institutions, as an example, was narrowly defeated, twenty-six to twenty-five.[30] Clearly some Republican delegates joined the Democrats on this vote. This gives important testimony regarding the wide sweep of anti-Negro sentiment in this conclave, seemingly a phenomenon beyond the range of Republican control.

In the last analysis, the resolution of the generic Negro question in territorial Kansas was not buttressed by black laws or by the sanction of slavery or by slavery extension; in all particulars it was a victory for antislavery. By the same token, neither the various constitutions nor the attendant debates established any bench marks of civil liberty for Negroes. Indeed, public policy at all levels and opinion in the private sector bore the stain of Negrophobia and prejudice. In this regard Kansas was truly one with the Union.

Negroes were not present in substantial numbers in Kansas between

28. Berwanger, *The Frontier Against Slavery*, 116–17.
29. *Kansas Session Laws, 1861* (Topeka, 1862), Chapter LXXVI, Article III, Section 1.
30. *Wyandotte Convention*, 175.

1854 and 1861. Nonetheless, Negroes were neither inconsequent nor ephemeral in the history of the territory. In spite of the clear repudiation of blacks, the Kansas crusade amplified the rhetoric of freedom. Abolitionism and the hope of civil liberty for Negroes seemed more assured by the antislavery verdict. Ostensibly the Civil War sustained that optimism. Topeka, Kansas, was an arena in which the political and social changes portended by the foregoing drama occurred. An analysis of the Negro community in Topeka, 1860 through 1865, will provide a more precise definition of the substance of the antislavery legacy.

The Free-State movement, from which Topeka derived its political heritage, also made anti-Negro sentiment a definitive element in the perception of race in the city. Indeed, concessions made to race prejudice by most Topeka delegates in successive political conclaves, 1855 through 1859, suggest that Negroes were not welcome. Topeka's endorsement of accompanying anti-Negro referenda further indicated pervasive private bias.

The furor over the Dred Scott case and the vindication of the antislavery cause, however, disturbed the inertia of race prejudice in Topeka. A few citizens actively, if secretly, showed concern for fugitive slaves. "The passions of the times," if not common cause with abolitionism, pressed some free staters into service as conductors on the Underground Railroad. The freedom line ran through Lawrence, Topeka, and thence into Nebraska and Iowa, "the shortest route to the North Pole." Avery Washburn, a banker, farmer, and philanthropist from Connecticut, and John Ritchie, a farmer and long an antislavery activist, originally from Ohio, were among the conductors at the Underground Railroad depot established in Topeka in 1857. Ritchie gave further testimony to his relatively progressive view of civil liberty for Negroes by voting down all anti-Negro resolutions as a Topeka delegate to the Wyandotte convention.[31]

None of the slaves who traversed Kansas "following the 'Drinking

31. Richard Cordley, *Pioneer Days* (New York, 1903), 128–35; "Kansas Underground Railroad," Cincinnati *Weekly Enquirer*, undated, in *Negro Clippings*, VII, hereinafter cited as *NC*; Richard Cordley, "Lizzie and the Underground Railroad," in Everett Rich (ed.), *The Heritage of Kansas: Selected Commentaries on Past Times* (Lawrence, 1960), 56; "Underground Railroad in Topeka," *Shawnee County Historical Society Bulletin*, No. 15 (December, 1951), 15; Cordley, *Pioneer Days*, 150–51.

Gourd,'" a euphemism for escaping north, elected to remain in Topeka in 1860. In fact, there were only eight Negroes in Shawnee County as a whole, the wife and children of Clement Shattio, living in Topeka Township. The interval between federal and state census periods, 1860 to 1865, witnessed the appearance of eighty-three Negroes in the city. There were an additional eighty-seven living in adjacent townships.[32] According to reports from Lawrence, emigrating slaves established freedmen's colonies in Wyandotte, Lawrence, and Topeka.[33] Although contemporary accounts from Topeka do not identify the earliest freedmen's colony in that city with any specificity, reports of their sojourn in Lawrence are informative. One source described their utility as a labor force: the Negroes were "strong and law abiding" persons whose willingness to work prevented them from becoming objects of charity.[34] Richard Cordley, a citizen of Lawrence and a thoroughgoing Garrisonian, proclaimed: "As they break their fetters they naturally strike out for the centers of abolitionism." The Free-State movement did not foster the liberal, egalitarian view of Negroes that Cordley described. However, the rejection of provisions for Negro exclusion in the Wyandotte Constitution by ascendant antislavery forces and the momentum of events leading to the Civil War were motive forces leading to black settlement in Kansas. The increase in the number of Negroes in Kansas between 1860 and 1865 reflected the accuracy of Cordley's assertion: "The Negroes are not coming. They are here. They will stay here. They are American born. They have been here for more than two-hundred and fifty years. They are not going to South America. They are not going to other parts of our own Land. . . . They are with us to stay. They are to be our neighbors, whatever we may think about it, whatever we may do about it."[35]

For the nascent black Topeka community, as for the nation, the pivotal

32. U.S. 1860 census; Kansas State Census Manuscripts, Shawnee County, 1865, in Microfilm Division, KSHS Archives, Reel 7.
33. Cordley, *Pioneer Days*, 137–38; Albert Castel, "Civil War Kansas and the Negro," *Journal of Negro History*, XXI (1936), 129–30; John D. Barker, *Sixty-eighth Session of Kansas Annual Conference of the A.M.E. Church and the Seventy-fifth Anniversary of St. John A.M.E. Church* (Topeka, 1943), hereinafter cited as *St. John Souvenir Program*.
34. Nell B. Waldron, "Colonization in Kansas" (Ph.D. dissertation, Northwestern University, 1932), 121–22, cites contemporary but anonymous impressions of Negroes in Lawrence in the early 1860s.
35. Cordley, *Pioneer Days*, 141, 149.

event of the years 1860 to 1865 was the Civil War. Partially through the efforts of Kansas Senator James Lane, Negroes appeared in the Union ranks earlier in the trans-Mississippi West than in the East. Lane began recruiting Negro troops in Kansas as early as 1861 without authority and against instructions from Washington. In no sense did his actions proceed from an egalitarian impulse. Lane believed that Negroes might just as well be "cannon fodder" as someone in his own family. In fact, Lane often drafted Negroes who did not share his enthusiasm for the war.[36]

Not uncommonly, Union troops returning north picked up a retinue of Negro hangers-on. At the head of a brigade composed of Kansas regiments, Lane made forays into Missouri in 1862, and several thousand slaves are alleged to have entered Kansas in the wake of his return.[37] That pattern persisted throughout the war. The Negroes came by land and by boat. In January, 1865, one Lieutenant Colonel Bassett took four boats down the Arkansas River from Kansas into Arkansas on a military campaign. On his return the boats had over 600 black refugees on board.[38]

Lane recruited and organized the 1st Kansas Colored Volunteer Infantry, which was officially recognized by the federal government in January, 1863. The *Official Military History of Kansas Regiments* indicates that the call for troops met a ready response from Negroes and that "within sixty days 500 men were ready to be organized into a battalion of six companies." Negroes showed in their response "a willing readiness to link their future and share the perils with their white brethren in the war of rebellion."[39] The roster of 27 men from Shawnee County in the first contingent of Kansas Negro troops contains the names of three persons from Topeka. None of those persons is found in the 1865 census tracts for Topeka, but they are enumerated in the 1870 census. The list of casualties for the 1st Kansas Colored contains the names of three

---

36. James M. McPherson, *The Negro's Civil War: How American Negroes Felt and Acted During the War for the Union* (New York, 1965), 164; Dudley T. Cornish, "Kansas Negro Regiments in the Civil War," *Kansas Historical Quarterly*, XX (1952), 417–19; Dudley T. Cornish, *The Sable Arm: Negro Troops in the Union Army, 1861–1865* (New York, 1966), 71, 74–75.

37. Zornow, *Kansas*, 111; Cornish, *The Sable Arm*, 47.

38. Kansas Adjutant General, *Official Military History of Kansas Regiments During the War for the Suppression of the Great Rebellion* (Leavenworth, 1870), 61–63.

39. *Ibid.*, 407; J. L. King (ed.), *History of Shawnee County*, 81.

Topekans; the majority, however, were from the southeastern part of the state. General James Blunt, appointed by the War Department as commissioner for the recruitment of Negro troops, organized the 2nd Kansas Colored Volunteer Infantry in June, 1863. Arthur T. Andreas asserted that the records of that contingent were lost in a military campaign. The roster and list of casualties of the 2nd Kansas Colored in the *Official Military History*, moreover, are incomplete. There were 2,080 Negroes alleged to have served in the army of Kansas. That figure is questionable, however, there being only 300 Negroes of military age in the state in 1860.[40]

By reputation and by deed, black Kansans acquitted themselves well and were mustered out "having nobly performed [their] duty and by [their] faithful service . . . demonstrated the capacity and the efficiency" of Negro men-at-arms.[41] Nonetheless, bigotry in the North hounded the Negro soldier with scarcely less fury than did the Confederates. The *Official Military History* provided at once an epitaph for the Negro soldier and an indictment of the Union: "An intolerant prejudice against the race denied . . . [him] the honorable position in society which every soldier is entitled to, even though he gained that position at the risk of his life in the cause of the Nation, which could ill afford to refuse genuine sympathy and support from any quarter."[42]

The number of black Topekans among the war dead is not known. Kansas, however, had 8,498 men killed, wounded, or missing in action. This was the highest number of casualties in percentage of state population in the Union.[43] That "last full measure" and the final vindication of the antislavery crusade became enduring emblems of Kansas' devotion to the northern cause; these too were gathered into the folds of myth and reality in Kansas' legacy to blacks.

In line with demographic shifts in the region brought about by the Civil War, in 1865 most black Topekans came from Missouri, with a smaller contingent coming from Tennessee as well as from states in the Deep South. The sex ratio was nearly equal. The median age was

40. Andreas, *History of the State of Kansas*, 200–202; *Official Military History*, 431–35; Zornow, *Kansas*, 108.
41. Andreas, *History of the State of Kansas*, 200–202.
42. *Official Military History*, 407–408.
43. Zornow, *Kansas*, 108.

twenty-seven for the heads of household and sixteen for the total population. This conformed to patterns described by David Katzman, Kenneth Kusmer, and Gilbert Osofsky in their studies of Negro migration to the urban North. The median figure for family size was six individuals, most of whom lived in single family dwellings inclusive of the head of household, his spouse, and children.[44]

The pattern of Negro and white dwellings, as they were enumerated in the census manuscripts, reveals that residential segregation was not the norm in Topeka. In 1868, however, many Negroes lived in a racially homogeneous neighborhood located on First Avenue, adjacent to the Santa Fe Railroad yards. Impressionistic evidence suggests that this was the site of employment for a portion of the 56 percent of heads of household who worked, most of whom were unskilled laborers. The majority of women and children were not employed. The city's corporate growth in the 1860s, moreover, did not create particular economic benefits for Negroes and there was no systematic recruitment of black labor.[45] Approximately one-fourth of the total black population was literate. The census of 1865 did not identify literacy rates for individuals under twenty-one. However, 82 percent of the children were in school.[46]

Kinship and informal relations in the enclave or the neighborhood largely defined associational behavior in fledgling black Topeka in 1865. There are no available records for the Shawnee Mission Lodge, a Negro fraternal order supposedly established in 1858 in Topeka.[47] Freedmen's Church, organized in 1863 as a mission of the white First Congregational Church, was the only religious organization for Negroes in the environs of Topeka before 1865. Freedmen's Church, however, was outside the western perimeter of the city in a region that was incorporated as Topeka's Third Ward after 1873. In 1863 and in all subsequent years,

44. Kansas 1865 MS census; Tables 2–4; David Katzman, *Before the Ghetto: Black Detroit in the Nineteenth Century* (Urbana, 1973), 63, 74–75; Kenneth L. Kusmer, *A Ghetto Takes Shape: Black Cleveland, 1870–1930* (Urbana, 1976), 39; Gilbert Osofsky, *Harlem: The Making of a Ghetto* (New York, 1966), 24.
45. Kansas 1865 MS census; Tables 5, 6; *St. John Souvenir Program*; Scott Greer, *The Emerging City: Myth and Reality* (New York, 1962), 111–13; Suzanne Keller, *The Urban Neighborhood: A Sociological Perspective* (New York, 1968), 19, 20. Greer and Keller provide some specificity to the definitions of *enclave* and *neighborhood*.
46. Kansas 1865 MS census; Tables 7, 8.
47. Andreas, *History of the State of Kansas*, 452. This source identifies officers only and gives no membership list for 1858.

moreover, Congregationalism attracted few Negro adherents.[48] Black Topeka's religious history, therefore, properly begins in the late 1860s, by which time there was a marked increase in the number of churches to serve the city's expanding Negro population.

There were no black institutions through which Topeka Negroes could formulate strategies for combating race discrimination, increasingly apparent in the city and throughout the nation at the conclusion of the Civil War. After 1865, however, protest against discrimination became institutionalized through informal political and social associations. In subsequent decades they comprised, with the church, the cornerstones of the Negro community. Significantly, organized agitation over civil rights and church activities put black Topekans in touch with the affairs of the nation and gave them common cause with Negro organizations outside the city.

After 1865, Negroes came to Topeka in increasing numbers, a migration pattern which culminated in the Great Exodus of black southerners to Kansas, 1879–1880. In that fifteen-year interim, old institutions grew within the matrix of the Second Ward; new ones appeared as the city's Negro residents dispersed into other wards. Organized protest, new churches, and more elaborate associational behavior provided the means by which Topeka's Negro enclaves developed into a viable community.

48. *Shawnee County Historical Society Bulletin*, No. 11 (June, 1950), 4–5; (black) Topeka *Colored Citizen*, June 7, 1879.

Chapter 2
Reconstruction, the Frontier, and Community Development 1865–1880

*C*lement and Ann Davis Shattio lived on the farm in Topeka Township in 1880 that they occupied in 1855 and on which they raised their two sons and three surviving daughters. With the exception of minor economic fluctuations, the Shattios fared well over that twenty-five-year interim and owned the farm free and clear. Ann Davis Shattio was a housewife. Evidently the family fortunes were stable enough so that she did not have to contribute a wage to supplement the family income.

In 1875, by which time all of the children had reached adulthood, the Shattio sons worked as farmers on their father's property. As of that date the daughters were married. Their husbands were all literate and gainfully employed. The new families established residence in Topeka Township.[1] With the exception of the daughter Laura, the lives of the Shattio family after 1875 will be allowed to merge with the broad categories of the census. Neither the newspapers nor the recollections of Shattio family descendants endowed their lives with marked significance. Indeed, Laura Shattio's particularity derives from an auspicious marriage. Laura's husband, Henry Clay Wilson, achieved considerable success in several business ventures.

---

1. U.S. 1860 census; Kansas 1865 MS census; Ninth Census of the United States, 1870, in National Archives, Microfilm 593, Kansas, Reel II, 442, Shawnee County; Kansas State Census Manuscripts, Shawnee County, 1875, in Microfilm Division, KSHS Archives, Reel 18; Tenth Census of the United States, 1880, in National Archives, Microfilm T9,

The exact date of Laura Shattio's marriage to Henry Wilson is of no consequence. In 1875, Laura and Henry had two children, Joseph, age three, and Ann, four months. Given the elder child's age and some allowances for propriety, the Wilsons probably married sometime in 1871, about a year after his arrival in Topeka.

Wilson spent his boyhood in slavery in Tennessee and came to Kansas "in a horse cart from Arkansas." Wilson claimed to be a Kansas Civil War veteran, which suggests that he was in the state before 1865. Suffice it to say, he was not reported as a resident of Shawnee County in 1865. In 1870, Henry Wilson lived in a rented room and identified himself as a "painter" who was unemployed that spring.[2]

On arriving in Topeka in his early twenties, Wilson probably had some flair and no little pluck. Seemingly in quick succession he won a bride, experimented with business, and emerged by 1873 as a "civic leader" and a member of Second Baptist Church. From 1875 through 1885, Wilson reported his occupation as "restaurateur." In later years he boasted of his "close association" with Cyrus Holliday, one of white Topeka's first citizens and a leading businessman, with whom he claimed to have "founded the Holliday House Restaurant."[3]

The Wilsons lived on Adams Street in the Second Ward, between 1875 and 1880, in a neighborhood that was two-thirds white. The eldest children, Joseph and Ann, were in school and could read and write. Ann and Ogeal, her younger sister, finished high school, but the extent of Joseph's education is not known. Laura Shattio Wilson's occupation was that of "housewife" in all census periods examined. Laura's existence is enlivened somewhat in the recollections of her daughter, Ann Wilson

---

Kansas, Reels 396, 397, Shawnee County. Clement Shattio is identified as head of household in the census manuscripts, 1860–80.

2. *NC*, VII; Kansas 1865 MS census; U.S. 1870 census. Differences in age and skin color preclude precise identification of Henry Clay Wilson with the one Negro household carrying the name Wilson, also from Tennessee and living in Topeka in 1865, as members of the same family. Henry Wilson's name is not found in the *Official Military History*, which enumerated black Kansans in the Civil War.

3. *NC*, VII; Kansas 1875 MS census; U.S. 1880 census; Kansas State Census Manuscripts, Shawnee County, 1885, in Microfilm Division, KSHS Archives, Reels 127, 128. Notably, Wilson was not listed in Samuel Radges, *Radges' Directory of Topeka and Shawnee County and Gazetteer of General Information*, 1875–85, a source which did identify Negro businessmen by race in 1880. Wilson also is not mentioned in any context in census materials relating to Cyrus Holliday's business activity.

De Moss. In that account Laura Wilson taught her children how to play the piano and also gave private lessons.[4]

Wilson's business activities gave him considerable prominence after 1900. In 1898, Wilson and his son Frank H. Wilson operated a diner and barbershop opposite the Santa Fe Railroad depot. They purchased and managed a coal company in 1912.[5] Between 1880 and the turn of the century, however, one is forced to rely primarily on family recollections as a bridge to the future of the Shattio-Wilsons. Unlike the Shattios in 1859, the Wilson biography does not illuminate the momentous events of the period 1865–1880: war's end, Reconstruction, and the Great Exodus of 1879. Wilson's name, moreover, does not appear on the membership lists of the political and race protest organizations which proliferated after 1880.

Yet, in significant ways, the Wilsons from 1865 to 1880 illustrate a favorable American theme: migration to the West and economic success through initiative and imagination. As befitted his income and station, Wilson's family had economic stability and education above the rudimentary level. Slim evidence of their associational behavior and use of leisure also suggests high social status. Black Topeka as a whole, of course, did not conform to the same socioeconomic profile. Few Topeka Negroes had a stake in the land, an inheritance, or could measure their tenure in the city in terms of generations. Most, moreover, were laborers as their descendants were destined to be.

Nonetheless, the Wilsons and the increasing number of Negroes in Topeka from 1870 to 1880 had important things in common. Most migrated from the Border South into the West to escape oppression and to move toward economic opportunity and success on the frontier; it was a black experience within an American design. In Kansas and in the nation at large, however, the desire of Negroes for an equitable share in the nation's covenant was largely unfulfilled. Therein exposed was an

---

4. Kansas 1875 MS census; U.S. 1880 census; interviews with Mrs. Ann Wilson De Moss, August 10, 1971, April 16, 1972. The Wilsons and my maternal forebears have been friends since the 1890s. Wilson and my maternal grandfather, Henry Shepard, the owner of Topeka's Negro theater in the 1920s and 1930s, also were business associates.

5. "Noted Colored Leader Operates 7 Acre Park," (white) Topeka *Daily Capital*, May 30, 1937, in *NC*, VII; (black) Topeka *Kansas State Ledger*, April 30, 1898; (black) Topeka *Plaindealer*, July 4, October 4, 1912.

intellectual dilemma which would affect the black experience for decades: how to resolve the manifold contradictions between freedom and race prejudice. Through a reasoned evaluation of issues and alternatives, Negroes began to plot a course toward civil rights and full equality. Thus, the irresolutions of Reconstruction and discrimination at the state and local levels caused Topeka Negroes to prepare for their common defense by joining forces with blacks throughout the state and nation in organized protest.

Despite the battle cry of freedom, race relations in Kansas to 1865 did not portend egalitarian fervor during Reconstruction. Nonetheless, Kansas quickly ratified the Thirteenth Amendment. Railroad development and agricultural production, however, were decisive concerns in the state after the Civil War. There was no discontinuity in territorial and Reconstruction themes; ideology remained a servant of enterprise. Comparatively, the affirmation of civil liberty for Negroes had less importance. Kansas' United States Senators James Lane and Samuel Pomeroy, both Republicans and declared Radicals, reflected the views of many in their constituency on those issues.[6]

Lane and Pomeroy were more concerned about their vested interests in railroads and land speculation than about Negro liberty; neither had the liberal pedigree of Thaddeus Stevens or of Charles Sumner. Noble Prentis, a chronicler of Kansas history, aptly described Lane as one "who had no single feature that would endear him to a Massachusetts heart." Likewise, "he had no New England habits or reverences." Pomeroy, "Subsidy Pom," earned a notorious reputation for chicanery in securing government appropriations to support his railroad interests.[7]

Formulas prescribed by Congress for the reconstruction of the South had limited significance as principle or as policy in Kansas. The same

---

6. Martha Belle Caldwell, "The Attitude of Kansas Toward the Reconstruction of the South" (Ph.D. dissertation, University of Kansas, 1938), 12–13, 38. Although dated, Caldwell's study provides valuable documentation of Kansas representatives' behavior from the *House Journal*, the *Senate Journal*, and the *Congressional Globe*. Zornow, *Kansas*, 111, 136–37, 266–71. For a dated but valuable quantitative analysis of economic and demographic development in Kansas with accompanying statistics and graphs, see Clark and Roberts, *People of Kansas*, 159, 162, Appendix; Daniel W. Wilder, *Annals of Kansas* (Topeka, 1885), 521; Giles, *Thirty Years in Topeka*, 88–89, 122–24, 240–44, 325–28.

7. Noble Prentis, "Jim Lane," *Kansas Miscellanies* (Topeka, 1889), 109; John Speer, *Life of General James H. Lane* (Garden City, Kans., 1896), 42; Zornow, *Kansas*, 121, 123, 127–31.

may be said of the Johnson impeachment fiasco, Kansas' United States Senator Edmund Ross's pivotal negative vote notwithstanding. The state's response to those crises was, by turns, conservative and fitfully radical. Government support for the railroads, which required the good offices of moderates who controlled patronage, helped to determine Kansas' political posture. For those reasons, Kansas joined ranks with the moderates and ratified the Fourteenth Amendment. When the Senate passed the Fifteenth Amendment, neither Kansas senator was present. For his part, Ross confessed "to a degree of humiliation at the failure" of Kansas to eliminate the race qualification for suffrage on its own initiative.[8]

Kansas officials in Washington were not imbued with the genuine liberalism characteristic of Radical Republicanism. They expressed a "laissez-faire hostility to reform," manifest as a desire to be rid of an increasingly burdensome race problem as Reconstruction ran its course.[9] Nonetheless, Kansas was not victimized by the virulent racism of the Old Northwest and race violence did not mar the state's history through Reconstruction. Economics, moreover, was not the sum of realities in defining what was important to Kansas' Radical Republicans at the state and local levels.[10] Several influential state officials attempted to combat racial discrimination in Kansas between 1866 and 1876.

Alarmed by the efforts of National Unionists and Democrats to label them as proponents of Negro suffrage, and with elections impending, Kansas Republicans at the state convention in 1867 opposed Negro suffrage. In his Annual Message to the legislature in the same year, however, Governor Samuel T. Crawford asserted that the increasing furor in Washington over Reconstruction made necessary some resolution of impartial manhood suffrage. Reflecting his personal views, Crawford saw "no reason in law or ethics" which should exclude Negroes from all rights that others enjoy "who are no more worthy, because of their race

---

8. Caldwell, "The Attitude of Kansas Toward Reconstruction," 38, 45, 63; (white) Topeka *Tribune*, August 17, 1866; Zornow, *Kansas*, 124. Edmund Ross replaced James Lane in the Senate after Lane committed suicide.

9. Lawanda and John Cox, "Negro Suffrage and Republican Politics: The Problem of Motivation in Reconstruction Historiography," in Kenneth Stampp and Leon Litwack (eds.), *Reconstruction: An Anthology of Revisionist Writings* (Baton Rouge, 1969), 156; Robert Cruden, *The Negro in Reconstruction* (Englewood Cliffs, 1969), 35.

10. L. and J. Cox, "Negro Suffrage," 160, concur with Kenneth Stampp in the admonition against viewing the "economic motive" as if one were "dealing with reality."

or color." Subjection of Negroes to discrimination was "unjust, unwise, and tyrannical and ought to have no toleration, either by parties or by legislative bodies."[11]

Samuel Wood, a member of the Kansas Senate and formerly prominent in the antislavery campaigns, denounced restricted suffrage in all of its guises. Accordingly, Wood organized the state Impartial Suffrage Association in Topeka in 1867 to provide an agency to disseminate information and to garner support for equal voting rights, "in the broad sense, without regard to sex, race, or color."[12] In tribute to Wood's advocacy, Charles H. Langston, a prominent black attorney from Kansas City, Kansas, asserted that the prospects for achieving that goal would "sink into inactive nothingness or unnoticeable insignificance without Wood's fostering care and powerful assistance." Langston, however, strongly opposed collateral consideration of sex discrimination as "absolutely incompatible . . . with the question of Negro suffrage." In an effort to quiet the furor over Negro suffrage in 1867, former governor Thomas Carney urged Kansas to lead "in the moral work as she had in the great martial work." Joining the crusade spearheaded by Crawford, Wood, and Carney, several prominent Republicans met in Lawrence to help in the campaign for Negro suffrage.[13]

Despite those valiant efforts, the Kansas electorate rejected an amendment to remove the racial qualification for voting in 1867. Of the forty-four counties in the state, only seven returned a majority in favor of the amendment and Shawnee County was not among them. As if the defeat of impartial suffrage in 1867 were not the measure of public attitudes, in 1869 Governor James M. Harvey proclaimed before the state legislature: "Uniformity in the civil and political rights of its citizens should be required of every government." There could be no justification, Harvey

11. Zornow, *Kansas*, 125; *Seventh Annual Message of Governor Samuel J. Crawford: Delivered to the Legislative Assembly of the State* (Reprint; Leavenworth, 1967); Frank W. Blackmar, *Kansas: A Cyclopedia of State History, Embracing Events, Institutions, Counties, Cities, Towns, Prominent Persons, Etc.* (2 vols.; Topeka, 1912), I, 481–83, provides an account of Crawford's administration and refers to the suffrage issue.
12. Zornow, *Kansas*, 124; Caldwell, "The Attitude of Kansas Toward Reconstruction," 57; Wilder, *Annals of Kansas*, 465, 480; "Events of Fifty-Six," *Kansas Historical Collections*, VII (1901–1902), 52–55. The latter source gives a brief sketch of Wood's legislative career.
13. Charles H. Langston to Samuel N. Wood, February 10, 1867, in Samuel N. Wood Papers, KSHS; Zornow, *Kansas*, 124; Caldwell, "The Attitude of Kansas Toward Reconstruction," 60.

concluded, "in the retention of a monopoly of political power in our own favored class of white male citizens." Therefore he urged the state legislature to ask Congress to prescribe uniform, national qualifications for voting.[14] The passage of the Fifteenth Amendment in 1870 took the suffrage issue out of Kansas' hands. Federal law, however, did not lead to the immediate removal of the race qualification for suffrage in the Kansas Constitution. In 1873, Governor Thomas A. Osborn identified that restriction as a "relic of barbarism" long overdue for removal. Although a dead letter after 1870, the word *white* remained affixed to the suffrage clause in the Kansas Constitution until 1888, a clear testament to the law's delay and the state's equivocation on civil liberty for Negroes.[15]

The Kansas statutes permitted race discrimination in the common schools. Local custom and the size of the city, however, determined how segregation was implemented. In 1865, Negro and white children in Topeka attended an elementary school located in a two-story building on Sixth Avenue between Kansas Avenue and Quincy Street. In 1866, however, the school facilities and instruction were segregated by moving the Negro children to the second floor. The teacher who formerly instructed the integrated group taught the Negro pupils. The school hired a new teacher for the white pupils, whose education continued on the ground floor.[16] Topeka, a city of the second class, instituted segregated education one year before the Kansas legislature gave boards of education in cities of that class the discretionary authority to maintain separate schools. The unfolding pattern of segregation did not proceed without dissent from Kansas educators. In 1866 the State Teachers Association sounded a liberal note. That body vowed to "use our best endeavors to overcome unreasonable prejudices existing in certain locali-

---

14. Blackmar, *Kansas: A Cyclopedia*, I, 482–83; Zornow, *Kansas*, 124; *Ninth Annual Message of Governor James M. Harvey: Delivered to the Kansas Legislature, January, 1869* (Topeka, 1869).

15. *Thirteenth Annual Message of Governor Thomas A. Osborn: Delivered to the Kansas Legislature, 1873* (Topeka, 1873); Wilder, *Annals of Kansas*, 480; Loren O. Pickering, "The Administration of John P. St. John," *Transactions of the Kansas State Historical Society*, IX (1905–1906), 382–83, n. 6 regarding Article III, Section 1, of the constitution.

16. Andreas, *History of the State of Kansas*, 268; Paul E. Wilson, "Brown v. Board of Education Revisited," reprinted from *Kansas Law Review*, XII (1964), 511; First through Ninth *Biennial Reports*, Kansas Superintendent of Public Instruction, 1877–1893 (Topeka, 1895). The statistics in the *Biennial Reports* did not designate race in the Kansas school population until 1893, and then by county only. Refer to Tables 7, 8.

ties against the admission of colored children as guaranteed by the spirit of the law of our state."[17]

Events during the ensuing eight years did not bring any respite from discrimination in that area of public accommodations. Segregation, albeit at the discretion of the board of education, would provide a focal point for black-white tensions in Topeka for decades. In January, 1874, Republican State Senator Jacob Winter identified members of the state legislature and of local boards of education who favored segregated schools as "moral dyspeptics who still have the scum and dregs of slavery deeply seated in their unregenerative natures." In fact, Winter censured discrimination in any area of public accommodations. It was unconscionable that "citizens of intelligence, culture, and moral worth are ejected from hotel tables, places of amusement, and ... treated with indignity for no reason other than that the Creator gave them a different color from ours." Perhaps he could be forgiven the subtle prejudice in his invocation to join in the "exalted work of redeeming and elevating fallen humanity"; it was a sustaining theme in the abolitionist crusade and in its postwar manifestations. Winter, moreover, dismissed concepts of Negro inferiority based on the doctrine of evolution: "I don't want Darwin here now to explain anything about them to me." His reference to Negroes as "the sons of Ham," however, is not readily explicable in liberal terms.[18]

Winter's polemic aside, segregation in the common schools remained the norm in Kansas. It was an area of discrimination untouched by the Fourteenth Amendment, and the issue was removed from the provisions of the Civil Rights Act of 1875. Education was the only area of public accommodations in which discrimination had the force of Kansas law. The state statutes of 1874 stipulated that, with the exception of the common schools, segregation in public facilities which required a state

17. Kansas 1865 MS census; Table 8; J. L. King (ed.), *History of Shawnee County*, 230; Wilson, "Brown v. Board of Education Revisited," 510–13; *Kansas Session Laws, 1861*, Chapter LXXVI, Article III, Section 1.

18. "Speech of Honorable Jacob Winter, Delivered Before the Senate of Kansas on Civil Rights, January 26, 1874," in *Kansas Legislative Documents, 1862–1899* (Topeka, 1901), 1–12. For a thorough analysis of how abolitionists invested their reform energies after the Civil War and of their paternalistic attitudes toward Negroes, see James M. McPherson, *The Abolitionist Legacy: From Reconstruction to the NAACP* (Princeton, 1976); Willie Lee Rose, *Rehearsal for Reconstruction: The Port Royal Experiment* (New York, 1964); Louis Harlan, *Booker T. Washington: The Making of a Black Leader, 1856–1901* (New York, 1972).

license was a misdemeanor.[19] Segregated schools and *de facto* discrimination in a myriad of manifestations caused black Topekans and Negroes throughout the state to organize in protest.

The retarded emergence of Negro freedom as a goal of the Civil War and the unrealized potentialities of Reconstruction provided the impetus for organized protest by Kansas Negroes. Such activities were not initiated or sponsored by black Topekans until the 1870s. Nonetheless, under the leadership of black Kansas City attorney Charles H. Langston, Negroes met in Leavenworth in 1863 to protest the legislature's rejection of a resolution to remove the racial qualification for suffrage. They contended that the service of Negroes in the Civil War gave a clear demonstration of their right to the full benefits of citizenship. The Kansas legislature took no action on that petition and reaffirmed its opposition to Negro suffrage in 1864, ostensibly because such action would inundate the state with Negroes.[20]

A convention of colored citizens, meeting in Lawrence in 1866, reiterated the demand for suffrage. Its pronouncements further established the terms of a general assault on discrimination. Accordingly, the convention resolved: "All political power is inherent in the people." It was neither the exclusive domain of class privilege, "an attainment, a reward of conduct, nor an incident of humanity." The right of suffrage, therefore, was not a "conventional privilege merely which may be extended to or withheld from any class of citizens at the will of the majority, but a right as sacred and immovable as the right to life, liberty, and property." The convention disavowed any interest in social equality, that being "a matter of taste and not of legislation." The conferees discussed every aspect of discrimination in Kansas. The vindication of the Union and the United States Constitution compelled them to conclude that the exclusion of Negroes from equal employment and from common carriers, among other public services, was "antidemocratic, inhuman, and unjust."[21] The convention's resolutions were ignored and the state legisla-

---

19. B. D. Reams and Paul E. Wilson, *Segregation and the Fourteenth Amendment in the States: A Survey of State Segregation Laws, 1865–1953* (Buffalo, 1975), vi, 183–86.
20. Caldwell, "The Attitude of Kansas Toward Reconstruction," 51, 52, citing *House Journal*, 1864, pp. 41, 78, 270.
21. *Proceedings of a Convention of Colored Citizens Held in the City of Lawrence, October 17, 1866* (Leavenworth, 1866). The number or identity of Negroes from Topeka at the Leavenworth and Lawrence meetings is unknown from the sources examined.

ture remained adamant in its refusal to remove the offensive stipulations.

Continuing irritation over segregation provided the initial spur for organized protest in Topeka. Before the passage of the statutes of 1874, Negro Topekans, meeting at St. John A.M.E. Church in February, 1873, asserted that segregation in education, in public accommodations, and in common carriers clearly belied the reputation of Kansas and of the Republican party for "complete liberty and exact equality."[22] Discrimination in the workplace was another problem which merited public discussion and joint endeavor. A group of black Topekans meeting at an "African Baptist Church" (Second Baptist) in August, 1872, were aware of that liability as they weighed the merits of supporting a bond issue for bridge construction in the city. William Brooks, a laborer, suggested that unity and a sense of civic pride and responsibility would enhance Negro employment opportunities. In that spirit black Topekans "should stand and work together. If we want employment we must work for the interests of the city and work to build it up." Other spokesmen echoed Brooks's optimism and looked with favor on the King Bridge Company, which had previously obtained a contract for bridge construction in Iola, a town in Shawnee County. John Carter, another laborer, asserted that in his experience the King Bridge Company did not merit a reputation for fair and equal employment of Negroes. Carter also alleged that the Santa Fe Railroad, which had a financial interest in the King Bridge Company, was no less guilty of discrimination: "We hear a great deal about their employing colored men. I am a mechanic, am a harness maker, but can't work at my trade in the shops because I am a colored man. Don't flatter yourself that you will get work. They may employ three or four hundred men, but I tell you there will not be any colored men there. They have dodged us once and they will do it again. Let's vote bonds to somebody who will help us."[23]

The black protest activity conducted under the auspices of the church in 1872 and in 1873 indicates that Topeka Negroes were not merely the passive victims of discrimination. In those forums their lively debates revealed an intelligent awareness of issues and alternatives. From such relatively inconspicuous beginnings, the city's Negroes developed other agencies through which they formulated strategies for race progress

22. *Commonwealth*, February 20, 1873, in *Shawnee County Clippings*, I; Table 5.
23. *Commonwealth*, August 9, 1872.

and for combating discrimination, a problem which did not abate in spite of the provisions of federal and state law. Expansion in the number and in the variety of institutions in black Topeka further strengthened community structure at home and facilitated contacts with Negro activities abroad.

The year 1865 was auspicious for black Topeka's institutional growth. Second Baptist Church, later called First African Baptist, issued its first call to worship from "a brush arbor" on First Avenue and Crane Street and thereby legitimately claimed to be the oldest Negro church organization in Topeka. In 1868, sixteen men and women formed the Prayer Circle and held religious services in a rented barn located in an alley between Harrison and Van Buren streets. That "free lance mission," having neither a denominational affiliation nor a pastor, became St. John A.M.E. Church in 1878 and was destined to be one of the most influential institutions in black Topeka.[24] The 1870s witnessed significant growth in the number of churches, with Methodists and Baptists enjoying the greatest increment. The location of most Negro churches, roughly within a seven-block radius in 1875, helped mold the nascent community into a cohesive unit. The Negro population spread into the several wards after 1875 and founded new religious congregations. Wesleyan A.M.E. Church and Second Colored Presbyterian Church were established in 1878 in the Third Ward. Shiloh Baptist Church, founded in 1880, ministered to the residents of Tennesseetown, an enclave in the Third Ward largely composed of Negro migrants who came to Topeka during the Great Exodus.[25]

The pace of church growth exposes additional phenomena vital for community development. By 1880 the churches provided institutional pillars which gave structural support for the Negro community beyond the immediate neighborhood and the sites of original black settlement in the city. The churches also provided channels for social interaction, social control, and mutual support. In addition, they stood in the breach

---

24. Andreas, *History of the State of Kansas*, 549–50; *Baptist Church Clippings*, I; "Second Small Beginning," (white) Topeka *State Journal*, June 19, 1915; *St. John Souvenir Program*.

25. "Wesleyan A.M.E. Church to Be Replaced by New Structure," *Daily Capital*, January 31, 1915, in *Methodist Church Clippings*, II; John D. Barker, *Souvenir Program of the Seventieth Anniversary of Shiloh Baptist Church, 1949* (Topeka, 1949). See Map 1 for the location of black Topeka churches.

to protect race interests. As early as 1872–1873, in the campaigns against discrimination, St. John A.M.E. and Second Baptist churches had given sanctuary to organized protest; they and other religious institutions would continue to do so in later crises.

By 1875, black fraternal orders increased in number and enjoyed considerable popularity. Occidental Lodge and Euclid Lodge were organized by Negroes in October, 1875, and met at the black Masonic Hall at 127 Kansas Avenue. The Great Western Lodge and the Good Samaritans, founded before 1875, held forth from a meeting hall on the second floor of 108 Kansas Avenue.[26] If the reason for different meeting halls in the 1870s is unclear, the proliferation of such institutions in the 1880s made separate headquarters a necessity. In the flurry of fraternal, social, and protest activity during the ensuing decades, the meetings of one or another organization were held each evening on a published schedule.[27] From the late 1870s through the turn of the century, church membership and social activity were major criteria for defining patterns of intraracial class differentiation. After 1880, affiliation with a political club or a protest group was an additional, important measure of status. Through the foregoing agencies a Negro leadership corps developed.

Thirty-three individuals for whom demographic data are available were identified as officials in church and fraternal associations or otherwise prominent in black Topeka, 1865 through 1875, according to the white local press and other sources. Negroes in Topeka, however, were without their own public voice until the late 1870s. The black press, whose commentary provides an important guide to associational behavior in all subsequent periods, was not established until 1878. Through 1875 no configuration of economics, prestige, and power, as basic determinants of social stratification, effectively distinguished Negro leaders from their fellows. Although there were clear signs of an emergent "interest group" consciousness, moral probity, participation in community institutions, literacy, and stable employment largely determined as-

26. *Radges' Topeka Directory*, 1875–1902; Andreas, *History of the State of Kansas*, 293; Map 1. Like the churches, black and white fraternal orders did not affiliate. No sources gave accurate accounts of membership in black social and fraternal organizations until after 1880. Sources examined to date do not reveal whether Negroes owned the lodge halls in which meetings were held.

27. *Radges' Topeka Directory*, 1875–92; Map 1.

cribed and achieved status; those standards were well within the reach of most.[28] The social-demographic profile of leaders conformed to that of black Topeka at large, thereby obviating the need to treat them as discrete categories.

In 1870 the Negro population in Topeka numbered 473, an increase of 470 percent since 1865, in a total population of 5,790. By 1875 there were 724 black Topekans in a total population of 7,272. That 53 percent increase, if less prodigious than in the previous five years, indicated steady growth. Approximately 25 percent of the population in 1875 had been residents in 1870. Clearly new growth was not the only determinant of demographic change. The lack of persistence indicated considerable flux in Topeka's Negro population. Sex ratio, age range, family size, literacy rate, and occupational profile, however, did not change markedly in black Topeka between 1865 and 1875.[29]

The heaviest concentration of Negroes continued to live adjacent to the Santa Fe Railroad complex near First Avenue in the city's First Ward, although geographical dispersion was one result of the increase in the black population. An additional, relatively smaller number was evenly distributed in the Second Ward, an area which was predominantly white. By 1870, approximately one third of the Negro population lived in the Third Ward in the southwestern part of the city, a region which became the site of migrant settlement during the Exodus of 1879–1880. Blacks and whites in the First and Third wards lived in racially homogeneous clusters within integrated neighborhoods. However, there were no appreciable differences in social, occupational, or economic patterns for Negroes in the several wards.

In 1875 the making of a ghetto did not seem to be an imminent prospect. Only 15 percent of Topeka Negroes lived in regional concentrations that were three-fourths black; in fact, most resided in areas that

---

28. Table 12; Arthur Vidich and Joseph Bensman, *Small Town in Mass Society* (Princeton, 1968), 49–52, 61–62, 76–77, 97, 259; Joseph Kahl, *The American Class Structure* (New York, 1956), 12–14, 159; Max Weber, *Essays from Max Weber*, trans. and ed. H. H. Gerth and C. Wright Mills (New York, 1946), 186–88. In fact, Kahl's reference to "interest group" theory nicely describes the development of class and class perception in Topeka's black institutions: "objective interests in common, recognition of that common bond, an evolving group or class consciousness, and finally, organization to promote the common advantage."

29. U.S. 1870 census; Kansas 1875 MS census; Tables 1–7, 9.

were only one-eighth black.[30] The occupational structure did not become more elaborate in the five-year period ending in 1875. Two ministers were the sum of professionals. Notably, those two individuals, nominally identified as clergymen in newspapers and business directories, were classified as laborers on the census rolls. There is every possibility that they wore both a clerical and a blue collar. The overwhelming majority of Topeka Negroes were common laborers, with fewer than 5 percent enumerated in skilled and service-entrepreneurial occupations.[31]

As in 1865, most Topeka Negroes in 1870 came from Missouri. The next largest number came from Kentucky, with some few from Tennessee and with considerably smaller numbers from the Deep South. By 1875, however, the census reveals an increasing number of Negroes from the Border and the Deep South.[32]

The tremors of demographic change in 1875 forecast the eclipse of Reconstruction and the Great Exodus. The Compromise of 1877 brought to a close nearly a decade of irresolution on the race problem in the South. The return of the Redeemers to power, a journey begun soon after the Civil War, caused an upturn in race-related brutality. Newly arrived black southerners in Topeka well may have apprised the city's Negro community of the building crisis. The development of organized protest as an institution and increasingly variegated associational behavior, moreover, prepared Topeka Negroes to join in the debate over alternatives to southern oppression, one of which was a planned migration to Kansas.[33]

30. With notable inconsistency, the census manuscripts do provide information regarding residence by ward and by street name with some demarcations roughly approximating a city block. Regrettably such information is not precise, being subject to the caprice and schedule of visits by the census taker. Where possible, within each of the designated "blocks," I approximated racial composition, thereby obtaining impressionistic information on ethnic segregation or heterogeneity.

31. *Radges' Topeka Directory*, 1875–76; "Census of the City," *State Journal*, December 29, 1900.

32. Tables 2, 6, 7 are particularly relevant.

33. Cruden, *The Negro in Reconstruction*, 165; John Hope Franklin, *Reconstruction After the Civil War* (Chicago, 1970), 149; Roland L. Warren, *The Community in America* (Chicago, 1963), 11, 162–64, says that the local community is not a discrete or autonomous unit existing solely by virtue of "vertical patterns" that govern the "functional relation of its various social units and subsystems to each other." "Horizontal patterns . . . clearly systematic relationships to extracommunity systems" provide "a strong tie between locally

The debate revealed an additional, critically important dimension of black public awareness which dictated Negro aspirations. As the discussion of economics, politics, and discrimination with regard to the King Bridge Company in 1872 attests, Topeka Negroes displayed a measure of civic pride and hopes for economic success, however circumscribed by discrimination. Their seeming confidence in the state's economic potential was warranted. Throughout the course of Reconstruction, Kansas' devotion to railroads and agriculture was rewarded with prosperity, marred only by the depression of 1873. Indeed, Kansas was a synonym for frontier opportunity. Topeka, moreover, competed favorably with its urban rivals in the marketplace. As a major center for agricultural trading and railroads, Topeka controlled the pace of economic growth in the cow towns on the Kansas prairie and in the agricultural hinterland in general.[34]

Political awareness helped Topeka Negroes measure their gains and losses, during the declining days of Reconstruction, relative to their southern brethren. The efforts of Kansas state officials to eliminate *de jure* segregation doubtless indicated moderation, if not thoroughgoing liberalism, with regard to race matters. By any terms, migration to Kansas emerged as a reasoned alternative to oppression against southern blacks and as a result of informed debate; therein, Kansas' vaunted economic abundance was an important auxiliary consideration. Thus the migration of blacks to Kansas and to Topeka between 1870 and 1880 was nearly as much a move toward frontier opportunity as an escape from deteriorating conditions in the South.

On a visit to Topeka in October, 1870, Horace Greeley, editor of the New York *Tribune*, observed: "Settlers are pouring into eastern Kansas

---

based units such as . . . governments . . . and social systems extending far beyond the confines of the local community."

34. Dykstra, *The Cattle Towns*, 4, 50; Daniel J. Boorstin, "Competitive Communities on the Western Frontier," in Kenneth T. Jackson and Stanley K. Shultz (eds.), *Cities in American History* (New York, 1972), 9–10; George L. Anderson, "Atchison and the Central Branch Country," *Four Essays on Railroads in Kansas and Colorado* (Lawrence, 1971), 8, 13. One of the limitations in the analyses by Dykstra and by Boorstin is the absence of comparative data on towns in regions other than southwestern and western Kansas. Anderson's comparison between Atchison and Topeka is informative, if weighted toward town founding as well as the geography and economics of antislavery activity.

by car loads, wagon loads, [and] horse-loads daily, because of the fertility of her soil . . . her admirable diversity of prairie and timber . . . and the marvelous facility wherewith homesteads may be created." George Marlowe, a Negro representing the State Labor Union, a black emigration agency in Louisiana, visited Kansas for eight days in August, 1871, and submitted the following glowing report: "What is raised yields more profit than elsewhere, and it is raised at less expense. The weather and the roads enable you to do more work than elsewhere. The climate is mild and pleasant. The winters, short and require little food for stock. Money plenty, and what you raise commands a good price. The country is well watered . . . [and] produces 40–100 bushels of corn and wheat to the acre and the corn grows 8 to 9 feet high."[35] The railroads also helped engender the belief that frontier opportunity was available to all. The Santa Fe Railroad published *A Sketch of the Garden of the West*, which gave information on agricultural productivity, land prices, and transportation, as well as testimonials to success in frontier Kansas. Bright promises were self-evident in publicity circulars and in chromographs of Negro farmers enjoying the fullness of the state's bounty. Similar types of promotional materials from the Santa Fe Railroad received wide currency in Europe. Likewise, Jay Gould and the Union Pacific Railroad encouraged emigration to Kansas. Such reports and promotions gave blacks, whites, and foreigners much to conjure with.[36]

The tendency to migrate has been a central component of the American experience. The validity of Frederick Jackson Turner's "safety-valve" hypothesis aside, Ray Allen Billington, the western historian, is correct: Americans "often popularly expressed [and] never questioned" the idea that westward migration provided a "social-psychological safety valve" for relieving class antagonism and economic disparity. That view

---

35. New York *Tribune*, October 18, 1870, cited in Wilder, *Annals of Kansas*, 532; *Howard Report*, 19.

36. "How and Where to Get a Living," *A Sketch of the Garden of the West* (Boston, 1876); "Exodusters," in Frank H. Betton, *First Annual Report of the Kansas Bureau of Labor and Industrial Statistics, 1886* (Topeka, 1887), 253; George R. Hovey, "How the Negroes Were Duped," *Journal of Negro History*, IV (1919), 55; undated, untitled newspaper article, in *Benjamin Singleton Scrapbook*; U.S. Congress, Senate, *Report and Testimony of the Select Committee of the United States Senate to Investigate the Causes for the Removal of the Negroes from the Southern States to the Northern States* (Washington, D.C., 1880), pt. 3, pp. 362–64, hereinafter cited as *Senate Reports*; *Howard Report*, 1–4. The *Senate Reports* make comparative reference to the inducements to blacks and to Europeans encouraging settlement.

was not based on measurable realities; it was an item of belief—a "proletarian philosophy," as it were.[37] The confrontation between blacks and whites, of course, turned on issues related primarily to racial animosity. In addition, however, there was a dimension of class antagonism and economic disparity in that conflict. By these terms, the impetus for black migration to the West may be viewed as a response to economic and social distinctions similar to those perceived by many Americans; it was not exclusively an "Anglo-Saxon" phenomenon. For Americans of both races, the collective representation of the West conveyed, in Henry Nash Smith's discerning analysis, "the power of the myth of the Garden over men's perceptions and imaginations."[38]

The State Labor Union, which sponsored George Marlowe's visit to Kansas in 1871, was part of a larger organized movement by blacks to investigate the prospects for western settlement. The Colonization Council, founded in Louisiana by Henry Adams in 1869, and the Tennessee Real Estate and Homestead Association, begun in Nashville by Benjamin "Pap" Singleton, Columbus M. Johnson, and Alonzo D. DeFrantz in the same year, were prominent agencies in that movement.[39] In May, 1874, in a "call for an Investigating Meeting," Singleton and

37. Everett Lee, "The Turner Thesis Re-Examined," in Richard Hofstadter and Seymour M. Lipset (eds.), *Turner and the Sociology of the Frontier* (New York, 1968), 66, 72, says that migration has been "a force of greatest moment in American civilization," whose significance is not diminished by modern social-scientific reevaluations of Turner's Frontier Thesis; Ray Allen Billington, *America's Frontier Heritage* (New York, 1966), 31, 33.

38. Robert G. Athearn, "Black Exodus: The Migration of 1879," *Prairie Scout*, III (1975), 92; Robert G. Athearn, *In Search of Canaan: Black Migration to Kansas, 1879–1880* (Lawrence, 1978), 3, 253–54, concedes that the motivations and incentives which spurred the Exodus were not different in kind from those which "attracted millions of immigrants to the West," but his collateral reference to the "emotional nature of the people involved" is devoid of historical or social-scientific content; Henry Nash Smith, *Virgin Land: The American West as Symbol and Myth* (Cambridge, 1950), 183.

39. Nell Irvin Painter, *Exodusters: Black Migration to Kansas After Reconstruction* (New York, 1977), 87–95, 113–16; *Senate Reports*, pt. 3, p. 380, and pt. 2, pp. 101–103. Painter provides the definitive analysis of social, intellectual, and political factors in the South which led to organized plans for black migration and concludes with the arrival in Kansas. The *Senate Reports* cited provide data on the Colonization Council and the organization of the Tennessee Real Estate and Homestead Association. Howard Bell, *The Negro Convention Movement, 1830–1861* (New York, 1969), 260; J. C. Hartzell, "The Negro Exodus," *Methodist Quarterly Review*, XXXIX (1879), 725; John Hope Franklin, "Reconstruction and the Negro," in Harold M. Hyman (ed.), *New Frontiers of American Reconstruction* (Chicago, 1966), 67. The foregoing sources support the view that migration as an alternative to race oppression had considerable tenure; it merited serious consideration in the Negro Convention movement in the 1830s. Hartzell asserts, moreover, that a "Baptist Association in Louisiana" actively promoted migration, as did benevolent and secret societies.

other spokesmen viewed emigration to Kansas as the embodiment of racial self-confidence and as an article of faith with strong millenarian overtones.[40] A fundamental element in plans for western settlement, however, was an urgent desire to get away from white mob violence as well as race-related civil and economic disorder in the South.

Plans for western settlement did not proceed without dissent. Divergent opinions regarding the merits of the Kansas emigration generated a lively debate among Negro leaders. The selection of emigration or political involvement as means of achieving substantive civil liberty during Reconstruction reflected intraracial antagonisms based on class and economic cleavage which existed before the war.[41] Invidious class distinctions between "political Negroes" and "the men who worked" were evident in the pronouncements of Singleton and Adams in advocating emigration. "Not a political Negro was in it," Singleton declared before the Senate committee investigating the migration. "Oh, no, it was the muscle of the arm, the men that worked that we wanted," Singleton asserted. As if to reemphasize the implicit class antagonism, Singleton concluded: "This thing was got up by an ignorant class of men." Henry Adams, no less than Singleton avoided identification with black politicians for reasons grounded in distrust and social distance. When asked by the committee about the involvement of politicians in the Colonization Council, Adams asserted: "No politicianers [sic] didn't belong to it, because we didn't allow them to know nothing about it, because we was afraid that if we allowed the colored politicianer to belong to it he would tell it to the Republican politicianers, and from that the men that was doing all this to us would get hold of it, too, and then get after us." It is significant that Republican office seekers, black as well as white, were equally subject to censure. "No; we didn't trust any of them," Adams

---

40. Nell Irvin Painter, "Millenarian Aspects of the Exodus to Kansas," *Journal of Social History*, IX (1976), 339; *Singleton Scrapbook*; Nashville *Republican Banner*, April 25, 1875, cited in Painter, *Exodusters*, 148. In 1875, Singleton published a circular, "To the Colored People of Tennessee," to dispel rumors of free transportation, supplies, and land in Kansas. The *Singleton Scrapbook* contains a variety of newspaper articles, brochures, and publicity materials on Singleton's activity with regard to Negro migration to Kansas, 1870–80.

41. Franklin, "Reconstruction and the Negro," 67; August Meier and Elliott Rudwick, *From Plantation to Ghetto* (New York, 1970), 91. The development of separate black-and-tan fellowship societies during the antebellum period roughly approximated distinctions based on color and class during Reconstruction.

reiterated. "Nobody but laboring men" were privy to the endeavors and proceedings of the Colonization Council.[42] The alienation of Singleton and Adams from Reconstruction politics and from black politicians in particular was largely self-induced. Their assertion of independence provided a means of putting the organized emigration effort beyond the reach of those whom they identified as agents of social control.

Negro emigration, however, was not without support within the ranks of the black political establishment. John Mercer Langston, a member of the abolitionist vanguard and a prominent statesman, identified the Exodus of 1879 as an expression of the freedmen's "exigent demand for independence without which no individual and no people can rise to the level of dignified and honorable manhood." Among other tangible benefits of emigration for the freedman, "contact with new men, new things, a new order of life, [and] new moral and educational influences will advance him in the scale of being in an incomparably short time, even beyond the expectations of the most sanguine."[43] Black political leaders such as Blanche K. Bruce and John R. Lynch, who rose to prominence during Reconstruction, believed that Negroes should remain in the South and that political action provided the best guarantee of civil liberty. Allegations of duplicity and vested interest, the basis for the indictment of black politicians by the emigration leaders, were exaggerated. Rather, as Billy D. Higgins asserts, "concentrations of protected black votes appeared to them indispensable for black successes." With their own tenure in office also at issue, however, the solutions proposed by Negro politicians "did not run toward dissipation of black constituencies through large-scale migrations."[44] Bruce and Lynch were no

42. *Senate Reports*, pt. 3, pp. 380–81, and pt. 2, p. 105.
43. John Mercer Langston, "Exodus Address," reprinted in *Freedom and Citizenship: Selected Lectures and Addresses* (Washington, D.C., 1879), 240, 251. There is something of Social Darwinism in Langston's reference to the Negro's place in the "scale of being." This suggests familiarity with period intellectual and social currents.
44. Sadie D. St. Clair, "The National Career of Senator Blanche K. Bruce" (Ph.D. dissertation, New York University, 1947), 167; Billy D. Higgins, "Negro Thought in the Exodus," *Phylon*, XXII (1971), 46; for additional information on Blanche K. Bruce, see *Dictionary of American Biography*, XIV, 61; *Appleton's Cyclopedia*, XIX, 357–58; (black) Topeka *American Citizen*, May 28, 1888. Higgins provides a well-written, informed analysis of the black intellectual crosscurrents regarding the merits and liabilities of the Negro migration to Kansas. In St. Clair's opinion, Bruce's absence from the Senate chambers when the vote was taken to convene the committee to investigate the Exodus indicated his "inability, if not his unwillingness" to exercise his influence on that controversial issue. The *American Citizen* article pushed for Bruce's candidacy for vice-president on the Republican ticket.

less committed to the cause of Negro liberty than were the emigration leaders. One suspects that anything short of their wholesale endorsement of emigration would have invited an accusation of political duplicity by Singleton and Adams.

Frederick Douglass was not actively involved in Reconstruction politics. Yet, he too believed that the emigration was inimical to the interest of southern Negroes: "Without abating one jot of our horror and indignation at the outrages committed in some parts of the southern states against the Negro, we cannot but regard the present agitation of an African Exodus from the South as ill-timed, and in some respects harmful." Endorsement of the Exodus of 1879 required "the surrender of a great principle," a concession that the government had no power to enforce the Constitution and the law. With unwarranted optimism, Douglass believed that in the 1870s, Negroes were "at the beginning of a grand and beneficent reaction," supported by "a growing recognition of the duty and obligation of the American people to guard, protect, and defend the personal and political rights of all the people of the states." A mass migration from the South would leave the Negro without moorings; "he is again, alas! in the deepest trouble without a home."[45]

In the last analysis, each spokesman articulated his perception of truth and the interests of the race. Faced with their own pressing realities and no less subject to wisdom, foolishness, and hope, southern Negroes in ever-increasing numbers were "linking their destiny for weal or woe with that of the young and thrifty states of the great Northwest."[46] Before the middle of the 1870s, the clarion call of the Tennessee Real Estate and Homestead Association, "Ho, For Sunny Kansas," gave vent to those collateral aspirations.

Singleton first visited Kansas in 1873 accompanied by two or three hundred settlers. They were bound for Cherokee County, in the southeastern corner of the state. Ostensibly that site was chosen in order to locate "as near the sunny South as possible." An indeterminate number in that party, however, opted for the city and moved farther north to Topeka. The city also was a staging ground for black migrants on their

---

45. Philip Foner, *The Life and Writings of Frederick Douglass* (4 vols.; New York, 1950–55), IV, 334–35, 327–28.
46. O. S. B. Wald to John Mercer Langston, September 16, 1879, reprinted in *Freedom and Citizenship*, 232.

way to Nicodemus, an all-black town founded in 1877 in Graham County, in the central part of the state, among other black colonies on the frontier.⁴⁷ Joel Williamson describes a similar momentum between town and country among South Carolina Negroes during Reconstruction. A search for employment and occupational mobility may have generated black population movement to and within Kansas. Stephan Thernstrom identifies that dynamic in the shifting residence of laborers between urban environments around Newburyport, Massachusetts, between 1850 and 1880.⁴⁸

Throughout the decade 1870–1880 the emigration of black southerners to Kansas gathered force. From scattered but organized beginnings, the streams of migrants became a torrent, culminating in the mass exodus of over 25,000 persons in 1879–1880.⁴⁹ The level of planning and preparation for the migration dropped off sharply after 1875. At all stages of the migration, however, the movement of black southerners to Kansas was neither "leaderless" nor "an unreasoned, almost mindless" pursuit of "some vague idea, some western paradise," as Robert G. Athearn concludes.⁵⁰ Declaring his just claim to opportunity on the frontier, one migrant provided a cogent rejoinder: "That's what white men go to new countries for isn't it? You do not tell them to stay back because they are poor. Who was the Homestead Act made for if it was

47. *Commonwealth*, March 25, 1879, in *Singleton Scrapbook*; Roy Garvin, "Benjamin, or 'Pap,' Singleton and His Followers," *Journal of Negro History*, XXXIII (1948), 6–11; Glen Schwendemann, "Nicodemus: Negro Haven on the Solomon," *Kansas Historical Quarterly*, XXXIV (1968), 16–19; Henry King, "A Year of the Exodus in Kansas," *Scribner's Monthly* (May–October, 1880), 212. Though lacking in documentation, Garvin's article is a valuable source for data on individuals and otherwise unreported events attendant to the Exodus. Schwendemann provides the best description of the economic conditions in Nicodemus colony and his ground-breaking, thorough research of the Exodus in general has been an important contribution. Henry King reported that the income of Negro farmers was $2.50 per head per annum, a figure that did not portend immediate success in agriculture.

48. Garvin, "Singleton and His Followers," 9; Joel Williamson, *After Slavery: The Negro in South Carolina During Reconstruction, 1861–1877* (Chapel Hill, 1965), 32–44; Stephan Thernstrom, *Poverty and Progress: Social Mobility in a Nineteenth Century City* (Cambridge, 1964), 90–92.

49. Carter G. Woodson, *A Century of Negro Migration* (Lancaster, Pa., 1918), 141; Painter, *Exodusters*, 256; Giles, *Thirty Years in Topeka*, 368; Andreas, *History of the State of Kansas*, 293. Woodson estimated that 60,000 southern blacks had arrived in Kansas by April, 1880. This figure is a bit exaggerated. Painter estimated that number at 25,000. In formal contemporary accounts, the number of Exodusters in Kansas between 1879 and 1880 varied from 20,000 to 40,000. One suspects that the spreading alarm made most contemporary estimates meaningless.

50. Athearn, *In Search of Canaan*, 4–5, 7.

not for poor men?" Proclaimed another newly arrived black southerner, "We are an integral part of the American people." In a fitting assessment of conditions in the South and a timely admonition to the nation, that spokesman concluded: "You can not oppress us without doing violence to yourselves." One wonders if white migrants had to reason out their alternatives with such acuity and rigor. Although the state's equanimity degenerated into alarm as the migration reached its height in 1879–1880, the *New West*, a journal which promoted settlement in Kansas, viewed the increase in Negro emigration in 1878 with guarded optimism: "Whatever befalls them in Kansas they at least have a chance to rise and fall on their own merits."[51]

The pattern of migrant settlement was split nearly evenly between urban and rural environments. Emigrating blacks were arriving in Topeka at a rate of 250 to 300 per month throughout 1879. Similar estimates were reported in local newspapers in cities along the Exodus route, through Wyandotte, Lawrence, and Topeka.[52] While the black population of Kansas increased 32 percent more than the white population from 1875 to 1880, the black growth rate in Topeka itself was 323 percent greater than the growth of the white population in this period. In fact, Topeka experienced a higher increase in Negro population than any other city in Kansas. By 1880, black Topekans numbered 3,648 in a total population of 15,528, a 404 percent increase since 1875; most in that new increment came between 1878 and 1880. Swollen numbers and demographic flux resulted, in part, from Topeka's importance as a conduit for migration to the western counties. Topeka, moreover, was the center for the activity of the Kansas Freedmen's Relief Association (KFRA), inaugurated to provide a system of social welfare and philanthropy for indigent Exodusters.[53]

51. *Commonwealth*, June 6, 1879; undated, untitled article, (white) Topeka *Tribune*, in *Singleton Scrapbook*; "Negro Migration," *New West*, II (April, 1878), 24–27.

52. Giles, *Thirty Years in Topeka*, 368; Andreas, *History of the State of Kansas*, 293; Glen Schwendemann, "Wyandotte and the First Exodusters of 1879," *Kansas Historical Quarterly*, XXVI (1960), 233; Clark and Roberts, *People of Kansas*, 74–75, 79. The percentage of Kansas' population living in cities rose steadily from 1860 through the turn of the century, spelled only by the rush for the farm between 1870 and 1880. The number of urban dwellers, however, climbed dramatically during that decade. And the number of cities having a population of 10,000 or more increased from one to three. The total population in those cities more than doubled, from 17,873 to 47,103.

53. Clark and Roberts, *People of Kansas*, 50; J. L. King (ed.), *History of Shawnee County*, 167; Kansas 1875 MS census; U.S. 1880 census; Table 1.

The population figures for black Topeka in 1880, 1885, and 1895 were obtained through a stratified random sample from the federal and state censuses. Selecting every fourth dwelling unit yielded 887 individuals out of a total black population of 3,648 in 1880. The 1880 federal census enumerated the Barracks, established by the KFRA to provide room and board for a selection of Exodusters, 127 of whom were in residence when the census was taken. The Barracks, however, was not a permanent residence; rather, it was a halfway house for migrants whose indigency or health did not permit immediate settlement in the community at large. With the exception of the Barracks, the 1880 census revealed the Exodus as an accomplished fact. The number of Exodusters in Topeka, of course, greatly exceeded the Barracks population. The following formula provided a means of identifying a selection of Negroes newly arrived in Topeka between 1879 and 1880. All black families within the random sample which contained a natural child two years of age or younger in 1880 and born in the South were identified as Exodusters. One hundred sixteen individuals fell into that category. Unavoidably, Exodusters who were single, childless, or who had adolescent children were not discernible in the Negro population. The lack of persistence makes more difficult the definition of the demography of black Topeka. Indeed, only 34 percent of the Negro population from 1875 is found in 1880.

Continuity prevailed in many social-demographic dimensions of life in black Topeka. In 1880, newly arrived and resident Negroes were fairly evenly distributed in Topeka wards, with the exception of the Fourth Ward, a sparsely settled region in the westernmost portion of the city. The increase in numbers, however, was manifest in greater racial concentration. In 1880, 15 percent of the total Negro population lived in all-black neighborhoods, a phenomenon not in evidence in 1875. Exodusters, moreover, lived in more dense racial concentration than did established residents. After 1880, Negro enclaves became clearly discernible. Among them were Redmonsville or Up in the Sands in the First Ward, and Tennesseetown in the Third Ward. That region was the site of heavy Exoduster settlement.[54]

---

54. Map 1; Tables 1, 10, 11. The restructuring of the city into four wards in 1873 established new physical, geographic patterns in the distribution of Topeka Negroes. The

The states of origin of the black population did not change by 1880; the Border South continued to contribute the greatest number. A majority of established residents and Exodusters lived in primary households. The low percentage of extended households across the board suggests that Exodusters had no greater propensity for moving in with relatives than did the established residents. By the same token, at least 50 percent of all elements in the black population lived in households containing one to five members. Unskilled labor continued to be the mainstay of the black occupational structure for all adult males and heads of household. To no less a degree than in 1875, the employment of women and children was not common. Without significant exception, those women who did work were domestic servants. Black skilled laborers in 1880 were a distinct minority. It is worth noting, however, that all of the carpenters and stonemasons in Topeka were Exodusters. It is conceivable that such skilled laborers found work at the state capitol, which underwent a continuous process of expansion and repair from 1869 through 1903. Although the number of service entrepreneurs and professionals who arrived during the Exodus was considerably smaller than that of laborers, they represented a manifold increase since 1875, and their presence gave a massive infusion of needed services to the black community. There were disparities in literacy among the several elements in the Negro population. The established residents were more literate than the Exodusters living in town; the latter, in turn, had higher literacy rates than migrants residing in the Barracks.[55]

The demographic, economic, and social distinctiveness of the Exodusters was incommensurate with the storm created by their presence in the city. The occupants of the Barracks and the Exodusters in general were censured by Negro and white Topekans alike. They and untold numbers of other new black migrants became the object of far-reaching

---

Second Ward encompassed the established Negro community and extended from First Avenue near the south side of the Kansas River to Sixth Avenue. The Third Ward covered a large geographical area embracing Tennesseetown in west Topeka. The Fourth Ward, adjacent to the Second Ward on the west, had no distinct black enclave.

55. Giles, *Thirty Years in Topeka*, 256–65; "Kansas and Her Capitol," *Kansas Industrial Development Commission Report* (Topeka, 1901); Katzman, *Before the Ghetto*, 111; U.S. 1880 census; Tables 2–7. The tendency of newly arrived migrants in Topeka to gravitate into menial employment, irrespective of their prior experience as skilled labor, also was observed by Katzman in Detroit.

programs of the KFRA, which attracted national and worldwide attention. White response to black, and black response to black in an atmosphere of neoabolitionism and prejudice set the tone for events in the Negro community through the 1880s.

Chapter 3
The Exodus

There was little evidence of either rancor or cordiality in Topeka race relations before 1879. The accustomed social distance between Negroes and whites continued, and Reconstruction defined the legal terms of that relationship. Like most Americans, whites in Topeka were grateful for the respite from the race problem signified by the Compromise of 1877. Negro Topekans acknowledged their gains and retained guarded faith in the benefits of Republican ascendancy. Discrimination in the franchise, in education, and in accommodations, however, caused blacks to gird themselves for a longer campaign for racial justice.

The gradual increase of the Topeka Negro population through 1878 caused no alarm among whites. The even pace of black migration since the Civil War brought diversity and welcome numbers to Topeka's black community. The swelling masses of Negroes swept into Topeka by the Exodus, however, generated controversy. Between April and August 1, reported one chronicler, "fully 7,000 refugees arrived in this state" of whom "at least 3,000 . . . passed through Topeka."[1] As the site of the only statewide, comprehensive social welfare and resettlement program, Topeka experienced the full impact of the Exodus. Irrespective of race, Topekans were disquieted by the arrival of the Exodusters. Indeed, there were significant parallels in their response to the migration. The white and the black press expressed the community's widening concern.

On April 25 the Topeka *Daily Capital* naïvely predicted that, in time,

1. Andreas, *History of the State of Kansas*, 292–93; *Commonwealth*, March 18, 1880; J. L. King (ed.), *History of Shawnee County*, 168.

the Exodus would resolve itself into relative obscurity: "The wonder will then be how sensible people could have allowed themselves to be excited and alarmed over a matter of such comparative insignificance as the arrival of a few thousand colored people." All appearances, however, suggested sharp contrasts between the newly arrived blacks and the established Negro community. Observing the flood of migrant blacks arriving in Tennesseetown, the Topeka *Commonwealth* reported with dismay, "The colored people who are or who have been in Topeka prior to Sunday are not of this lot." On July 13 the *Commonwealth* reiterated the implicit distinction between the Exodusters and the city's resident Negro population: "For the past four or five years colored people in considerable numbers have been coming to this state but their coming attracted no more attention than that of other nationalities until, when they in large numbers and in destitute condition, brought their coming directly before the people of the State in such a manner as to produce considerable excitement, and, in some quarters a great deal of bad feeling was excited and decided opposition was expressed."[2]

In a matter of a few months, commentary on the Exodus in Topeka's Negro press went from ardent support to caution. The Topeka *Colored Citizen* (November 30, 1878) celebrated the "First Phase" of the Exodus and pronounced an anathema on the Redeemers: "Our advice then is to the people of the South, Come West, Come to Kansas . . . in order that you may be free from the persecution, and cruelty, and the deviltry of the rebel wretches."[3] The fame of the state, proclaimed the *Colored Citizen* (March 29, 1879), "has gone abroad and poor white men and poor black men by the thousands have for years been pouring into the state and will continue to pour in until her lands are all taken." In view of the black southerners' diminishing alternatives, the *Colored Citizen* concluded: "If they come here and starve, all well. It is better to starve to death in Kansas than be shot and killed in the South." As early as May, however, an article in that newspaper revealed black Topeka's in-

---

2. *Daily Capital*, April 25, 1879; *Commonwealth*, May 25, July 13, 1879, in *NC*, I.
3. Glen Schwendemann, "The Negro Exodus to Kansas: The First Phase, March–July, 1879" (M.A. thesis, University of Oklahoma, 1958). His term, "First Phase," is merely a chronological reference point for early events attendant to the migration. The (black) Topeka *Tribune* and the (black) Topeka *Kansas Herald*, Topeka's other two Negro newspapers published between 1878 and 1881, are available only for discontinuous dates in 1879–80. For more detailed reference to black Topeka newspapers, see Chapter 4.

creasingly equivocal response to the migrants: "The reports circulated . . . that the colored people coming to Kansas would receive a home free or anything else free is false." The Exodusters would be well advised to "remember that in Kansas everybody must work or starve. This is a great state for the energetic and industrious, but a fearful poor one for the idle or lazy man; root hog or die is the motto here."[4] The same theme was evident in the white press. In the view of the Topeka *Weekly Times*, "Nothing will elevate the [Negro] race more than to be thrown upon their own resources, and taught by experience to think, act and provide for themselves." Accordingly, "the better nature of a man" is achieved by the awareness that "he has his own future to hew out; that upon his own individual efforts alone he must depend."[5]

A proprietary interest in the established community and a sense that the new black arrivals had to earn their place and keep defined Topeka's response to the Exodus. Topekans of both races practiced some variant of discrimination against the migrants. However dire their condition and legitimate their cause, the migrants seemed to contradict the ideal of self-reliance, an ethos endorsed by white and Negro Topekans.[6] A decisive factor in shaping public opinion was that the Exodusters were poor and alien. The journalist Henry King's description of the Exodusters who congregated in Wyandotte reflected the prevailing impression of migrants in cities along the Exodus route: "They were of all ages and sizes, and every modulation of duskiness, these newcomers; their garments were incredibly patched and tattered, stretched and uncertain; their 'plunder' as they called it, resembled the litter of a neglected backyard; and there was probably not a dollar in money in the pockets of the entire party."[7] One Exoduster's description of the stark conditions at an unidentified migrant encampment in Kansas became a poignant supplication: "We are here with women and children, starving and freezing, we want you to help us, we will die if you don't. We can get no house or work. We live in tents and are not allowed to burn wood. Please help us . . . God in Heaven knows we are suffering." "It is in fact a pauper

---

4. *Colored Citizen*, March 29, 1, May 3, 1879. The rumor of "forty acres and a mule" received wide circulation in the South. Railroads, the Tennessee Real Estate and Homestead Association, and other agencies were accused of encouraging the migration.
5. (White) Topeka *Weekly Times*, March 11, 1881, in *Shawnee County Clippings*, III.
6. Athearn, "Black Exodus," 92; Athearn, *In Search of Canaan*, 253–54.
7. H. King, "A Year of the Exodus in Kansas," 211.

immigration," reported the *Nation*, "and as such it is not heartily welcomed by the people of Kansas."[8] Philanthropy was a clear and pressing need, but from whom?

Municipal officials were steadfast in their objection to the expenditure of public monies or the use of municipal facilities to aid the migrants. Michael C. Case, mayor of Topeka and a Republican, did not believe that the city's 15,500 inhabitants could be expected to underwrite the expense of caring for the Exodusters. Time and money would be better spent sending the migrants back to the South. Case dismissed oppression by the Redeemers as a just reward for those Negroes "who were always talking politics."[9]

A review of state laws regarding indigency sheds some light on the response of municipal and county government to the Exodus. The mayor and the town council of incorporated cities, empowered to act as "Overseers of the Poor," were required to "enter into a poor book all names of indigent persons in the Township." An additional duty of the overseers was "to examine in the name of the poor complaints that the poor have not been sufficiently provided with 'the common necessities of life.'" If a poor book was kept, no such record survives. Although six months' residence defined legal settlement, state law made the following provisions: "It shall be the duty of the Overseers to the poor, on complaint made to them that any person not an inhabitant of their township is lying sick therein, or in distress without friends or money, so that he or she is likely to suffer, to examine into the case of such [a] person and grant such temporary relief as the nature of the same may require."[10] The stated predisposition of Mayor Case in this matter and the absence of any expenditure of municipal funds to aid the Exodusters indicate the abdication of legal responsibility by local government.

The board of county commissioners was required to "relieve and support all poor and indigent persons lawfully settled therein." That

---

8. T. H. Well to Governor John P. St. John, undated, in *Exodus Matters*; E. L. Godkin, "The Flight of the Negroes," *Nation* (April, 1879), 242.

9. *Senate Reports*, pt. 3, pp. 18, 20; Athearn, "Black Exodus," 90. Irrespective of the current crisis, Mayor Case and the Topeka black community were at odds over a wide range of issues.

10. C. F. W. Dassler, *Compiled Laws of the State of Kansas* (St. Louis, 1879), Chapter XXIX, Sections 1, 9, 10; *Kansas General Laws, 1862* (Topeka, 1863), Chapter CLXIII, Sections 10, 4, 24.

agency, moreover, "may raise money for the support and employment of the poor." "Any attempt to directly or indirectly send or cause to be sent out of the county any pauper or persons who are likely to become the objects of public charity" was a misdemeanor punishable by a fine and/or imprisonment.[11] Conceivably, the use of the word *may* permitted the board of county commissioners to act at its own discretion in refusing to raise monies or otherwise aid the Exodusters. Nonetheless, there is no indication of efforts to expel the Exodusters from the county. The only action indicating the positive support of the law was the employment of ten Exodusters in the construction and repair of the state capitol. The archives yield little regarding Topeka's response to poverty in 1880. Jail records are spotty and the designation of race is inconclusive for the Exodus period. The census, which identifies race in institutional populations in 1885 and 1895, is rudimentary on that issue in 1875. The 1880 census also provides no precise measure of social welfare recipiency. Henry King, however, gives a summary analysis of the official response, city and county: "The fact is worth recording here that not a dollar of public funds has ever been expended in any way for the colored immigrants in Kansas; even the sick and infirm have been taken care of without municipal or county help."[12]

A brief comparison of the response of Kansas government to the Exodus and to the Grasshopper Plague in 1874 is revealing. The state quickly harnessed its resources to meet the distressed conditions in 1874, and Governor Thomas A. Osborn convened a special session of the legislature to pass emergency appropriations, to grant extensions on farm mortgages, and to float state relief bonds. Public money, moreover, was expended through private citizens and organizations. Notably, the federal government made available surplus stocks and supplies to aid the victims in 1874.

According to the Topeka *Commonwealth* (April 19, 1879), the state leg-

11. *Compiled Laws, 1879*, Chapter XXIX, Sections 4, 39, 40; Grace Browning, *The Development of Poor Relief Legislation in Kansas* (Chicago, 1935), provides a comprehensive, if dated, survey of the history of social welfare in Kansas. That source, however, contains no specific references to the Exodus period.
12. *Kansas Herald*, January 30, 1880; Index, Topeka City Jail, 1875–85, in KSHS; Kansas 1875, 1885 MS census; Kansas State Census Manuscripts, Shawnee County, 1895, in Microfilm Division, KSHS Archives, Reels 142, 143, 144; H. King, "A Year of the Exodus in Kansas," 212.

islature would not be in session for two years and, unless a special session were convened, no state funds could be appropriated. No explanations have been discovered for Governor St. John's not taking this course of action. It would be conjectural to compare the relative extent of economic dislocation in the two crises. The Grasshopper Plague was a greater economic calamity. The contrasts in the pattern of state action in 1874 and in 1879, however, suggest race prejudice.[13]

Topeka's escape from civic responsibility for a sustained relief effort was no less evident in other Kansas cities. Mayor J. S. Stockton of Wyandotte received some attention through an appeal to Washington for aid.[14] In April, Kansas Senator John J. Ingalls responded to Stockton's request and introduced Senate Bill 472 for the relief of "destitute colored persons now migrating from the southern states." The senator sought an appropriation of $100,000 to be expended by George W. McCrary, secretary of war. Ingalls gave a litany of problems regarding Exoduster relief and settlement, identifying the crisis as a national responsibility requiring "immediate and efficient action." The bill, however, was defeated.[15] During the same month, McCrary refused the request of George W. Shelley, mayor of Kansas City, Kansas, for provisions and the use of the facilities at Fort Leavenworth to aid the migrants. Representative James A. Garfield of Ohio introduced House Resolution 523 requesting an appropriation of $5,000 and an authorization for the secretary of war to issue tents and rations to the freedmen. As with other requests, the Garfield resolution was defeated.[16] In rejecting an appeal for relief requested by Kansas Governor John P. St. John, Kansas

13. *House Journal*, 1874, contains Special Session Laws (see Chapter VI, Sections 1, 2), Governor Osborn's message, and "Proceedings of Governor Thomas A. Osborn," 3; see also Governor Osborn's message, *House Journal*, 1875, p. 21.; James C. Carey, "People, Problems, Prohibition, Politicos, and Politics, 1870–1880," in John D. Bright (ed.), *Kansas: The First Century* (4 vols.; New York, 1956), I, 298.
14. Schwendemann, "Wyandotte," 233–36, 242–46, and "The Negro Exodus to Kansas," 84, 88–89. Although there was no overt violence in Topeka during the Exodus period, incidents were reported in Wyandotte; see Glen Schwendemann, "The Exodusters on the Missouri," *Kansas Historical Quarterly*, XXIX (1963), 39. Garvin, "Singleton and His Followers," 14. On Mayor Stockton and the response of Wyandotte to the Exodus, also see Athearn, *In Search of Canaan*, 38–39.
15. *Congressional Record*, 46th Cong., 1st Sess., pt. 1, pp. 620, 661, also cited in Schwendemann, "Wyandotte," 241.
16. *Commonwealth*, April 18, 1879, in *NC*, I; *Congressional Record*, 46th Cong., 1st Sess., pt. 1, p. 620.

Representative D. C. Haskell contended that legislative appropriations would tend to diminish private contributions.[17] Government reports, private correspondence, and newspaper commentary make it abundantly clear, however, that because of the blatant sectional overtones of the Exodus controversy, the Democrats, in control of both houses of Congress, blocked efforts to provide emergency appropriations in Congress.[18]

The urgent need for relief did not fall completely on deaf ears in Washington. Senator William Windom of Minnesota, who had credentials as a Radical Republican, acknowledged the nation's responsibility for aiding the migrants. With the help of like-minded legislators, Windom organized the National Refugee Relief Board. The relief board sought to convene a national committee of prominent individuals to inaugurate a program of philanthropy. In addition to the committee, the relief board established a branch office in Chicago, Illinois. In subsequent months Chicago emerged as a major site for the solicitation of funds for the Kansas Freedmen's Relief Association. Although there was no formal affiliation between the relief board and the association, the KFRA largely superseded the work of Windom's organization. Paul Jones and Edwin P. McCabe, Negroes then residing in Chicago and affiliated with Senator Windom's relief board, brought a carload of food and clothing and a certified check for $2,000 to Governor St. John to aid the migrants.[19] Jones and McCabe eventually settled in Kansas and exercised considerable influence in black Topeka.

Relief programs inaugurated by local churches were weak and ineffective. As an example, in April, 1879, the Board of Church Extension of the Kansas Conference, Methodist Episcopal Church, assembled in Topeka and addressed issues and problems attendant to the Exodus. No funds or relief material were solicited at the conclave. The predominant concern was "how shall they be educated and christianized and pre-

17. D. C. Haskell to John P. St. John, April 28, 1879, in St. John, Correspondence Received, Box 10, KSHS.
18. The *Senate Reports* are replete with claims of Republican duplicity and counterclaims of Democratic depravity. This document must be viewed in that light.
19. Garvin, "Singleton and His Followers," 19; Ella Lee Blake, "The Great Exodus, 1879–1880, to Kansas" (M.A. thesis, Kansas State College, 1942), 43; undated, untitled newspaper article, in *Singleton Scrapbook*; P. Foner, *Frederick Douglass*, IV, 551; Godkin, "The Flight of the Negroes," 242.

pared for honorable citizenship."[20] Notably, the Reverend James E. Gilbert, pastor of First Methodist Church in Topeka, was a member of the State Central Relief Committee, organized by St. John, and served as president of the association. Neither the contributors' lists nor the records of the association, however, reveal support from any level of Kansas Methodism. A survey of these sources also indicated similar delinquency in other denominations in Kansas.

The receipt of money and relief material through public and private subscription was inadequate, and the arrival of the Exodusters in Kansas continued unabated. It was clear that municipal, state, and federal authorities were not willing to shoulder the major responsibility for the welfare of the Exodusters. That initiative was left to Governor St. John. "We trust," asserted the *Commonwealth*, "that the Governor will take such steps as may be deemed the best to devise a plan which will . . . effect the object desired." That note of confidence was well founded. An avowed proponent of women's rights and temperance, St. John was every inch a reformer. To one observer he had "something apostolic in his faith as well as in his name." Indeed, he once described himself as "an old, once despised and persecuted abolitionist." St. John's Republican credentials, political acumen, and administrative skills were well suited to the task of bringing order to the chaotic relief effort.[21] Accordingly, on April 20, 1879, St. John called for a meeting of sixty prominent citizens to be held at the Topeka Opera House. They founded the State Central Relief Committee.

In a keynote address, St. John alluded to Kansas' association with the cause of Negro liberty and its present duty to fulfill that historic responsibility.[22] Since it was conceded that "the state government affords no

---

20. *Commonwealth*, May 7, 1879, in *Methodist Church Clippings*, I. Neither the KSHS nor the Baker University (Baldwin, Kans.) collection of materials on Kansas Methodism revealed any support for the Exodusters. The records of the Presbyterian Historical Society (Philadelphia, Pa.) indicate that Kansas Presbyterians paid scant attention to the relief problem.

21. *Commonwealth*, April 19, 1879, cited in Schwendemann, "Wyandotte," 238; Elizabeth Comstock, "Kansas," KFRA *Broadside* (Topeka, 1881); Pickering, "The Administration of St. John," 381.

22. *Daily Capital*, April 21, 1879; *Commonwealth*, April 22, 25, 1879, in *NC*, III; Schwendemann, "The Negro Exodus to Kansas," 121; Athearn, *In Search of Canaan*, 49, 117, asserts that St. John was "deeply concerned about the problem of human relations." However, such "humanitarian qualities were advertised as his political stock in trade."

means of extending special aid to immigrating freedmen," the thrust of the committee's concerns was as follows: "It is not their purpose or desire to meddle in politics, to induce immigrants to come into the state, or do anything but help the needy temporarily, and put them into the way of supporting themselves. Humanity and the good name of the state demand this." In a brief flush of generosity, those attending the meeting donated $533.[23]

From backroom offices in the City Building, the committee administered a statewide relief effort. St. John appointed an executive committee composed of public officials and private citizens. Among them were Topeka Mayor Michael Case, the Reverend Thomas W. Henderson, a Negro Topekan and pastor of St. John A.M.E., as well as representatives from counties throughout the state. The cross section of Kansas officials and biracial representation on the various committees did not indicate any new sense of common cause and responsibility. Rather, they were "procrustean bedfellows"; public sponsorship provided a means of shifting direct responsibility away from local citizens and government.[24] "But for the Central Board" and the subsequent development of the KFRA, the *Commonwealth* reported, "Shawnee County would have had to spend a great many thousands of dollars."[25]

Various city and county aid societies helped administer the relief effort. A ladies' auxiliary, which included the wives of Central Committee officials, tried to drum up support from Topeka civic groups. The practical goal of the coordinated committee activity was to procure employment for the migrants and to direct their settlement within and without the state. Newspapers and *House Journal* reports of Central Committee proceedings and activities, however, do not provide a precise indicator of the extent or effectiveness of that endeavor.[26]

Committing the resources of the state to welfare for the Exodusters, moreover, did not meet with favor "in a basically Anglo-Saxon frontier agricultural community."

23. *Commonwealth*, April 22, 1879, in *NC*, III; *Daily Capital*, April 21, 1879.

24. *Commonwealth*, May 3, 1879; "procrustean bedfellows" was coined by C. Vann Woodward, *The Origins of the New South: 1877–1913* (Baton Rouge, 1971), to describe a similarly stressful partnership.

25. "The Facts of the Case," *Commonwealth*, March 24, 1880, in *Shawnee County Clippings*, III.

26. *Daily Capital*, April 21, 1879; *Commonwealth*, April 22, 1879, in *NC*, III; Schwendemann, "The Negro Exodus to Kansas," 121. The Central Committee tried to obtain information from A. S. Johnson, a land agent for the Kansas Pacific Railroad, regarding

The agency within the Central Committee which exercised the most enduring influence was the Committee of Twelve. It was charged with responsibility for receiving money and relief material from an expanding number of "charitable citizens in all parts of the country." The appeal for funds generated by the Committee of Twelve helped create a national network of philanthropy.[27] The publicity gained thereby attracted the attention and support of reformers who had a long-standing interest in the freedmen's cause.

At a meeting on May 2, the Central Committee endorsed the idea of incorporation under state law. "This course," reported the *Commonwealth*, "gives greater responsibility than can exist in a voluntary organization." Although St. John stayed on in an unofficial advisory capacity, a new board of directors was selected on which private citizens replaced public officials and the Central Committee dissolved. Custody for the relief program was remanded to the Kansas Freedmen's Relief Association, incorporated May 8, 1879.[28] The association, in Henry King's view, undertook its duties "as an organized and distinct Christian charity having no political taint or affiliation and relying solely on religious generosity." As stated in the articles of incorporation, the association sought "to do and perform such . . . acts of charity and benevolence as the necessities of the . . . freedmen, refugees and immigrants may require and humanity suggests."[29]

Christian stewardship provided a motivation for KFRA endeavors. The

---

the classes and the ages of the immigrants and the railroad's machinations in encouraging settlement (see Schwendemann, "The Exodusters on the Missouri," 39, and "Wyandotte," 238; *Senate Reports*, pt. 3, pp. 106–210; *Commonwealth*, April 20, 1876).

27. *Daily Capital*, April 21, 1879; *Commonwealth*, April 22, 1879, in *NC*, III; Schwendemann, "Wyandotte," 238. Some early contributors who responded to St. John's national appeal were Jay Gould, of the Union Pacific Railroad, who donated $5,000 and a shipment of food and clothing (he was not so generous subsequently); Robert Ingersoll, from Chicago, who gave $1,000 and a shipment of supplies and, according to the *Colored Citizen* (April 19), further committed "half of his income for the next five years if necessary"; P. D. Armour, owner of a Chicago meat packing company, who collected $12,000 from Chicago business firms (see H. King, "A Year of the Exodus in Kansas," 212; Athearn, *In Search of Canaan*, 112).

28. *Commonwealth*, May 7, 1879; "Articles of Incorporation," *Second Semi-Annual Report of the Kansas Freedmen's Relief Association* (Topeka, 1880), Articles 2, 3 (there was no first report in the KSHS Archives); KFRA Minutes, September 29, 1879, in KSHS; *Daily Capital*, May 3, 5, 10, 1879; Blackmar, *Kansas: A Cyclopedia*, I, 685–86.

29. H. King, "A Year of the Exodus in Kansas," 213; *Second Report KFRA*, 3.

charitable and humane offices of Quakerism, the principles of abolitionism, and paternal social control completed the working mechanism.[30] Poverty as the evidence of sin and depravity, a traditional frame of reference for charity work in America, affected but did not debilitate the programs of the association. Rather, the evidence of a casework method and a careful accounting of the nature and causes of indigency were more definitive. The association also applied then-current techniques in the administration and implementation of social welfare. The channels for philanthropy from the eastern states and from Europe facilitated a rich exchange of information on systematic relief work.[31] The association also attempted to separate the "honest poor" from the charlatan.[32] Public opinion and limited resources made it incumbent upon the association to structure its services so as to avoid chronic pauperism and dependency.

The blueprint for social welfare employed by the association was in common use in the development of the West. Midwesterners, moreover, had long experience with economic hardship and the need for organized charity.[33] But the association enjoyed neither support nor acceptance in Topeka; in fact it received particular censure. A short discussion of that institution, its personnel, ongoing services, and its reception in general will help illustrate the shape of interracial relations in Topeka in the 1880s.

---

30. James M. McPherson, *The Struggle for Equality: Abolitionists and the Negro in the Civil War and Reconstruction* (Princeton, 1964), Chapter 17, pp. 386–416, and Rose, *Rehearsal for Reconstruction*, identify the programs and the principles employed by abolitionists to mitigate the influences of slavery and to prepare blacks for citizenship. The association adopted similar formulas to address the problems of the Exodusters. Clifford S. Griffin, *Their Brothers' Keepers: Moral Stewardship in America* (New Brunswick, 1958), 23, 27, indicates that social control was implicit in the efforts of reformers and religious leaders to bring settlers in a succession of western frontiers to the Lord and to civic virtue.

31. For a general survey of the development of systematic social welfare in the United States, see Ralph and Muriel Pumphrey, *The Heritage of American Social Work* (New York, 1961); Leah Feder, *Unemployment Relief in Periods of Depression* (New York, 1936); Nathan Cohen, *Social Work in the American Tradition* (New York, 1958); Auguste Jorns, *The Quaker as Pioneer in Social Work*, trans. T. K. Brown (New York, 1931). Essays by Stephan Thernstrom and Bayrd Still in Alexander B. Callow (ed.), *American Urban History* (New York, 1964), are informative.

32. KFRA, *Instructions to Visitors* (Topeka, 1880).

33. On the development of social welfare and related issues in Kansas and the trans-Mississippi West in the nineteenth century, see reference to Mother Mary Breekerdike and the Grasshopper Plague of 1874, in Carey, "People, Problems, Prohibition," 379; Browning, *The Development of Poor Relief Legislation*, 73–79, 81.

The major responsibility for the association's relief effort fell to John M. Brown, general superintendent; Laura Haviland, secretary; Elizabeth Comstock, correspondent; and William O. Lynch, member of the board of directors. Brown, Haviland, and Comstock shared residence in a two-story house at 260 Kansas Avenue. Records do not indicate that the association owned that property. The head of the household was one John M. Watson, identified in the census as "Secretary of Kansas Religious Affairs" but not affiliated with the association. Lynch, his wife and six children, lived at 524 Quincy Street.[34]

John M. Brown, a black Topekan, emigrated from Mississippi in 1877. While in Mississippi he held political office and taught school. One surmises that Brown came to Kansas with money saved because in 1880 he owned property on the outskirts of North Topeka where the KFRA facilities were located. "A man of unusual cultivation and executive ability," Superintendent Brown was responsible for the management of the Barracks as well as the resettlement of the migrants. Well-received in the black Topeka community, Brown also was a member of the Colored State Emigration Board, formed by Negroes in the city,[35] about which more will be said later.

At St. John's invitation, Laura Haviland, a Quaker philanthropist from Adrian, Michigan, came to Kansas in November, 1879, for the express purpose of assisting with the relief effort. She was reputed to have given "a good portion of her life to the work of ameliorating the condition of the colored race." In Michigan before the war her home was an outpost of the Underground Railroad. During the war she was an "angel of mercy to our sick and wounded soldiers in hospital and in camp." As secretary of the association, Haviland was responsible for the solicitation, the receipt, and the recording of all relief materials and money received. Haviland also provided yeoman service in obtaining the support of the Society of Friends at home and abroad.[36]

---

34. U.S. 1880 census; KFRA Expenditures, Minutes, and Reports, May, 1879–April, 1881 (when the corporation terminated), in KSHS.

35. *Senate Reports*, pt. 3, pp. 351, 358–59; U.S. 1880 census; Elizabeth Comstock, "A Day Among the Kansas Refugees," KFRA *Broadside* (Topeka, 1881); *Commonwealth*, April 25, 1879, in *NC*, III; KFRA Minutes, March 3, 1879, March 1, 1880.

36. KFRA Minutes, July 6, 1879; *Second Report KFRA*, 8; Laura Haviland, *A Woman's Life Work: Labors and Experiences of Laura S. Haviland* (Cincinnati, 1881), 482–508; H. King, "A Year of the Exodus in Kansas," 216; U.S. 1880 census; Mildred Danforth, *A Quaker*

Elizabeth Comstock, "a widely known Quaker preacher" from Rollin, Michigan, came to Kansas at the request of Laura Haviland "to minister to the destitute and suffering refugees." No less than Haviland, Comstock had impeccable credentials as a humanitarian and long association with the abolitionist crusade. Although Comstock had no official position in the association and received no remuneration except her board and travel expenses, she adopted the title correspondent. Comstock gave invaluable assistance to the relief effort by securing liberal contributions in the United States and in Europe. Her extensive contacts and voluminous correspondence with the Society of Friends and other philanthropists quickened interest in the migrants' plight.[37]

William O. Lynch, a Negro pastor of Asbury A.M.E. Church in North Topeka, came to Kansas in 1878 from Marion County, Alabama. In addition to his pastorate, Lynch was a presiding elder in the black Kansas Conference, Methodist Episcopal Church, and formerly held a similar position in Alabama. Lynch was charged with responsibility for setting up migrant encampments in Kansas and in other states.[38] Largely through the efforts of these four stalwarts, the KFRA programs of philanthropy, social welfare, and resettlement were conducted with efficiency and with humanitarian resolve.

The association's most pressing need after the arrival of the migrants in Topeka was for shelter and a locale from which to initiate the relief effort. This problem was inherited from the Central Committee and it triggered a major confrontation with the community. In April the Central Committee quartered a contingent of Exodusters at the Topeka Fair Grounds. After little more than a month, the board of county commissioners, in charge of that facility, ordered the Central Committee to vacate, ostensibly because the buildings were in need of repair. Although the record is clouded, the committee is alleged to have obtained permission to use the Fair Grounds from one Charles Curtis, a member of the

---

Pioneer: Laura Haviland, Superintendent of the Underground Railroad (New York, 1906), 201–206, 249–50.

37. Elizabeth Comstock, *Statement* (Topeka, 1880), 5; Comstock, "Kansas"; *Second Report KFRA*, 8; U.S. 1880 census.

38. KFRA Minutes, March 1, May 3, 1880; U.S. 1880 census; *Colored Citizen*, June 28, 1879.

board. Perhaps responding to pressure from the community, the board reneged on that agreement. The board made an alternative suggestion: since most of the migrants were arriving on the Kansas Pacific Railroad in North Topeka, they should be housed in that section of the city. An indeterminate number of migrants already were settled there, living "in tents, dugouts, and in other makeshift shelters."[39]

In June the association, then in charge of relief work, erected a temporary shelter called the Barracks near the junction of the Kansas Pacific and Sante Fe tracks, adjacent to the Kansas River in North Topeka. Rumors of contagious diseases carried by the migrants, an often-heard complaint, caused alarmed North Topeka residents to tear down the Barracks and to throw the lumber in the Kansas River. Census materials and KFRA records indicate that, indeed, whooping cough among children and the sundry ills and infirmities of the old were rampant in Exoduster encampments. An epidemic of yellow fever, then raging in Tennessee, was the bane most feared by Topekans. There were, however, no reported outbreaks in the city.[40] H. H. Stanton, manager of a hotel-restaurant complex for the Kansas Pacific Railroad, expressed the increasing discontent of North Topeka residents regarding the settlement of migrants in that region: "I think I may safely say that there is no man in the First Ward of Topeka who thinks it best for them to come here. When they threw those barracks in the river . . . it was the best businessmen of the place that did it, and advocated its being done."[41]

The Reverend J. Barrett, pastor of North Topeka Baptist Church, identified an additional element of community hostility: "It is doing the colored people and the white people great injury to offer relief under the circumstances." The Barracks, moreover, provided an incentive for the Exodusters to stay, and were it not for the complicity of the association, "most of the migrants would just as soon return home." Reported

---

39. *Senate Reports*, pt. 3, pp. 290, 690; Schwendemann, "Wyandotte," 246–47; Blake, "The Great Exodus," 50, 56.

40. (White) North Topeka *Times*, June 30, 1879; *Senate Reports*, pt. 3, p. 290. For a sample of newspaper accounts of issues related to the health of the migrants, see *Commonwealth*, May 6, 1879, and New York *Tribune*, July 11, 12, 1879.

41. *Senate Reports*, pt. 3, pp. 96–99. It is worthy of note that the railroads were accused of complicity in encouraging southern Negroes to come to Kansas to preempt railroad lands. "How and Where to Get a Living," *A Sketch of the Garden of the West*, is illustrative of railroad activity in that regard.

one resident, "There is not a house in Topeka that can be rented for the accommodation of the refugees."[42] Summarily rejected, the association set up the Barracks, three fourths of a mile north of the city line, on land owned by John M. Brown.

There are, however, some discrepancies in both ownership of the land and the location of the Barracks. Throughout the tenure of the association, Brown was paid for varying amounts spent in behalf of the migrants. No financial records indicate sale or the payment of rent on the land occupied by the Barracks. It is worth noting, in view of the controversy regarding the association's financial management, that by law, incorporated benevolent societies could erect buildings and obtain "the loan of funds for the purchase of real property."

Curiously enough, the Barracks was said to be located on "two city lots . . . owned by a colored refugee" who received $5 monthly for rent. By strict definition of the Exoduster *qua* "colored refugee," Brown's arrival in 1877 places him one year shy. In any case, it seems unlikely that Brown would be so addressed, in view of his position with the association. The confusion is compounded further, by Brown's suing in 1881 one L. Johnson for trespassing. A basis for the suit was that Johnson claimed title to the land when the association's lease was up.

According to the 1880 census, the Barracks was located on Adams and Washington streets in North Topeka. The preponderance of evidence suggests, however, that the final site of the Barracks was on Brown's land.[43]

From that base of operations, the program of services moved into high gear. The KFRA made contact with the migrants upon their arrival at the Kansas Pacific Railroad depot in North Topeka. A committee of twenty visitors, appointed by the association, was instructed to determine the migrants' physical condition and family status and to ascertain the nature and level of their needs. Thereupon the visitors advised the migrants of written regulations governing relief. After presenting each

42. *Senate Reports*, pt. 3, pp. 106–210; Elizabeth Comstock, "The Exodus," KFRA *Broadside* (Topeka, 1880), is in the transcript of a letter written by Mrs. Caroline De Greene of Topeka, January 26, 1880, in KSHS.
43. KFRA Expenditures; KFRA Inventory of Property, August 6, 1881, in KSHS; *Compiled Laws, 1879*, Chapter XXIII, Section 3; *Second Report KFRA*, 26, 28; *Commonwealth*, September 15, 1881.

family with a card listing the vital information and the type of relief needed, the visitors trooped the Exodusters to the Barracks.[44]

The 1880 census enumerated residents in the Barracks. Figures for that population, however, fluctuated widely. Between December, 1879, and January, 1880, when the migration was at its height, there were four hundred occupants. During peak periods, Comstock asserted, "some of the children have to sleep five in a bed, and whole families are obliged to sit up at night for want of sleeping room." In the winter of 1880/81, when the migration subsided, there were substantially fewer occupants.[45]

In October, 1879, the *Colored Citizen* identified "a party of 120 . . . refugees, a part of whom were white" in the Barracks. In August, 1880, the Topeka *Tribune* reported that approximately sixty destitute Mennonites were admitted to the Barracks to "be cared for until they can get away." In a solitary reference, Henry King mentioned "blacks and whites" who attempted to obtain association services. With the aforementioned exceptions, no reference to white recipiency was found. The 1880 census, moreover, enumerated no white occupants in the Barracks.[46]

The Barracks was a complex which contained all relief facilities. The most prominent structures were dormitory buildings designed to house two to five hundred individuals. Compartments accommodating three to four families had eight double bunks and a cookstove. In the immediate vicinity of the dormitories were a hospital, a commissary, and a two-story structure housing the offices and a warehouse. The Barracks was constructed by the Exodusters themselves; approximately 100,000 board feet of lumber, donated to the association at various times, provided the building material. Many of the Exodusters, Comstock reported with pride, "are good mechanics and can build well." The mi-

---

44. Comstock, *Statement*, 9; *Commonwealth*, April 14, 1880, in *NC*, III; KFRA, *Instructions to Visitors*.
45. John P. St. John to Horatio N. Rust, January 16, 1880, in Lambert Tree Collection, Newberry Library, Chicago; U.S. 1880 census; Comstock, "The Exodus"; for a sharp increase in received contributions of heavy clothing, bedding, and lumber during the winter, see KFRA Minutes and Expenditures, September, 1879–April, 1880; *Second Report KFRA*, 28; Comstock, "A Day Among the Kansas Refugees"; KFRA Monthly Reports and Minutes, carried by the *Commonwealth*, September, 1880–January, 1881.
46. *Colored Citizen*, October 25, 1879; (black) Topeka *Tribune*, August 26, 1880; H. King, "A Year of the Exodus in Kansas," 212; U.S. 1880 census.

grant carpenters, moreover, were paid by the association for their labor.[47]

The warehouse, site of much ongoing activity, contained a distribution room for relief materials. A registry book recorded the number and type of goods received and the name of the contributing party. The distribution room also stocked "Bibles and Testaments" donated by the Bible Association of Friends in America; there were no formal religious services at the Barracks. Nonetheless, with some semblance of Puritan rigor, the officials in charge of the distribution room checked on the dormitory residents "in the morning before the rooms are opened and at night after they are closed." By that means, "few imposters have received help from the Association." By all accounts, order and efficiency were the keynote of operations at the Barracks.[48]

An indeterminate number of Exodusters for whom the KFRA provided services resided in the city proper. The association bought "tracts of land, carefully selected" in Tennesseetown, an established black enclave in a section on the city's western perimeter called King's Addition. Frye W. Giles, who chronicled the history of Topeka, asserted that a large number of lots from a bankrupt estate in King's Addition became available at a "very low price."[49] According to association reports, the tracts of land were "divided into house lots and sold at cost to the refugees. On these they erected small frame houses." Those Exodusters remained eligible for association services. Migrants residing in town who tended garden plots brought fresh produce to the warehouse in exchange for clothing and relief materials.[50] It is impossible precisely to distinguish those Exodusters who obtained homes through the KFRA from those who acted independently using their own resources. No lists

---

47. Comstock, "A Day Among the Kansas Refugees," and *Statement*, 8; *Commonwealth*, November 27, 1879, in *NC*, III; Elizabeth Comstock to Horatio N. Rust, February 5, 1880, in Quaker Collection, Huntington Library, San Diego, Calif.; undated, untitled item in *NC*, III, and in *Shawnee County Clippings*, III.

48. Susan T. Perry, *A Peep at the Warehouse of the K.F.R.A.* (Topeka, n.d.); *Commonwealth*, April 14, 1880, in *NC*, III; Comstock, "A Day Among the Kansas Refugees." No registry book was discovered. KFRA Monthly Reports and Expenditures, however, give a fair indication of contributions.

49. KFRA Expenditures, May, 1879–April, 1881; Comstock, "A Day Among the Kansas Refugees"; Giles, *Thirty Years in Topeka*, 367, 386.

50. KFRA Expenditures and Minutes, undated; Comstock, "A Day Among the Kansas Refugees."

of individual names survive in association records and the 1880 census does not record real or personal property.

Association materials indicated that the largest proportion of Exodusters were from Tennessee and Mississippi and lived in Tennesseetown.[51] The 1880 census, moreover, identified a heavy influx of migrants from Tennessee and Mississippi in the black population as a whole. The relative concentration of Exodusters in Tennesseetown, moreover, was no higher than in other established Negro enclaves in the First and Third wards. Patterns of residence also indicate no heavy concentration of migrants from the same state of nativity within Negro enclaves; with the exception of a few clusters, they were dispersed throughout black Topeka. Giles confirmed that the migrants "established dwellings in the outskirts of Topeka—some to the East, some to the Northwest, but more to the West."[52]

All of the Exodusters receiving association services did not remain in the city. Design and necessity dictated plans for resettling migrants throughout the state. Accordingly, the association established Exoduster colonies in Wabaunsee, Graham, and Morris counties.[53] The fortunes of those migrants are of no direct concern here. Notably, however, a trace

---

51. Comstock, "A Day Among the Kansas Refugees"; a retrospective on the founding of Tennesseetown (*Daily Capital*, November 1, 1943, in *NC*, VII) indicates that Martin Oglesvie and Cal Picket, leaders of an emigrant group from Tennessee, founded the enclave in 1879. They were Exodusters, but it is likely that they merely set up residence in an already established black settlement. Benjamin "Pap" Singleton, president of the Tennessee Real Estate and Homestead Association, directed Negro migrants toward settlement in King's Addition, popularly known as Tennesseetown as early as 1873; see Garvin, "Singleton and His Followers," 8, 13. The Kansas 1875 MS census and other materials consulted indicate that Tennesseetown was founded no later than 1875.

52. Tables 10, 13; Giles, *Thirty Years in Topeka*, 367–68.

53. J. L. King (ed.), *History of Shawnee County*, 168, 292; *Second Report KFRA*, 28. One surmises from a survey of available association records that the Barracks population averaged 60 arrivals and 40 departures per month over a six-month period ending April 15, 1880. Inclusive of all recipients, 120 families received association services over that period; there were no companion figures for individuals. The focus of this study precludes reference to such settlements as Nicodemus, an all-Negro town in Graham County, Kans., established before the Exodus but a locus for migrant settlement, 1878–81. KFRA Minutes and Expenditures throughout the tenure of the association indicate the expenses and activity attendant to the maintenance of installations outside of Topeka. On Nicodemus, see: Schwendemann, "Nicodemus"; Orval McDaniel, "A History of Nicodemus, Graham County, Kansas" (M.A. thesis, Fort Hays State College, 1950); "When Nicodemus Was a Thriving Village," Concordia *Kansan*, undated, in *NC*, VII; "Freedmen Notes," *Commonwealth*, July 8, 1879, in *NC*, III; "She Helped Settle Second Colony of Nicodemus," *Daily Capital*, August 29, 1937, in *NC*, VII.

of several Topeka Exodusters over two census periods (ending 1895) indicates that a stint on the farm in a prairie county and a return to Topeka were not an uncommon pattern.[54]

An employment bureau at the Barracks, supervised by Laura Haviland, provided one point of entry for the Exodusters into the life of the city. As a means of fostering independence and reducing the drain on limited relief supplies, the employment program ranked high among the association's concerns. The association required that "those who lodge here are expected to go out each day and get jobs . . . and so provide their own food and that of their families." An unknown number of migrants obtained employment in Topeka as day laborers and as gandy dancers on the railroad, in addition to those employed on public works projects.[55] The 1880 census identified common labor as the prevailing occupation of the migrants and of the black Topeka work force as a whole. Commonly, Negro women in both populations who worked were employed in some area of domestic service. On the average, employed Negroes in Topeka worked approximately seven months per year in 1880. The degree to which the pay rate for Exodusters and blacks in general adhered to prevailing wage scales in 1880 is not known. The Kansas census of 1875 listed the going wage for common laborers as $1.25 per day. The *Annual Labor Report, 1886* of the Kansas Bureau of Labor and Industrial Statistics, the only other reference point, identified the annual wage rate for black laborers in Wyandotte as $212.75 and for whites as $333.09; there were no companion figures for Topeka.[56]

Frye W. Giles asserted that upon arrival in 1879–1880, the Exodusters "at once became very valuable . . . in the grades of labor requiring little mechanical skill, and at the end of five years they show a degree of achievement in all conditions of life." "Many of them," moreover, "have become good mechanics." It is possible that the expanding labor force during the Exodus period had an immediate depressing effect on wages

---

54. Fluctuating persistence rates have greater significance in the 1890s, when many black Topekans migrated to Oklahoma. See Stephan Thernstrom, *The Other Bostonians: Poverty and Progress in the American Metropolis* (Cambridge, 1973), 225–27.
55. Comstock, "A Day Among the Kansas Refugees"; *Commonwealth*, March 21, April 14, 1880, in *NC*, III; *Kansas Herald*, January 30, 1880.
56. Betton, *Annual Labor Report, 1886*.

The Exodus

for black common laborers in the city; potentially this was a catalyst for black hostility toward the new arrivals.[57]

The employment bureau received numerous applications for laborers from employers throughout Kansas and from other states. Governor St. John, for example, identified some interest among migrants in resettling in Illinois, and "a few were sent to Iowa and Nebraska." Comstock offered an optimistic appraisal of Chicagoans' willingness to "open their gates in Illinois to 50,000 of these long-oppressed, long-suffering people."[58] The association urgently sought "to remove the migrants as rapidly as possible to colonies or places where employment may be found." The KFRA Minutes in particular are replete with references to the transportation of migrants out of Topeka for employment. Haviland encountered difficulty in complying with the numerous requests for single males and females to work outside the city. Most migrants came in family groups and unless the employer was willing to retain or find accommodations for the entire family, his request was refused. Haviland admonished: "In the cursed bondage of the past the breaking up of families was the most bitter trial of their hard lot and now they shrink from anything that looks like separation. Put yourself in their place." As an incentive to obtain rural employment and to keep families intact, however, Haviland suggested that giving a home, fuel, and provisions to the family would "provide an easy way for paying quite a portion of their wages." The association subscribed to the idea that "we must adopt so much of their old plantation as will give them a home by themselves, close by that of their old masters."[59] If not by design, that view had the earmarks of the share-tenant system which led to debt peonage in the South.

Haviland requested that railroad fare be provided by the employer if

57. Giles, *Thirty Years in Topeka*, 367–68; see Tables 5,6; *Colored Citizen*, October 4, 1879; Conference on Research in Income and Wealth, *Trends in the American Economy in the Nineteenth Century* (Princeton, 1960), Vol. XXIV of *Studies in Income and Wealth* (44 vols.; Princeton, 1937—); Edgar O. Edwards, "Notes on the Pattern of United States Economic Growth," in Simon Kuznets (ed.), *Economic Growth and Structure: Selected Essays* (New York, 1965), 305.

58. St. John to Rust, January 16, 1880; "The Exodus Fund," undated, in *NC*, III. There are no concrete figures or estimates of the number of migrants in Topeka who then moved on to other states.

59. KFRA Minutes, March 6, September 12, 1879–July 5, 1880; Laura Haviland, "Open Letter," *Senate Reports*, pt. 3, pp. 371–72; Pickering, "The Administration of St. John," 388, quoting Haviland; *Commonwealth*, March 21, 1880, in *NC*, III.

arrangements were finalized.⁶⁰ The records, however, indicate that transportation costs were often paid by the association. As an example, there were numerous receipts, varying from $3 to $85, payable to the Topeka Transportation Company throughout the year 1880–1881. The Santa Fe Railroad also was paid for such services in similar amounts over that period.⁶¹

To illustrate the migrant's circumspect behavior and fitness for employment, Comstock assured employers and potential contributors that the Barracks did not contain "a single colored tramp . . . not one refugee has been arrested for stealing. Very little profanity has been heard among them. Of those for whom occupations and homes have been found . . . we have very good reports. As a class these refugees are orderly, sober, honest, and industrious and very glad to get work if they can." One surmises that this aspect of the program achieved some measure of success. By January 16, 1880, the association took credit for securing jobs for 10,000 Exodusters.⁶²

James L. King reported that "most of them are fieldhands, but they adapted themselves to the new conditions and found employment as mechanics, laborers, teamsters, and in other branches of industry." Reports of migrant experiences as agricultural laborers on white-owned farms in rural counties are mixed. The migrants enjoyed relatively greater economic success in the independent Exoduster colonies and in the all-Negro town, Nicodemus, in Graham County. A review of newspapers in adjacent towns and KFRA materials did not reveal outstanding antagonisms between migrants and whites in the area.⁶³

Henry King asserted: "Exodusters work in desultory fashion for white farmers and herders . . . doing the best they can but are powerless to get ahead . . . without considerable assistance." Schwendemann, in "The Negro Exodus to Kansas," contends that Negro land ownership was un-

---

60. Pickering, "The Administration of St. John," 388; *Commonwealth*, March 18, 1880, in *NC*, IV.
61. KFRA Expenditures, 1880–81; Pickering, "The Administration of St. John," 381.
62. Comstock, "The Exodus"; St. John to Rust, January 16, 1880.
63. J. L. King (ed.), *History of Shawnee County*, 168; Schwendemann, "Nicodemus," 18, 28; "Freedmen Notes," *Commonwealth*, July 8, 1879, in *NC*, III, contains comments by Thomas Beaumont of Hill City, a white town near Nicodemus, which describe the economic relations between the black and white settlements; "The Kansas Refugees," Atchison *Daily Champion*, September 25, 1879, in *NC*, IV, describes the relations between whites and the Exoduster encampment in Hodgeman County, Kans.

common and the white farmer was squeamish about having Negroes "eating at his table and sleeping in the house. Manual farm labor, therefore, was closed." As a result, many blacks were forced to obtain employment and settlement in the towns. To no less a degree, and for similar reasons, Topeka provided a locus for black settlement from its hinterland, Shawnee County. Notably a similar ordering of economic relationships prevailed for white small farmers caught in the grip of speculators and the consolidation of large farm holdings. There were few documented cases of violence between whites and Exodusters in the rural counties. The one reported lynching of a Negro in Fort Scott in 1881 did not clearly indicate Exodusters' involvement.[64]

The migrants reached Topeka, having accomplished a long journey, arduous in all seasons, but particularly so during the winter months. Even during the relatively mild winter of 1879/80, many migrants died of exposure because accommodations at the Barracks were insufficient. The incidence of whooping cough, pneumonia, and other respiratory ailments was higher at the Barracks than among Exodusters and other blacks in the community at large.[65]

That "we have no city hospital or alms-house for them" exacerbated the problem, Comstock declared. Thus, it was necessary to establish a hospital at the Barracks. Through the agency of association supporters in Chicago, one Daniel Adams, "a reliable and worthy" physician in that city, was supposed to have come to Kansas. There is no record indicating his service to the refugees in Topeka.[66] The association had a contract with two Topeka physicians, Doctors John B. Hibbin and E. B. Ramsey, who charged a fee per patient and who were paid $1 per visit and 50¢ for a prescription. Hibbin successfully sued the association for the recovery of $650 in unpaid medical fees; this suggests many visits to the

64. H. King, "A Year of the Exodus in Kansas," 214; on white farm tenancy, see Paul Wallace Gates, *Fifty Million Acres* (Ithaca, 1954), Chapters 1–3; Paul Wallace Gates, *Landlords and Tenants on the Prairie Frontier* (Ithaca, 1973), Chapters 2, 8; James C. Malin, *Grasslands: Prolegomena* (Ann Arbor, 1948), 312–15; *Colored Citizen*, August 22, 1881; *Commonwealth*, August 31, 1881, in *NC*, V.
65. Comstock, *Statement*, 3, 5; *Second Report KFRA*, 30; *Senate Reports*, pt. 3, p. 118; Haviland, *A Woman's Life Work*, 506. The U.S. 1880 census identified disease. The figures in the *Second Report* were derived by comparing the Exodusters with the established Negro population.
66. Comstock, "The Exodus"; St. John to Rust, January 16, 1880; Arthur Little to Horatio N. Rust, January 14, 1880, in Charles L. Hutchinson Collection, Newberry Library, Chicago.

Barracks and widespread sickness. Clearly, for Hibbin as for most Topekans, the plight of the Exodusters did not inspire benevolence or charity. Expenses for coffins and burials further attest to the seriousness of health problems.[67] Neither KFRA records nor newspapers indicate that Seth Vernella, a West Indian and a recent arrival as well as Topeka's first and only Negro physician, provided any service at the Barracks.

The records do not so indicate, but the association is purported to have established educational facilities for the migrant children and a night school for adults at the Barracks. Most commonly, however, association expenditures for educational materials and facilities were for Exoduster colonies in rural areas.[68] It is likely that migrant children residing in the city proper received a public education. The construction of two new schools for Negroes in Topeka between 1880 and 1885 may be attributed to *de jure* segregation and to an increase in the black school-age population brought on by the Exodus. In addition, one Mr. Kimberlin, a white man, "opened a night school at 205 Kansas Avenue for colored people. The tuition is low and the teacher is thoroughly qualified, and all should improve their opportunity."[69]

The Freedmen's Educational Society, founded in February, 1880, also sought to redress the "extreme ignorance" of Kansas Negroes and to meet their "great desire for knowledge, both of books and of business." Lawrence and Leavenworth, however, were the principal locales of the society's activity. Although "there have been a few terms taught in Topeka," the impact of that agency on black education in the city was minimal.[70]

After the KFRA phased out operations in May, 1881, Comstock and Haviland founded the Agricultural and Industrial Institute in Columbus, Kansas, on 400 acres paid for by the Society of Friends. The purpose of the institute was "to meet the needs of this long-abused race in

   67. *Minutes of the Board of Directors Meeting, April 14, 1881* (Topeka, 1881); KFRA Monthly Reports, *Commonwealth*, June, 1879–March, 1880; Office of District Court for Shawnee County to KFRA, April 15, 1880; Notice of Garnishment from the District Court, April 20, 1880; Attachment Order from the State of Kansas, Third Judicial District; KFRA Expenditures; Purchase Order no. 968 for coffins, signed by L. Haviland, 1881. All materials are in KSHS Archives.
   68. J. L. King (ed.), *History of Shawnee County*, 168.
   69. *Colored Citizen*, December 6, 1879; for comparative figures on literacy for the established and the Exoduster populations, see Tables 7, 13.
   70. *First Annual Report of the Freedmen's Educational Society* (Topeka, 1881), 2, 6.

helping them to help themselves by systematizing labor for them and connecting it with education." Among the trades taught were farming, mechanics, carpentry, and blacksmithing.[71] The activities of the institute, designed to facilitate rural settlement, had no measurable bearing on the history of black Topeka; as subsequent events will demonstrate, however, controversy over that venture spelled the end of the association.

Members of the Society of Friends and others long associated with the abolitionist crusade responded to the association's effort in behalf of the Exodusters. It was a late skirmish in what Kenneth Stampp calls "the last great crusade of the nineteenth century romantic reformers." James McPherson cogently argues, however, that the abolitionist legacy had longer tenure as a seminal force for integrationist protest through the turn of the century. One abolitionist elder statesman supported the Exodus but with misgivings. William Lloyd Garrison thought that an end to southern rapacity would obviate the need for migration. It is worth recalling that Frederick Douglass shared that view. Nonetheless, Garrison gave valuable support to the association endeavor. Relief materials from Boston were channeled through "Wm. L. Garrison, 137 Federal Street, Boston, Mass."[72]

Laura Haviland acknowledged the valuable service of those who followed the association's example and organized: "The efforts of the Association at Topeka have been nobly aided by auxiliary organizations . . . whose work has been done as cheerfully and with as careful economy as that of the laborers here." Horatio N. Rust, a well-to-do Quaker busi-

---

71. *Industrial Institute for People of Color* (Columbus, 1881); Elizabeth Comstock, *Announcement* (Columbus, 1881); *Agricultural and Industrial Institute Financial Statement* (Topeka, 1881). The philosophy and the programs of the institute in Columbus had much in common with Hampton Institute in Virginia. Comstock's correspondence indicates that the association entertained and rejected a plan for sending Exodusters to the Sandwich Islands, under care of a resident missionary, General Samuel Armstrong, who founded Hampton (Elizabeth Comstock to Horatio N. Rust, January 10, 1881, in *Horatio N. Rust Scrapbook*; Horatio N. Rust to John P. St. John, December 18, 1880, in St. John, Letter Volumes, both in KSHS). This evidence provides no explicit link between the two institutions or an indication of an exchange of ideas on Negro education. Armstrong merely agreed to "spy out the land." From all indications, that issue received neither debate nor further mention in correspondence in succeeding months. It was under Armstrong's tutelage and sponsorship that Booker T. Washington established Tuskegee Institute in Alabama.

72. Kenneth Stampp, *The Era of Reconstruction, 1865–1877* (New York, 1967), 101; McPherson, *The Abolitionist Legacy*, 103; P. Foner, *Frederick Douglass*, IV, 327–28, 334–35; *Commonwealth*, May 27, 1879; Elizabeth Comstock, "The Colored Refugees in Kansas," KFRA *Broadside* (Topeka, 1880).

nessman in Chicago, wrote St. John: "I am anxious to get an organization started upon so broad a base that we can meet any demands the Exodus makes from any direction." So pledged, Rust and like-minded philanthropists in Chicago organized the Southern Refugee Relief Society, incorporated February, 1880. The Chicago society existed, as was emblazoned on its stationery, "For the Purpose of Relieving the Great Want Growing Out of the Negro Exodus."[73] Joshua L. Baily, a Quaker merchant and philanthropist in Philadelphia, helped organize the Quaker Kansas Relief Association of Philadelphia. The KFRA also received contributions and correspondence from a Quaker organization called the Emigrant's Friend in England.[74]

Substantial contributions from private citizens filled the association's coffers and warehouse. John Hall, a Pennsylvania Quaker, gave $1,000. Clearly the religious overtone did not retard contribution to the relief effort: Robert Ingersoll, the nationally famous agnostic, sent $1,000 and a shipment of supplies for which he paid the transportation costs. P. D. Armour of Chicago, who responded to an earlier appeal by the State Central Relief Committee, remained steadfast and collected $1,200 from Chicago business firms for the association. Amounts as small as 50¢ were duly recorded in association reports of contributions.[75]

The attitude of most Kansans toward the migrants and the association suggests and the records confirm that contributions from within the state were insubstantial. The "List of Contributors," for the year ending March 31, 1880, indicates that only $84 was contributed by Kansans or Kansas organizations. Cross-checking the names of the five contributors from Topeka confirmed that none was a Negro or a government official. Curiously enough, a report of association contributions in a local newspaper lists "Topeka Collections" in July, 1879, amounting to $476.14. No corroborating evidence from association receipts for July confirms that figure. Through St. John's influence, however, the Fowler family,

---

73. Laura Haviland, "Report to the Board of Directors," *Second Report KFRA*, 10; Horatio N. Rust to John P. St. John, January 20, 1880, in St. John, Letter Volumes, KSHS; news report, undated, Chicago *Inter-Ocean*, in *Exodus Matters*.

74. Elizabeth Comstock to Joshua L. Baily, February 23, 1880, in Joshua Baily Collection, Haverford College, Haverford, Pa. (reference obtained from James McPherson); *Second Report KFRA*, 9–13.

75. "List of Contributors," *Second Report KFRA*, 9–13; H. King, "A Year of the Exodus in Kansas," 214.

owners of a Topeka meat packing concern, contributed material and monetary aid through the association.[76]

By March 31, 1881, the association had over $28,000 deposited in the bank. Among the states which enlisted in the relief effort, New York was first with a "magnificent contribution" of over $6,000; smaller but substantial amounts came from Pennsylvania, Massachusetts, and Illinois.[77] Haviland gave the following summary of contributions received: "Over seventy thousand dollars worth of supplies have passed through my hands... between September 1879... and March 1881. Thirteen thousand dollars of this amount came from England."[78]

The cost of shipping supplies to Kansas required funds which the association believed could be better spent for philanthropy. Railroad companies often charged an extra fee when there was a delay in the unloading of relief supplies.[79] The receipt of materials from Europe imposed greater difficulty. One British steamship line, Mark Whitewell and Company, agreed to a free shipment of relief goods, but that did not fully relieve this pressing problem.[80] In the association's view, "the charitable people of Europe and this country have a right to expect that our government shall be magnanimous and liberal in all that affects the welfare and alleviates the wants of our destitute citizens." From that optimistic premise, it followed that relief materials should be shipped duty free. Accordingly, the association resolved to apprise Kansas legislators in Washington of the difficulty and request that the matter receive congressional attention.[81]

Thomas Ryan, Republican congressman from Topeka, introduced a bill for relief of Exodusters in January, 1880, to remove the duty on shipments. The bill was long held up and eventually defeated owing to the objections of Fernando Wood, a notorious wartime Copperhead and chairman of the Ways and Means Committee, ostensibly because the

76. *Second Report KFRA*, 9–13; *Commonwealth*, July 13, 1879.
77. KFRA Minutes, July 7, 1881; Blake, "The Great Exodus," 39; Laura Haviland, *Circular—1880* (Topeka, 1880); "List of Contributors" and Haviland, "Report to the Board of Directors," *Second Report KFRA*, 9–13, 10; "An Appeal for Aid," New York *Tribune*, June 23, 1879, refers to the "excellent work" of the association and alludes to the crisis of southern Negroes.
78. Haviland, *A Woman's Life Work*, 506.
79. *Commonwealth*, March 18, 1880.
80. Comstock, *Statement*, 8.
81. KFRA Minutes, November 3, December 11, 1879.

measure would cause a drain on the federal treasury. Comstock, in a letter to Rust, could hardly contain her displeasure:

> If thou hast any influence in Washington, better use it now. Let our gov't know that while they are too weak to protect the lives and the liberty of the poor in the land, they are avaricious enough to grasp nearly half of what I have begged our English friends for. . . . Let Fernando Wood know that while he postpones the passage of that [Ryan] bill, poor people here are perishing and freezing for lack of things the Gov't holds in bond for duties . . . things have already been held . . . 3 or 4 weeks in N. York and are now delayed longer.[82]

The association, however, did not obtain redress from the government and shipment costs remained an expense.

Clearly, financial affairs dictated much of the course of KFRA activity. It was as if the headquarters in Topeka were a countinghouse. The shadow of public criticism and the exigencies of the relief work made accurate, efficient record keeping a necessity. A review of association accounts revealed items as various as the payment of "$20.00 to obtain a wooden leg for one Jordan Lamb," insurance policies with four different companies covering the Barracks, "shoes, dry goods, and kitchen utensils," and sundry other items. If Topekans were reluctant to contribute to the relief effort, they readily took advantage of an opportunity to do business with the association. Most perishable foodstuffs as well as consumer goods were bought from Topeka firms.[83]

Nonetheless, throughout its existence the association was dogged by accusations of misusing relief funds and encouraging the migration. Comstock, having no official status with the association, received particular abuse. Former governor Charles Robinson had misgivings about the financial management of the association and demanded public disclosure of its records: "Either Mrs. Comstock is acting independently and clandestinely or there is a wheel within a wheel which will need an

---

82. *Commonwealth,* January 15, 1880; Elizabeth Comstock to Horatio N. Rust, January 15, 1880, in Quaker Collection, Huntington Library, San Diego, Calif.

83. *Minutes of the Board of Directors Meeting, April 14, 1881;* KFRA Expenditures and unbound, uncatalogued bills and receipts contain insurance policies with Springfield Fire and Marine Insurance Company (Springfield, Mass.), Niagara Fire Insurance Company (New York, N.Y.), The Phoenix Insurance Company (Hartford, Conn.), Insurance Company of North America (Philadelphia, Pa.); KFRA Expenditures show, among the bills paid to Topeka business firms, "J. M. Steel, Butcher—$10, 1881" and "J. Thomas and Co. Lumber and Coal Dealers—$15.30, 1881."

explanation." For his part, former governor Charles Anthony viewed the association's relief work as "a piece of political buncombe." A comprehensive review of published materials, association proceedings, and correspondence reveals no indication of malfeasance. The association, moreover, was at pains to inform the public that "its officers are worthy of the heartiest commendation and entitled to the unqualified confidence of the most critical and exacting of a scrutinizing and impartial public."[84]

Quite possibly the extensive publicity involved in the subscriptions for contributions generated part of the complaint. In that regard, there was dissension within the association. George W. Carey, a judge and vice-president of the association, alleged that Haviland and Comstock put out publicity circulars of which the association did not approve. In one called "The Exodus," Comstock accompanied the appeal for funds with several testimonials affirming her integrity and that of the association. St. John supported her assessment of the need for contributions: "The statements of Mrs. Comstock are as nearly correct as it is possible to make them." As if some further defense were necessary, Comstock inquired of her friend Rust, "Will my circular at all remove the wrong impressions given?"[85]

The magnitude of the relief problem alone precludes the possibility that the association deliberately encouraged the migration. As for any personal complicity, said St. John, "I beg leave to state that nothing could be farther from the truth than to say that I, either directly or indirectly, am connected with the present movement of the blacks so far as encouraging them to come to Kansas is concerned."[86] Superintendent Brown, in testimony before the Senate committee inquiring into the causes of the Exodus, reported that the association's activity was not intended in any way to encourage further immigration. The thrust of the program ensured that the migrants "would not become a burden on the corporation of Topeka." Under instructions from the association, William O. Lynch wrote an open letter, to be published in southern jour-

84. "An Open Letter from Ex-Governor Robinson," in *Exodus Matters*; untitled article, *Prairie Empire*, May 29, 1879, in *NC*, III; *Second Report KFRA*, 7.
85. *Senate Reports*, pt. 3, p. 396; Comstock, "The Exodus"; Comstock to Rust, January 10, 1881.
86. J. M. Cavaness, "Governor St. John and the Exodus," *Commonwealth*, April 4, 1880, in *NC*, IV.

nals, strongly urging the migrants to "go into other Northern states, where labor is more needful and wages are higher; no one has anything to do with a man when he is depending on charity." On several occasions the association sent Lynch to other states in search of sites for Exoduster settlement.[87] As a KFRA official and assistant editor of the *Colored Citizen*, the Reverend Thomas W. Henderson tried to assuage public alarm in an editorial (April 26, 1879) wherein he disclaimed migration as a means of stemming southern oppression and advised "poor Negroes not to come expecting windfalls of philanthropy."

Columbus Johnson and Alonzo D. DeFrantz, charter members of the Tennessee Real Estate and Homestead Association, settled in Topeka in 1878. Their intimate awareness of issues and events attendant to the migration did not prevent them from denying complicity in the Exodus: "As for us providing houses for them, it is all a mistake, though we did obtain them shelter until we could get transportation for them. . . . We have never proposed to look after any emigrants but those of our own . . . from Tennessee."[88]

In a scarcely veiled early warning to the association, a "meeting of colored citizens" in June, 1879, condemned "those who intend to Africanize the state and [to] create racial divisions." Such attitudes became more strident and pointed in the black Topeka press in succeeding months. During the winter of 1879/80, when the pressures of relief were extreme, the black *Kansas Herald* alleged: "Perhaps the Relief Association doesn't comprehend the scope of the movement they are supposed to guide and direct." The association, moreover, catered to "individual interest" and "contributions are not being used in the interest of these people [Exodusters] exclusively." Without ascertainable grounds, the *Kansas Herald* joined the chorus of those claiming malfeasance: "Where is that promised report regarding the finances of the Refugee Board. We think it high time that it was given the public who have been held in suspense long enough." Though somewhat less harsh and derogatory, similar attitudes were manifest in the *Colored Citizen*.[89]

There were no reported contributions from black Topekans to the

87. *Senate Reports*, pt. 2, pp. 351–59, 364–67, and pt. 3, pp. 368–69; (black) Topeka *Tribune*, July 1, 1880; KFRA Minutes, March 1, May 3, 1880.
88. *Commonwealth*, March 22, 25, 1879, in *NC*, I.
89. *Ibid.*, June 8, 1879, in *NC*, I; *Kansas Herald*, January 30, February 6, 13, 16, 1880; *Colored Citizen*, January–February, 1880.

KFRA; this was a clear manifestation of their disapproval. The association did receive $400 from Negro individuals and organizations in New York and Pennsylvania. Lesser amounts came in from black churches and fraternal orders all over the country.[90] The Exodus, however, posed a particular dilemma for black Topekans, one common to ethnic minorities regardless of race and culture; they feared that increased numbers might cause an outbreak of indiscriminate hostility from the larger community against old and new Negro residents alike. Thus, charity was not its own reward. There were, however, no overtly racial incidents in Topeka during the Exodus period.[91]

The cumulative impact of public censure and internal dissension over the direction of the relief effort led to the breakup of the association. In published proceedings, the association terminated operations on April 4, 1881. The facilities were to be "closed against all newcomers on and after May, 1881." Pressures from without and from within were abundantly clear: "The dissolution of said Association was brought about not so much from a sense that the objects for which it had been created were accomplished, as from a feeling on the part of some of its directors that there had been a somewhat reckless management in the conduct of its affairs, funds, etc., having been diverted and likely to be diverted from the use intended by original donors." The precipitating issue, however, was not malfeasance but an imbroglio over the Agricultural and Industrial Institute and its funding.[92] As early as September, 1879, the association debated the question of founding educational facilities in the hinterland: "Shall we ask for funds to establish schools in locations where free public schools cannot be established?"[93] Evidently, freedmen's education continued to generate controversy. In February, 1880, the association approved the organization of an educational society for

90. *Second Report KFRA,* 9–13; *Commonwealth,* July 13, 1879, in *NC,* III.
91. All Negro newspapers in Topeka clearly expressed that concern. Moses Rischin, *The Promised City* (Cambridge, 1962), 95–111, identified a similar pattern of conflict between established and newly arrived Jews in New York City. Allan H. Spear, *Black Chicago: The Making of a Negro Ghetto* (Chicago, 1969), 168, 201–202; Osofsky, *Harlem,* 43–45, 131–35; David Gerber, *Black Ohio and the Color Line, 1860–1915* (Urbana, 1976), 295; Kusmer, *A Ghetto Takes Shape,* 252–53, all identify class antagonism between established and newly arrived Negroes. In the last analysis, the threat to established patterns of relations with the larger community was the decisive issue, irrespective of race, ethnicity, and locale.
92. *Daily Capital,* June 15, 1881; *Minutes of the Board of Directors Meeting, April 14, 1881; Compiled Laws, 1879,* Chapter XXIII, Section 3.
93. KFRA Minutes, September 29, 1879.

the freedmen. Unfortunately, this issue was not clearly resolved in records of subsequent meetings. The institute, in any event, was supported primarily by the Society of Friends and there was no evidence of a transfer of association money to the institute.[94] That Haviland and Comstock may have influenced contributors toward the institute, if not away from the association, is a plausible but unconfirmed explanation. Be that as it may, the association and the migration largely disappeared from the newspapers and thence from public commentary after 1881. There were scattered reports of new black migrants arriving in North Topeka in March, 1882, but the tone was more temperate: "The emigrants were evidently poor people, but not without the ordinary necessaries of life. They had boxes and trunks without number, and some of them had small amounts of money."[95]

The permanent impasse between the association and the established black community precluded any exchange of techniques in social welfare and reform. Topeka Negroes did not experience much success in their own jerry-built social welfare program. A synopsis of that activity illustrates the tepid response of most black Topekans to the problem of Exoduster relief.

Before community attitudes hardened against the migration, the *Colored Citizen* (April 7, 1879) asserted: "Topeka Negroes could not but render all the assistance in our power in aiding our persecuted brethren." In that spirit, black citizens met at Second Baptist Church in Tennesseetown on April 19 and formed the Colored State Emigration Board. Columbus M. Johnson, "the old colored pioneer" and former general agent for the Tennessee Real Estate and Homestead Association, was chairman of the meeting. John M. Brown, president, and the Reverend Thomas W. Henderson, corresponding secretary, brought experience in organized charity owing to their membership on the Central Relief Committee. William L. Eagleson, editor and publisher of the *Colored Citizen*, and Seth Vernella, Topeka's Negro physician, served on the board of directors.[96]

---

94. See *Industrial Institute for People of Color*, for complete accounts of contributions; Comstock, *Announcement*.

95. *Commonwealth*, March 8, 1882, in *NC*, V.

96. *Colored Citizen*, April 21, 1879; *Commonwealth*, April 23, 1879, in *NC*, III.

A recitation of sins perpetrated on southern blacks dominated the discussion. Talk of stemming the tide of the Exodus generated some consensus but not without a dissenting voice. One delegate, Charles H. Langston, expressed a desire to see Kansas "as black as midnight" rather than have southern Negroes submit to further depredations.[97] Concrete plans for Exoduster relief were formulated in the following resolution: "We feel it our duty to at once contribute of our means to the aid of the suffering." Contributions were to be solicited at "stated periods" to create a "permanent fund" to be used as needed. The board pledged to work in conjunction with the Central Relief Committee inaugurated by Governor St. John. The $37.05 collected at the meeting was turned over to the committee "to be disbursed under its direction."[98] Thus, during its short life, the board was not an independent agency.

When the members of the board discussed the impact of the Exodus, however, the political potential in the increasing numbers of new black citizens received relatively more attention than did plans for supporting the relief effort. The black press, moreover, was quick to remind the former black southerner, now Topekan: "It was the weakness of Republican policy reaching back to the Mississippi election of 1875 that is one of the leading causes of his having to abandon his home in the South." The gambit of power politics took the form of a progressive concern for voter education and registration. In order to secure a broad base of political action, black newspapers in Topeka published the requirements for the exercise of the franchise under state law.[99]

The migrants were better served by Negroes in cities along the Exodus route. Black Samaritans in St. Louis were particularly helpful and well organized. Although some few migrants settled in St. Louis, in the main the Exodusters were Kansas-bound transients who posed no permanent threat to the community social structure. Negroes in other Kansas cities also founded relief societies. Negro churches in Wyandotte performed noteworthy service in behalf of the Exodusters. Still, black-sponsored philanthropy in Wyandotte, in Leavenworth, and in Law-

97. *Colored Citizen*, April 21, 1879.
98. *Commonwealth*, April 23, 1879, in *NC*, III; *Colored Citizen*, May 3, 1879.
99. *Colored Citizen*, April 21, September 20, October 25, 1879; Topeka *Tribune*, October 30, 1880. The *Colored Citizen* (September 20) and the *Tribune* articles are the only extant record of the Colored Emigration Board in the black Topeka press.

rence did not have appreciably more success than did efforts in Topeka.[100]

By all evidence black institutions in Topeka contributed staff but no material support to organized relief efforts. There were few dissenting editorials in Negro newspapers to counterbalance the increasingly shrill reportage against the continuing migration. Nonetheless, black Topekans readily endorsed the idea that the causes and the effects of the migration merited discussion in a nationwide forum. Accordingly, under the auspices of the KFRA, the Reverend Thomas W. Henderson attended the National Convention of Colored Men, held in Nashville, Tennessee, May 7–9, 1879, as Kansas' only representative.[101]

In its broadest aspect, the convention met to evaluate the Negro's relative gains since the convention's first conclave held in 1863. John R. Lynch of Mississippi and P. B. S. Pinchback of Louisiana, two major political figures in the vanguard of black Reconstruction, set the tone for the proceedings. A definitive concern was the organization of a national black political caucus to recapture the evanescent mind and mood of Reconstruction; the Kansas Exodus was merely one part of that larger compass of issues. Although formally welcomed by the chair, Henderson sat on no committees and offered no resolutions.[102] Notably, when the impetus to black migration was building in 1878, Lynch and Pinchback disavowed the Exodus as a means of halting southern oppression.[103]

100. The Missouri State Historical Society, St. Louis, has numerous newspaper items, broadsides, and pamphlets identifying philanthropy inaugurated by the Colored Relief Board; the work of Charles H. Tandy, a black St. Louis lawyer, was particularly prominent (*Senate Reports*, pt. 3, pp. 36–37). John H. Johnson, also a Negro official with the Colored Relief Board, was often in conflict with Tandy over the thrust of the black relief effort in St. Louis (*Senate Reports*, pt. 2, p. 289). Notably, the response of William Overholtz, St. Louis mayor, closely reflected the view of Mayor Case of Topeka and Mayor Stockton of Wyandotte. Exodusters also had trouble gaining access to the Bryan Mullanphy Fund, a private St. Louis-based charity for settlers moving into the west (Bryan Mullanphy Fund—Materials and the St. Louis *Globe Democrat*, April, 1879, February, 1880, in Missouri State Historical Society; Schwendemann, "The Exodusters on the Missouri," 25–26; New York *Tribune*, June 2, 1879). B. F. Watson, a Negro pastor in Kansas City, Kans., describes the black relief effort in that city (*Senate Reports*, pt. 2, p. 338; see Athearn, *In Search of Canaan*, 20–23).

101. *Colored Citizen*, May 3, 1879; *Kansas Herald*, May 8, 1879. Both newspapers endorsed Henderson's attendance.

102. For Henderson's report on the convention, see *Commonwealth*, May 16, 1879, in *NC*, III; Athearn, *In Search of Canaan*, 101.

103. See *Senate Reports*, pt. 2, pp. 245–46, for a synopsis of events and issues at the convention; St. Louis *Globe Democrat*, May 7, 1879, refers to Exodus concerns at the convention.

Nonetheless, the convention resolved: "That . . . the great current of migration which has for the past few months taken so many of our people from their homes in the South, and which is still carrying hundreds to the free and fertile West, should be encouraged and kept in motion until those who remain are accorded every right and privilege guaranteed by the Constitution and laws." No plans for relief or philanthropy were forthcoming, nor were contributions solicited to aid the migrants. Rather the convention designated the Windom Committee, under whose auspices the Senate investigation of the Exodus convened, as a "permanent national executive committee on migration." Reflecting attitudes previously echoed in black Topeka, the convention urged migrants to exercise "great care" and to have "money enough to pay their passage and enable them to begin life in their new homes with [a] prospect for ultimate success." "As best I could," Henderson reported to his fellow Kansans upon returning home, "I told the people and the Conference what Kansas was and was not. That while our doors are open . . . we did not seek to induce men to come to our borders; that people had to do here as they had to do everywhere else, work, labor, and suffer til they get a start."[104]

Exodusters did "get a start" in Topeka, often after experiencing considerable economic hardship. Overt poverty was evident among many migrants in the city. On April 26, 1879, the *Commonwealth* reported that a Negro woman and her four children were encamped on the sidewalk in front of the State House after having been brought there at her own request. The woman asserted that neither she nor her children had eaten for two days. Her husband had emigrated to Topeka "nearly a month" earlier and was able to care for his family if he could be found. The tone and the substance of the article did not suggest that he had deserted them. Rather, the unnamed man and his family were separated in the general chaos of settlement in a new environment.

The evidence of discontent in the established black community about the Exodusters among them is scant and impressionistic but revealing. First Avenue, one site of migrant settlement and a locale of established black residence, developed pockets of poverty. The black press treated this issue as if it were a new problem brought on by the presence of the

---

104. *Senate Reports*, pt. 2, pp. 245–46; *Commonwealth*, May 16, 1879, in *NC*, III.

migrants. The *Kansas Herald* bristled with self-righteous indignation in reporting the case of a Negro boy, not identified as an Exoduster, caught begging from a white man: "We accosted the boy and succeeded in finding out from him that he lives on First Street; that his father has been dead for some time and that his mother sends him out to beg for nickels. Now we have traced this matter home, and we know the family, and should this thing ever occur again we shall publish the names of the child's parents. There is no need for anyone begging in Topeka, and nuisances of this kind must and shall be abated." There is no evidence that the black newspapers deliberately served a diet of scandal to the reader. They did reinforce commonly accepted doctrines of propriety and race progress. Reports of prostitution, petty theft, and hooliganism were frequent in 1879. "The race can do better without them," asserted the *Colored Citizen*, and "we most sternly protest against such conduct on the part of colored people, for we have enough to battle against."[105] The imprecise definition of race and the inconsistent designation of residence in jail records precludes their use to identify crime patterns in black Topeka. In general the records of Kansas state institutions suffer from the same deficiency through 1885.

Significantly, in 1879 St. John A.M.E., one of Topeka's oldest black churches, moved from its original location to a new building on lots purchased on Second and Madison streets, where comparatively fewer Exodusters were settled. Second Baptist Church, also located on First Avenue, was destroyed by fire in 1879, "and as the locality was considered undesirable, the decision was made to purchase lots at the present location" on Second and Jefferson streets.[106] A *Colored Citizen* editorial condemned "that crowd of lowflying wretches who congregate in front of our churches every Sunday night to curse, dawdle . . . smoke, and in general disturb the decent people who go to church to worship God."[107] The shift in the location of two institutional pillars of the black community strongly suggests that geographical distance, however slight, connoted social distance from the Exodusters. The Exodus, however,

105. *Kansas Herald*, February 27, 1880; *Colored Citizen*, May 10, July 12, November 29, December 12, 1879.
106. *St. John Souvenir Program*; article in *Baptist Church Clippings*, I; *Colored Citizen*, October 10, 1879.
107. *Colored Citizen*, April 10, 1879.

had a more decisive impact on the institutional and social structure of the Negro community. As a result of the migration, black Topeka received an infusion of new leaders with new ideas that put an indelible stamp on organized protest and on the development of political and nonpolitical institutions.

Chapter 4
Social Order and Social Structure 1880–1896

*T*he Great Exodus left its mark on the demography of black Topeka. After the manifold increase from 724 to 3,648 between 1875 and 1880, the twenty years ending in 1900 saw black numbers leveled off sharply to only 4,807. The states of nativity remained much the same in 1900 as in 1875; most Topeka Negroes not born in Kansas came from the Border South. There was an accretion in the number of Negroes born in the state as a result of natural increase. Household structure and size as well as sex ratios did not change appreciably over that period. By 1895, however, 80 percent of the black Topeka population was literate and relatively more children attended school. The occupational structure became more varied throughout the eighties and nineties owing to the great number of professionals and service entrepreneurs who came during the Exodus period. As in all decades, however, most black Topekans were laborers.

At the turn of the century, Negroes could be found in all of the city's five wards. As in previous decades, this was not an indicator of interracial harmony. Rather, black residence conformed to distribution patterns established when the Negro population was diffuse and small. Nonetheless, under the onslaught of the Exodus, established Negro neighborhoods emerged as definite Negro enclaves in which the concentration of blacks was between 50 and 75 percent. Most resided in the First, Second, and Third wards, which traditionally had been regions of black settlement. The most important enclave adjoined the black business district located on the first three blocks of Kansas Avenue, Jackson

Street, and Quincy Street in the Second Ward.[1] This was the hub of the black community's active social and business life. Railroad shops and yards, as well as agricultural processing plants in the immediate vicinity, provided economic supports. Real estate and other service concerns, sundry small businesses, and the offices of an expanding cohort of professionals were additional building blocks in the corporate structure of black Topeka from 1880 to 1896.

Throughout the 1880s and 1890s new neighborhood churches developed and established congregations showed an increase. A fundamentalist sect, a faith healer, and one or two other purveyors of miscellaneous doctrines gave variety to religious expression. In the 1890s, black Episcopalians offered new spiritual and social alternatives. St. John A.M.E., Shiloh Baptist, and Second Baptist churches, however, remained the major institutional pillars of the community. Several fraternal orders, meeting in one or another of two Negro-owned lodge halls, represented one dimension of social behavior. Still another was the presence of two saloons, one owned by a Negro, the other by a white. Of critical significance, between 1880 and 1896, black Topeka claimed six newspapers, which reflected the many facets of Negro life in the city and provided a link to affairs in the state and in the nation. This wealth of Negro enterprise, social activity, and communications indicated a viable community whose goods and services increasingly came from fellow blacks, many of whom were recent arrivals.

The establishment of the black Topeka press was one of the signal events of the Exodus period. The press became a major institution which knit the Negro community into a whole in the ensuing decades. In April, 1878, Topeka welcomed its first black newspaper, albeit secondhand. William L. Eagleson was editor and publisher of the *Colored Citizen* in Fort Scott, a small town in southeastern Kansas, long a stopping place for blacks en route to Kansas from Missouri and points farther south. Eagleson closed his press and moved the operation to Topeka. Thomas W. Henderson, Eagleson's assistant editor, emigrated with him. There seemed to be no outstanding discontent for either man. Perhaps the quicker pace of business and social life in Topeka, the state

1. Tables 1–7, 11; Map 1; Kansas 1865, 1875, 1885, 1895 MS census; U.S. 1870, 1880 census; *Eleventh Census of the United States, 1890*, Vol. I, Pt. 1 (Washington, D.C., 1893); *Radges' Topeka Directory*, 1879–1900.

capital, promised rewards commensurate with its greater size and power. Their own designs for race progress, boundless confidence, and considerable talents found an audience, to the mutual benefit of the men and the city.[2]

The *Colored Citizen* proclaimed "fidelity to Republican principles, a free ballot and a free press," and steadfast adherence to "the goal of race progress." As expansive as his proclamation, Eagleson gained easy entry into the social and political life of the black community. Though unsuccessful, Eagleson's bid for the post of assistant doorkeeper in the Kansas House in 1881 indicated his interest in public service.[3] Henderson, an A.M.E. minister and an activist, participated in black and white philanthropic efforts during the Exodus. As grand secretary for the Freemasons' regional office and as a member of numerous Republican councils, Henderson had a well-rounded public life.[4] E. H. White arrived from Tennessee in 1878. In 1880 he founded the short-lived Topeka *Tribune*, which complemented the *Colored Citizen* in editorial policy with somewhat more attention to social affairs. Through the 1890s, White further served his community as a teacher at the Quincy School; he was an alumnus of Oberlin College. Membership in the Freemasons and in the Shawnee County Colored Horse Fair Association completed his limited social activities. White's association with black Republicans and with the state conventions of colored men was relatively more prominent.[5]

The *Colored Citizen*, the *Tribune*, and the *Kansas State Ledger*, among other black newspapers, provide an indication of class alignment as well as of the processes of decision making and the distribution of power in

---

2. Blacks began to settle in Fort Scott just before the Civil War. Missouri blacks readily escaped from slavery by emigrating there. It is possible that Negroes found employment in the coal and zinc mines near Fort Scott. See Clark and Roberts, *People of Kansas*, 159, 162; Zornow, *Kansas*, 289–91; Athearn, *In Search of Canaan*, 55, 182, 236.
  3. *Colored Citizen*, April 19, 1878, January 11, 1879, November 23, 1881.
  4. Andreas, *History of the State of Kansas*, 548–49; *Colored Citizen*, June 28, September 27, 1878, August 23, 1879.
  5. Kansas 1885, 1895 MS census; U.S. 1880 census; *Colored Citizen*, August 2, 1879; *Commonwealth*, July 31, 1881, in *NC*, V. The Shawnee County Colored Horse Fair Association is a delightful enigma about whose origins or supply of animals nothing has been found. One surmises that the organization was established before 1878 and was a bastion of the Old Guard. For its meetings, see *Colored Citizen* (cited above); *Daily Capital*, May 31, 1882; *Commonwealth*, June 1, 1882, in *NC*, V.

political and nonpolitical institutions.[6] Negro newspapers also provided a measure of men in black Topeka, displaying their occasional prejudice and narrowness as well as their frequent courage and vision. Of decisive importance, black Topeka newspapers from 1878 to 1882 provide information on the dynamics and structure of the Negro community before and after the Exodus.

Ascribed and achieved status in black Topeka between 1865 and 1880 was based on stable employment, circumspect moral behavior, and membership in community institutions. Impressionistic evidence suggests that skin color and literacy had no marked relevance to class position. Biographical sketches of some established residents, the Old Guard, will illustrate the interplay of status determinants. Likewise, the range of values ascribed to the Old Guard is evident in their social activity. The following are among the few whose records provide a fairly complete social-demographic profile.

Whenever David Ware went downtown in the 1880s, people would salute him as Cap'n Ware in recognition of his service in the 1st Kansas Colored. Ware had been in the state for a long time. Born a Missouri slave, he fled to Kansas, enlisted, and at the end of the war settled in Topeka. In 1865, Ware's prospects did not look outstanding; he was an illiterate laborer with no property to speak of. Ware's fortunes improved and in 1873 he secured a highly valued job as the janitor at the State House. That conferred high ascribed status because government employment provided relatively greater security than the run of manual labor. Good steady employment and membership in Second Baptist Church from its founding helped secure his place in the community. Ware, not prominent in political affairs, was a member of the Great Western Lodge and the Shawnee County Colored Horse Fair Association. Further, his presence at most social functions suggests wide acquaintance with the comings and goings of the community. When Ware died in 1888, the flag at the capitol flew at half-mast as the assembled

---

6. On the beginnings and terminations of black Topeka newspapers, see William E. Connelley, *History of Kansas Newspapers* (Topeka, 1916), 293, 295; William M. Tuttle and Surendra Banaha, "Black Newspapers in Kansas," *American Studies*, XIII (1972), 123; Samuel P. Hays, "Social Analysis of American Political History," *Political Science Quarterly*, LXXX (1965), 375.

legislators observed silence.[7] Without doubt, Ware's familiarity with government affairs enhanced his prestige in black Topeka during his lifetime.

Solomon G. Watkins came from Tennessee to Kansas in 1871. Although no information is available regarding his training, Watkins was one of Topeka's first Negro teachers. Both he and his wife taught at the black Quincy School. Less active in the social swirl than Ware, Watkins was more the political activist. His Republican principles, honed in black political caucuses at the city and state levels, made him aware of the decline of Republican resolve regarding racial matters. Accordingly, he joined the Populist-Democrats in 1892. Watkins also served prominently with the Colored League, organized in 1887 to combat discrimination. Watkins tested the political winds by running unsuccessfully for justice of the peace in 1893. He joined forces with E. H. White in 1880 as associate editor of the Topeka *Tribune*, a forum for his political concerns.[8]

Tolliver Byrd, an illiterate laborer and a founding member of the Prayer Circle, which later became St. John A.M.E., came to Topeka from Missouri at the time of Quantrill's raid in 1863. One surmises that Byrd and his wife lived quietly, and, except for church activities and membership in the Freemasons, he avoided the rarer atmosphere of social and political affairs. As was the case with Ware, Byrd's employment as a custodian at the State House conferred some status. And upon Byrd's death in 1893, the capitol flag was lowered to half-mast.[9] Conceivably, for both men, state employment prevented their active involvement in the politics of protest.

Henry Clay Wilson came to Topeka from Tennessee sometime between 1865 and 1870. During the early years, Wilson was variously employed as a house painter, a restaurateur, and a barber. After 1885, Wilson operated a fifteen-chair shop across from the capitol, a location sure to attract influential white customers. By the 1890s, Wilson also had controlling interest in a recreation park on the eastern outskirts of Topeka,

---

7. Kansas 1865, 1875 MS census; U.S. 1870, 1880 census; *Colored Citizen*, November 23, 1878, November 22, 1879; *American Citizen*, December 7, 1888.

8. Kansas 1875, 1885, 1895 MS census; U.S. 1870, 1880 census; *Kansas State Ledger*, March 3, 1893; *Commonwealth*, July 31, 1881, September 6, 1883, in *NC*, V.

9. Kansas 1865, 1875, 1885 MS census; U.S. 1870, 1880 census; *St. John Souvenir Program*; *Colored Citizen*, August 2, October 18, 1879.

a site for numerous church outings and community affairs. Business, membership in Second Baptist Church, and participation in black Topeka social life, if not political activism, qualified Wilson for the role of leader.[10]

The Old Guard was uniformly distributed in Topeka's four wards. Black Topeka's earliest churches, St. John A.M.E., Second Baptist, and Shiloh Baptist, enjoyed proportionate representation in the Old Guard. The Exodus, however, portended manifold changes in all facets of the black Topeka community. The upper level of the social structure underwent particularly significant change.

By 1880, black Topeka was alive with New Men. They were southern born and in their thirties. New Men displayed organizational skills, initiative, and imagination. They were Republican to a man and took the goal of race progress seriously. Their emigration to Topeka between 1876 and 1880 was not solely a result of outraged fortunes in the white-dominated South. The active involvement of New Men in black Topeka politics and protest from 1878 through the turn of the century suggests that their emigration signified a move toward and not a retreat from public affairs as a forum for racial matters. Their social and economic behavior over a comparable period indicates that self-advancement vied with principle; New Men also had an eye for the main chance.

James H. Stuart, Topeka's first Negro lawyer, hailed from Tennessee and set up residence and practice in 1878. Stuart quickly made his mark, successfully defending his first case, a civil suit involving a black Topeka merchant, in November, 1879. In advertisements in the black press, Stuart billed himself as a specialist in real estate transactions, deeds, and titles. Although no information is available regarding his academic training, Stuart was schooled in the social graces; his name was often included on the guest and membership lists of the Topeka black elite. No less adept as a speaker, Stuart gave "a masterly address" at a Thanksgiving Day dinner in 1879, before "a large and elegant gathering of the best class of people," sponsored jointly by St. John A.M.E. and Second Baptist churches. Stuart's knowledge of the law and acquaintance with public affairs contributed to his selection as Topeka's representative at a statewide meeting of black Republicans to press for

10. See *Daily Capital*, May 3, 1937, in *NC*, VII, for an article about Wilson's business activity.

Negro representation on the state ticket in 1882. Stuart continued to exercise influence in black Topeka in subsequent years.[11]

John J. Jennings came to Topeka from Indiana at an unknown date between 1876 and 1879. Jennings is identified as a "professor" as well as a "tonsorialist" who operated a barbershop on Kansas Avenue adjacent to the Taft House, the largest hotel in town. Seemingly, Jennings' several occupations provided a good income; in 1879 he purchased five lots in east Topeka. Throughout the 1880s, Jennings was regarded as a gentleman of property and standing.[12]

C. L. de Randamie was born in Dutch Guiana and came to Topeka in 1877. De Randamie rivaled Jennings in business acumen. Topeka's first black real estate agent, he advertised in the local black press: "If you want to invest in cheap city lots go to de Randamie—106 E. Kansas Avenue," his business and home address. De Randamie tried to encourage fellow black Topekans to go into business in 1879 and led an effort to organize a cooperative brick manufacturing company. That venture ended after an initial subscription of thirty shares of stock. Undaunted, de Randamie opened a wood and coal yard on Tenth and Kansas avenues in 1880. Economic and social status were complementary, and de Randamie was equally comfortable in polite society and in a political meeting.[13]

Alonzo D. DeFrantz from Mississippi and Columbus M. Johnson from Washington, D.C., came to Kansas between 1877 and 1880. Johnson and DeFrantz occupy a special category in the ranks of New Men; both were intimately associated with the Great Exodus. DeFrantz joined forces with Benjamin Singleton and set up the Tennessee Real Estate and Homestead Association, an agency which laid the groundwork for the emigration to Kansas as early as 1875. Seemingly, DeFrantz was not affected by the indictment of the Exodus; he plied his trade as a barber in Topeka, and his name appeared frequently as a participant in a variety

---

11. *Colored Citizen*, November 15, 1878, November 8, 29, 1879; *Daily Capital*, May 31, 1882, and *Commonwealth*, June 1, 1882, in *NC*, V; U.S. 1880 census.

12. Kansas 1885, 1895 MS census; U.S. 1880 census; *Colored Citizen*, January 26, April 29, 1879; *Commonwealth*, March 9, 1883, in *NC*, VII; *Daily Capital*, May 31, 1882; *Commonwealth*, June 1, 1882, in *NC*, V.

13. Kansas 1885, 1895 MS census; U.S. 1880 census; *Colored Citizen*, November 15, 1878, October 28, November 29, 1879, October 23, 1880; *Commonwealth*, March 9, 1883, in *NC*, VII.

of social and political activities. In 1878, with Singleton, DeFrantz founded the United Colored Links, a quasi-political organization broadly concerned with race uplift and "the colored laboring masses." Johnson never ascended the occupational scale beyond the level of manual laborer. Nonetheless, he enjoyed some measure of influence as president of the Southern Kansas Colonization Society, organized in 1881 to encourage migration to various black settlements in that section of the state. Organizations advancing such ideas were popular in the 1890s and sponsored the migration of Topeka blacks to the Oklahoma Territory. DeFrantz and Johnson were members of the Colored State Emigration Board, black Topeka's ill-starred effort at organized philanthropy during the Exodus. Significantly, both men also were present at the meeting at which black Topekans condemned the Exodus as an effort to "Africanize" the state.[14]

The rejection of the migration by men who were themselves new arrivals is one of the enduring ironies of the Exodus experience, despite its explanation in terms of social distance and institutional development. The relative successes of New Men indicate that identification as an Exoduster was determined by a complex of factors, only one of which was tenure in the city. Clearly the Exodus brought more than indigent masses to Topeka; it also brought a needed infusion of professional services and new leadership. A review of social affairs from 1878 to 1882 reveals that the Old Guard and the New Men found common cause as well as grounds for conflict; this helped define the nature of social stratification in black Topeka through the turn of the century.

Events on black Topeka's social calendar indicate the presence of a cross section of established residents and new arrivals who, by virtue of frequent interaction, shared standards, and exclusivity, constituted a social class. At the twentieth wedding anniversary celebration of Mr. and Mrs. David Ware, Dr. and Mrs. Seth Vernella, Mr. and Mrs. John Jennings, and Mr. and Mrs. William Eagleson were among the new Topekans in attendance.[15] And the guest list at the party commemorating the seventh anniversary of Dr. and Mrs. Seth Vernella included Mr. and Mrs. David Ware and other old and new notables. An exchange of gifts

14. "The Colored Links Convention," undated, in *Singleton Scrapbook*; *Weekly Times*, March 25, 1881, in *NC*, V; *Commonwealth*, June 8, 1879, in *NC*, III.
15. *Colored Citizen*, November 23, 1878.

and a sumptuous fare—oysters and champagne, among other delicacies—suggest that ostentation and some attempt at gentility were characteristic of those affairs. Musical entertainment provided by the Shawnee Cornet Band of Topeka, organized by "leading colored musicians" of the city, added variety to social events. At a dance given by the Young Men's Independent Club in November, 1879, "the first of the season," the assembled divided their attention between David Ware, who demonstrated his specialty, "the pigeon wing," and one Mr. Milan, a "neat dancer who changes kid gloves every set." The social liaison between old and new prevailed on more sedate occasions; James H. Stuart, the newly arrived black lawyer, was a guest at the Tolliver Byrds' reception for a visiting A.M.E. minister.[16] Without significant exception, these and other social events indicate mutuality of recognized status between the established and the recently arrived. "The elite," moreover, was the standard frame of reference in black newspapers for gatherings of this coterie. The issues of social class, associational behavior, and the distribution of power appeared in more complex array after 1890.

Like other citizens, black Topekans were interested in improving their position in the marketplace and rising in the city's esteem. The black community urgently sought to make good its boast that "as a race we are making commendable progress. Our growing intelligence and refinement, our enterprise and prosperity are noticeable to the unprejudiced on every hand."[17] New opportunities and old liabilities for professionals, businessmen, and farmers as well as for skilled and unskilled laborers indicated an increasingly diversified occupational structure and economic growth at the close of the nineteenth century. Black women, too, engaged in important business, civic, and social activities.

After the dramatic increase in the number of black professionals during the Exodus, a miscellaneous group of individuals in that occupational category continued to emigrate to Topeka and opened offices or taught school. Most were from the Upper South and had been educated at black undergraduate and professional schools in Tennessee, although some had been undergraduates at Oberlin.

As was the pattern among blacks during the period, service businesses

---

16. (Black) Topeka *Tribune*, October 7, 1878; *Colored Citizen*, July 26, 1878, November 22, 29, October 18, 1879.

17. (Black) Topeka *Colored Patriot*, May 11, 1882.

were most numerous, with barbers and caterers heading the list. Advertisements and other news items indicate that in the 1890s, many were self-employed or owned their own establishments. The distinction between ownership and operating a facility owned by someone else, by no means clear in the newspapers, is made more questionable by the frequently accompanying title of manager. Probably more barbershops, restaurants, and service businesses located in Negro neighborhoods were owned by blacks than were their counterparts in public buildings in the white business district. The relative differences in economic success are unknown.[18]

By 1890 the number of black entrepreneurs in service to a Negro market increased. Among them were several grocers, barbers, salesmen, retailers, restaurateurs, two coal and grain dealers, a notary public, a professional typist-stenographer, two printers, and three licensed real estate agents. A newspaper advertisement for the Washington Investment Company, whose base of operations and ownership are unknown, also suggested new occupational opportunities: "Wanted—Men and Women, white and colored for the sale of Building and Loan stock on the industrial plan, no experience necessary, can make good wages." In 1879, Topeka blacks planned to establish an insurance company, but the plans never came to fruition. Nonetheless in that year, the Chicago-based International Industrial Association, designed to "unite colored persons regardless of sex . . . for mutual benefit, to assist in finding employment, support while sick, and a decent burial after death," had three black Topeka agents. The association was organized as a lodge to which each member paid a fifty-cent initiation fee and monthly dues of fifteen cents.[19] Black fraternal orders and burial policies carried through churches probably covered the largest part of that need. The extent of black coverage through white firms is unknown. Most commonly, moreover, Topeka Negroes were buried in Mount Auburn, the segregated cemetery donated to the black community in 1881 by Colonel John Ritchie, deceased landowner and abolitionist.

Black prosperity spread to the agricultural hinterland around the city.

18. Katzman, *Before the Ghetto*, 115–17, 127–34; Spear, *Black Chicago*, 111–12; Tables 1, 4–6.
19. Tables 1, 4; *Kansas State Ledger*, May 17, 1895, April 23, 1897; *Colored Citizen*, November 11, 1897.

In 1897 the *Colored Citizen* proclaimed that "colored farmers in common with white farmers rejoice over the prospects of a good corn crop which with the wheat, cattle, and hogs will bring considerable money." The press was full of accounts of black farmers who owned rural acres as well as lots in town.[20] Black farmers in the Topeka area would figure prominently in the activities of the National Negro Business League (NNBL) after 1900.

Racism, however, continued to hound Negroes in the labor market. "In short," observed the white Topeka *Daily Capital* with unaccustomed candor, "capital, labor, and the trades . . . are against him and . . . prejudice declares that he must be kept" on the bottom rung.[21] Because of competition with white workers and subjection to the whims of white employers, the economic impact of race discrimination was probably more severe for Negro laborers than for black professionals or businessmen.

In 1895, common laborers constituted 45 percent of the black labor force. Usually the black laborer was a literate head of a single household containing three children and an employed spouse. Laborers' households could be found in all five wards. Greater density, however, was manifest in clusters located in the industrial region near the Kansas River in the Second Ward and in Tennesseetown in the Third Ward. The names of men identifiable as laborers dotted the membership lists of churches and fraternal orders, with a particular concentration in the latter.[22] Limited comparative data on white laborers in racially mixed or contiguous neighborhoods do not reveal stark social or economic differences. Although depression in the 1890s constricted economic development for laborers in general, racism and discrimination created the decisive disparities.

Matters were particularly troublesome in municipal employment. In 1894, 125 Negroes on a municipal work site were laid off and the black press ventured the bleak forecast that, for those men, "it will be almost impossible to find work." Things improved in the following year: "a large number of colored men" could be found in municipal work gangs.

    20. *Kansas State Ledger*, June 19, 1897; *Colored Citizen*, August 12, July 29, 1897; (black) Topeka *Baptist Headlight*, August 1, 1894.
    21. *Daily Capital*, January 3, 1886, in *NC*, VI.
    22. Kansas 1875, 1885, 1895 MS census; U.S. 1880 census; Tables 3, 4, 7.

Yet there did not seem to be grounds for satisfaction with that employment; "some of these men are only working for the purpose of having something to do while others are compelled to break rock for a livelihood."[23] Wages for common laborers averaged $1.43 per day and $6.15 per week. Domestic service, still the mainstay for employed women, paid an average of $1 per day.[24]

Blacks made some inroads in the private sector of the job market. In 1898 the black press reported "a small strike" by whites because of the employment of a black man at a construction site. The contractor retained the Negro against the protests of the white men, who "threw down their shovels in protest." The whites were paid off and not rehired. "All that is needed," Eagleson observed, is "to let that class of men know that the colored man also must live from the proceeds of his labor."[25]

Black Topeka's experience with labor unions was varied and contradictory. Widely prevalent discrimination dictated opposition to organized labor because it excluded Negroes irrespective of their qualifications. Eagleson queried, "Why should Negroes be excluded from places where common laborers are employed? . . . Who is responsible for the signs, 'Negroes Need Not Apply,' attached to the factory and foundry doors everywhere? No one except the labor organizations."[26]

On their own initiative in 1897, Negro waiters formed a union "for the increase of wages during conventions. They request $1.50 a day." Topeka blacks organized the Colored Labor and Trade Union "for the purpose of bringing all the mechanics of the city into a compact body to protect their own interests." That William Eagleson and John M. Brown, neither of whom was a laborer, were members of a standing committee of the Colored Union indicates their collateral interest in reform.[27]

The conditions for blacks in organized labor improved somewhat by 1900. The previous year, the Topeka City Council decided to employ

23. *Kansas State Ledger*, May 25, 1894, February 8, 1895.
24. Leroy A. Halbert and M. L. Sherman (comps.), "Tennesseetown Census, 1898," in KSHS; "Tennesseetown Surveyed," (white) Topeka *Daily Capital-Journal*, March 3, 1883; Kansas 1895 MS census.
25. *Kansas State Ledger*, April 9, 1898; *Colored Citizen*, April 14, 1898.
26. *Colored Citizen*, November 18, 1897.
27. *Ibid.*, March 10, 1897; *Kansas State Ledger*, August 7, 1898. Unfortunately, single reports in the black press listing the officers are the only available records of the two unions.

only union labor in the construction of the new municipal auditorium. The local contractor engaged for the project made a stated commitment "to employ an equal amount [of] white and colored laborers, hence there will be no friction among them for employment."[28]

Perhaps no better indicator of improved fortunes for black laborers could be found than their employment with the Santa Fe Railroad, traditionally noted for racial discrimination. Scattered reports between 1894 and 1898 indicate that, indeed, the hiring policy at the Santa Fe became more liberal at several occupational levels. A Negro porter was promoted to "cook" and placed "in charge of Special Car Number 114." A black press editorial in 1898 proclaimed, moreover, that "the colored men in the employ of the Santa Fe in this city all own their houses and are steady and influential citizens." In part, that affluence may be attributed to the pay, $1.97 per day in 1894, which was more than 45¢ higher than the prevailing rate for common laborers. There also was diversity in the types of employment available for blacks. Three Topeka Negroes, identified as carpenters, helped build fifty houses for that railroad in Illinois. In addition, the Santa Fe retained black Topekan Dr. J. M. Jamison as a company physician.[29]

In 1898 the black press enumerated nine Negro "carpenter-contractors," three "painter-paperhangers," seven "stone mason-contractors," two "brick-masons," one "stone-cutter," one "plumber," two "mattress-makers," and two "carriage builders," among other subspecialties of skilled labor. The wage rates for skilled laborers averaged $1.30 per day higher than those for the unskilled.[30] As with common laborers, skilled workers in the 1890s were able to obtain employment through white contractors. There is every possibility that home improvements and new construction work in the black community were accomplished by Negroes. Both skilled and unskilled workers were employed for approximately eight months per year.

Women established beachheads in public affairs and in business. Lutie Lytle, fledgling lawyer and seasoned Populist campaigner, was admitted

28. *Kansas State Ledger*, November 30, 1899, January 6, 1900.
29. *Ibid.*, January 5, 1894, August 30, 1895, January 24, 1896, December 4, 1897; *Colored Citizen*, October 21, 1898.
30. *Kansas State Ledger*, April 2, 1898; *Colored Citizen*, March 31, 1898, July 27, 1900. There were no noteworthy disparities in demographic or household characteristics which bore an ascertainable relationship to one's position as a skilled or unskilled laborer.

to the bar "without question" in Kansas and in Tennessee. Pearle McNeal, Topeka born, had ample clerical skills and access to political patronage. Through the agency of John Wright, black deputy county clerk, she secured an appointment as a stenographer in the county clerk's office. Lena Thompson "some time ago . . . placed on the market a homemade bread and for a while it did not take too well, but she continued to push a good thing along and today the demand is greater than her supply." Additional retail sales through black grocers increased her profits and enhanced racial economic solidarity. Millinery and dress shops, beauty parlors, and a fortune-teller or two completed the evidence of women's enterprise. Most black Topeka women who worked labored at less glamorous, more menial occupations.[31]

A rash of home and business improvements in the 1890s was not merely appearance for appearance' sake but an emblem of economic progress. Irrespective of occupation, many blacks were imbued with such enthusiasm. Dr. Seth Vernella placed "two magnificent hitching stones" in the front yard of his home, which was "supposedly worth $10,000." Mack Walker, a barber, purchased new furniture for his recently remodeled shop. William Schroud, a janitor at the State House, purchased four lots "with a neat four-room cottage." Black news items, moreover, indicated a rise in home ownership. According to one report, in all of Topeka's Negro enclaves, "most of them own their own homes, humble though they be as a rule." A measure of civic pride also was evident. It is no wonder that Topeka "has an attraction for visitors among our people." Who would not be impressed by "our perfect electric car system extending in every direction, our well paved streets and electric lights, and our public housing?"[32]

The dimensions of social class in black Topeka's economic and social order became more complex in the 1890s. The determinants of class included income, occupation, locale of residence, possessions, and associational behavior.[33] Names appearing in news accounts of social af-

---

31. *Kansas State Ledger*, September 11, October 9, 1897, February 26, 1898, October 7, 1905, January 27, 1906; Table 6.
32. *Kansas State Ledger*, November 27, 1897; *Colored Citizen*, June 17, July 29, October 7, August 12, 1897.
33. Vidich and Bensman, *Small Town in Mass Society*, 49–52, 61–62, 76–77, 97, define social class as a "configuration" in which social and economic behavior as well as patterns of consumption and interaction make it possible to distinguish groups of individuals

fairs and traced through records of the federal and state census, however, do not indicate that skin color had redeeming social importance. Advertisements for skin lighteners, which frequently appeared in the black press, are of equivocal value as a gauge for determining color consciousness. William Eagleson believed that given the insidious nature of color consciousness and discrimination in society as a whole, one would expect Negroes themselves "to resent and remove this unreasoning and unyielding prejudice." Resulting intraracial distinctions based on color, he warned, "if suffered to grow ... will make us an easy victim of our enemies who would divide and devour."[34] To whatever degree it was applicable, color consciousness was merely one of several influences on social behavior. From the vantage point of the 1880s, length of residence in Topeka, independent of occupation and income, was not an important indicator of high status, primarily because many of the leaders were new arrivals. Until 1900, moreover, tenure in the city did not have a measurable influence on social behavior.

Education was an important but inconsistently applied criterion for position and advancement. Throughout the eighties and the nineties, education of the "head and hand" was an often-used metaphor for race progress. Although cleavage into competing ideologies was imminent, in the view of the *Colored Citizen* in 1897, both talents were required for the present, as "there is no other road open for us but by combination." After all, cautioned Eagleson, "as society gets daily more complicated, a much greater amount of general as well as specific information is needed in order to give one a fair start in life." In the 1890s, moreover, black Topekans endorsed the value of both general and specific information and tested their mettle "in competition with other races in the

---

from each other. Of equal importance, social class is an indicator of "the individual's or group's self-perceived notion of position or rank relative to each other and to the particular community within which social interaction occurs." Styles of life, therefore, are "related to preferences in expenditures of time, energy, and money." Weber, *Essays*, 168–88, analytically divides social stratification into economic class (*i.e.*, access to market economy and production of goods), prestige class (*i.e.*, consumption patterns, possessions, associates), and power (*i.e.*, ability to control behavior of others, sometimes defined as effective decision making). While not equivalent, such variables are usually highly correlated. Kahl, *The American Class Structure*, 158–59, separates the large concepts into several indicators of social class (occupation and income, possessions, associates, and values), which permit more subtle treatment of the interrelation of class variables.

34. *Colored Citizen*, August 12, November 18, 1897.

mercantile world."[35] The foregoing characteristics of social and economic class were intricately interrelated. Work, play, education, and worship were parts of the same equation.

On the average, black professionals had a spouse and three children. When not occupying a manse or maintaining living and office quarters in the same place, they lived throughout the wards in neighborhoods that were neither occupationally nor racially segregated. The Seth Vernellas and the James H. Guys, among other notables, black and white, lived between Fifth and Seventh streets on Buchanan and Western avenues, making that a locale where particular people congregated. By 1895, thirty educators, six physicians, seven lawyers, four newspaper editor-publishers, and one pharmacist served the 4,500 Negroes in Topeka. One surmises from black newspaper advertisements that phrenologists and nostrum peddlers also did a lively business. Black businessmen and professionals as an economic group had a similar social, demographic, and residential profile. There were no marked differences among them in household characteristics or distribution through the community. Black businessmen were literate as a rule, but there was relatively less information or emphasis on educational attainment. By any criteria, however, the wide variety of goods and services available through Negro businessmen attests to their abundant and various talents.

A black newspaper editorial asserted that the 1890s was "essentially an age of leagues, brotherhoods, and associations," whose cultural, intellectual, and social concerns defy separation into discrete categories of class or social interests. The Pleasant Hour Literary Circle, meeting under the sponsorship of St. John A.M.E., had an equal number of old and new residents. The Coterie, a popular black women's club, had in 1895 a diversified schedule: church suppers, whist parties, literature selections, relief work, and a guest lecture by Ida Wells Barnett, "The Evils of Lynching."[36] Public affairs, moreover, had an urgency which riveted

35. *Ibid.*, July 15, August 19, 1897. In the August 19 article, however, Eagleson reached the arresting conclusion that "machinery is crushing the hand." Thus "common labor, honest though it be, is battling against machinery at a terrible disadvantage and machinery wins every time." *American Citizen*, January 25, 1889; (black) Topeka *Evening Call*, June 19, 1893.

36. *Baptist Headlight*, September 15, 1893; *American Citizen*, March 18, 1888, April 5, 1889; *Kansas State Ledger*, June 14, 1895.

black Topeka's attention to the present and the future. For most, the legacy of slavery, the end of Reconstruction, and the Great Exodus were not grounds for nostalgia. Nonetheless, the Ex-Slaves Pension Association and the Colored Civil War Veterans Club met irregularly and innocuously through the 1890s. Benjamin "Pap" Singleton and the United Colored Links, intimately associated with the Exodus, also represented an age cohort of social interests. Although Singleton continued to enjoy some veneration and occasional public remembrance, in the 1890s the Links occupied a shadowy ground between the old and the new order and thereafter went into eclipse.[37]

The Interstate Literary Association, founded in 1892 and active through the turn of the century, provided an outlet for black Topekans and a few individuals from other cities in Kansas and in Missouri with academic, intellectual leanings. Numbered among its members were many prominent Topeka educators and professionals as well as their wives. At meetings the assembled were treated to discussions, "The Relation of Higher Education to the Professions," "The New England Period of Literature," and "Black vs. White—The Needs of the Hour." A program of classes, promotions, and graduation certificates indicated the association's pedagogic function. There were also Shakespeare, Beethoven, and Handel clubs as well as art appreciation societies. Black Topekans believed that no apologies were needed for their interest in refinement and cultivation, as such activities "tend to benefit us socially, intellectually, and morally." Negroes were not at a loss for popular entertainment. "Professor" George W. Jackson's New Military Band entertained at large black social functions and at the opening-day ceremonies for the municipal auditorium in 1900.[38]

Lavish entertainments with exotic menus, an orchestra, and a guest list of two hundred or more were not uncommon at the homes of attorney James Guy and Dr. Seth Vernella. The Robert Buckners, also among the socially prominent, gave a reception for forty "visiting ladies" from

37. (Black) Topeka *Benevolent Banner*, August 27, 1887; *Commonwealth*, April 27, August 2, 1881, in *NC*, V; J. L. King (ed.), *History of Shawnee County*, 81; *Daily Capital*, August 26, 1894, in *NC*, VI; *Kansas State Ledger*, February 14, March 13, 20, 1896, May 14, 1898; *Colored Citizen*, March 10, August 11, 18, 1898; Painter, *Exodusters*, 118–19, 121–23.
38. (Black) Topeka *Times-Observer*, November 28, 1891–January 9, 1892; *Kansas Herald*, April 9, 1880; *Colored Citizen*, July 1, 1897, September 21, 1900; *Kansas State Ledger*, May 25, 1894, January 1, April 9, 1898.

Washington, D.C.: "As the moments fled by the bright stars in turn appeared on the society horizon, each endeavoring to outshine the other." Excursions by socially prominent families to Denver, Los Angeles, and Chicago also were fashionable.[39]

Similar patterns of consumption and types of entertainment, if of a more modest order, were evident in the organized social activity of unskilled laborers in Tennesseetown. The Odd Fellows, numbering many unskilled laborers in its membership, "ran an excursion of two railroad coaches to Lawrence, Kansas."[40] Among social recreations, "bicycle riding has become popular among coloreds. All those who do not have them may rent them." Games, such as "Pump, Pump, Pull Away," "King William," and "Crack the Whip," were standard fare at garden parties. "Those wishing to . . . perfect matters for a tennis set" were instructed to call the office of the black Topeka *Times-Observer*. Black Topeka had its own baseball team, the Mascots. Apparently, there were more "razzberries" than usual when they played a visiting black team from St. Joseph, Missouri, in 1898: "As do all colored ball games . . . it ended in a squabble," and the Mascots had to forfeit the game.[41]

The values of the late nineteenth century, material wealth and successful competition, caused Topeka blacks to determine their progress by standards in force in society at large. Nonetheless, imitation of white models was not essential to black social development.[42] The race problem did permeate many areas of public life and it influenced social affairs. Although there was some evidence of class antagonism, consensus among social and protest groups in combating Jim Crow and promoting

39. *Colored Citizen*, August 27, 1897, October 12, November 4, 1898; *Kansas State Ledger*, November 16, February 15, 1894, June 7, 1895, August 27, 1897, October 12, 1898.
40. *Kansas State Ledger*, August 13, 1894; Kansas 1885 MS census; *Colored Citizen*, May 5, 1898.
41. *Kansas State Ledger*, August 24, 1894; *Times-Observer*, June 25, 1892; *Colored Citizen*, May 26, 1898.
42. Mary White Ovington, *Half a Man: The Status of the Negro in New York* (New York, 1911), 171, contends that black social and protest organizations developed in accordance with a "distinctly American ambition." Although achieving civil rights on a par with whites was the desired end, it does not follow that imitation of white models was the major determinant in the success or failure of such endeavors. The difficulties in Ovington's argument are also evident in Nancy J. Weiss, "From Black Separatism to Interracial Cooperation: The Origins of Organized Efforts for Racial Advancement, 1890–1920," in Barton J. Bernstein and Allen Matusow (eds.), *Twentieth-Century America: Recent Interpretations* (New York, 1972), 54–85.

racial progress was the definitive pattern in organized social behavior, irrespective of class alignment.

Black Topekans occasionally lived beyond their means. Such ostentation was unwarranted, in the view of the *Colored Citizen*. No one else does "what we are doing with impunity on such slender resources." The *Kansas State Ledger* voiced that complaint: "With Winter . . . just over the fence," some Negroes unemployed all summer took "what little money they had . . . [and] are eager to spend it rusticating up and down our railroads pleasure seeking."[43] Employment in the lairs of wealthy whites, "rich Pullman Palace Cars and private dwellings," created among blacks a desire for conspicuous display "wholly unsuited to their true social condition." This behavior only "gives false notions of life . . . frequently leading to the commission of offenses against law and morals, [thereby] wrecking many lives and creating unfavorable public sentiment."[44]

Popular use of the term *class* in period news accounts clouds technical definition of class as a system of hierarchical stratification. Nonetheless, the latter, more precise frame of reference for social class and the impact of racism are implicit in the following *Colored Citizen* editorial: "We are all said to look alike, [but] there are as many differences among us as among the whites." Thus, all blacks suffer unfairly from the iniquity of Negroes who, "dead to all sense of decency or self-esteem," are no better than a "millstone around the necks of the better class."[45]

By definition, invidious class and social distinctions consigned some black citizens to the bottom of the social pyramid. Eagleson detected a "feeling of unfriendliness" on the part of the "average individual" who, "by reason of social disadvantage, feels scorned by the more socially favored classes." "Although untrue," he editorialized, this attitude produces "a hostile course of action towards the other as if it was."[46] Likewise, at the upper end of the scale, competition bred losers who fell from atop the social order to be replaced by others. Nonetheless, rapid turnover was not the norm, and a few families were able to preserve their good name and the community's good offices across two genera-

43. *Colored Citizen*, June 17, 1897; *Kansas State Ledger*, August 7, 1896.
44. *Kansas State Ledger*, April 2, 1895; *Colored Citizen*, July 19, 1897.
45. *Colored Citizen*, July 19, 1897.
46. *Ibid.*, November 25, 1897.

tions; Henry Clay Wilson, James Guy, and John Lytle are cases in point. The 1900s, however, provide the best vantage point for observing social and occupational mobility.

Certain physicians, lawyers, businessmen, ministers, and educators provided vital services to the black community and gained a measure of acknowledged prestige. Status, however, was based on more subtle, intangible factors than occupation and wealth. Moral probity and participation in community institutions such as the church indicated respectability and helped define one's social standing. A few black Topekans, fulfilling most of those criteria for status and prestige, ascended to positions of authority in many organizations and, thereby, constituted a leadership elite. Thus, in significant ways, "leadership accumulated leadership."[47] William Eagleson, James Guy, the Reverend William L. Grant, Seth Vernella, and Robert Buckner, among others, conformed to that pattern.

Politics and the church provided a platform for launching black Topeka leaders. Political activity placed a Negro, regardless of occupation, in the vanguard of the race's confrontation with white decision makers. Black clergymen represented a formidable institution charged with responsibility for guarding the community's social and spiritual forces. The Reverend William L. Grant, as an example, had a short but effective tenure at Shiloh Baptist. By reputation, he was "a great pulpiteer . . . organizer, and orator of renown." In addition to political activism, Grant "had the ear of the people of the other race as no other Negro minister of the day."[48] Although few reached Grant's public stature, most ministers were ardent proponents of social welfare, reform, and community service. Some were not ennobled by their calling. The Reverend George Olden, pastor of Second Baptist in the late 1890s, was nearly hounded from his pulpit for alleged misappropriation of funds—by no less a paragon of virtue than Nick Chiles, whose notoriety as a gambler and tavern owner tarnished his more respectable reputation as a responsible journalist and community leader.[49]

---

47. Vidich and Bensman, *Small Town in Mass Society*, 259, describe the patterns of leadership in one institution expanding to a spectrum of influence in public affairs.
48. *Shiloh Souvenir Program*; *Daily Capital*, April 11, 1898; *Colored Citizen*, August 11, September 15, 1898.
49. *Baptist Church Clippings*, I; *Daily Capital-Journal*, June 19, 1915.

New construction and expansion were the norm for the established churches, St. John A.M.E. and Shiloh Baptist churches in particular.[50] Through the early 1890s, St. John A.M.E. had the largest number of elites and decision makers, although Shiloh had many members with high social and economic status. In 1890, St. Simon's, the fledgling black Episcopal church, was a mission with no regular priest, sheltered under the wing of white Topeka's Grace Cathedral. By 1900, however, membership in St. Simon's denoted class and color consciousness. Although there was no wholesale defection from established denominations, by 1905 James Guy, lawyer, Solomon G. Watkins, teacher, and John Wright, accountant, had left St. John A.M.E. for St. Simon's. As a badge of ascribed status, moreover, those men and their families occupied pews closest to the altar.[51]

A healthy ecumenism prevailed at church-sponsored religious and social functions. Musical aggregations and speakers from St. John A.M.E., Shiloh Baptist, and St. Simon's often shared the same platform and audience.[52] Whatever one's inward grace, membership in one or another of those churches was an outward sign of social success. Prominence in the church and in social affairs provided a measure of influence in the black community as a whole. This confirms the validity of the hypothesis that "leadership in non-political institutions is as much a public fact as leadership in party politics or public administration, for it is a crucial feature of decision-making and the distribution of power."[53]

Press reports indicate that most members of Second Baptist Church were "poor washer women . . . who only know how to wring clothes and collect their small mite." Some families in that congregation, moreover, were "frequently in need of assistance from the city or the county during the winters." Primitive Baptist Church, noted for its fundamentalism and the practice of "washing the feet," had a small congregation that constituted "a very good class of working people."[54]

---

50. Kansas 1875, 1885, 1895 MS census; U.S. 1880 census; *Colored Citizen*, July 22, 29, August 19, 1897.
51. Interview, August 8, 1973, with Dr. Henrietta S. Cox, whose family has been affiliated with St. Simon's since 1905.
52. *Kansas State Ledger*, July 3, 1897; *Colored Citizen*, December 9, 1897.
53. Hays, "Social Analysis of American Political History," 375.
54. *Kansas State Ledger*, September 4, 7, 1894; *Daily Capital*, May 4, 1886, in *Baptist Church Clippings*, I.

The church clearly reflected the dimensions of ascribed and achieved status as well as the growth of the Negro community. In 1910, black Topeka had thirty churches distributed throughout the city.[55] By the turn of the century, however, the church was only one among several institutional pillars in the expanding community. Nonetheless, as the site of many secular activities, the church maintained its preeminence in defining social structure and order.

Exclusion and preference determined membership in secret societies and fraternal orders and, therefore, provided an indicator of status. Those organizations also created "quasi-kinship bonds," which served as one basis for social identity. Burial and insurance policies carried through the lodges helped create new opportunities for services in that quarter by black businesses, though discrimination set the terms for development. Similarly, black fraternal orders originated because of racism. "Even to this very hour," T. Thomas Fortune observed in 1887, white organizations "refuse to fraternalize with or to recognize the legality or regularity of the orders their actions caused colored men to establish."[56] Nonetheless, the Masons and the Knights of Tabor, among other fraternal orders and their women's auxiliaries, enjoyed considerable popularity.

Thus, the church, the marketplace, and the clubhouse were arenas for the community's active social life. In the 1880s and 1890s an abundant enthusiasm permeated economic and public affairs. In 1897 the *Colored Citizen* justly proclaimed: "Our young men and women are up to date in every particular," politicians and businessmen court us, and "the scholarly find attraction in our literary people, societies and libraries."[57] By all terms, the concept of race progress was the basis for institutional, social, and economic development of black Topeka. As it evolved, that concept fused institutions, ideas, and men into a community.

The goal of race progress assumed many guises. Migration to Oklahoma, for example, fired the imagination of black Topekans in the 1890s. Going to Oklahoma was not an escape from oppression but a

55. *Colored Citizen*, August 17, 1910.
56. Vidich and Bensman, *Small Town in Mass Society*, 22–25; *Benevolent Banner*, September 10, 1887, reprint from New York *Age*.
57. *Colored Citizen*, August 12, 1897.

move toward economic opportunity on a new frontier. That migration, however, resists comparison with the Great Exodus, both in terms of magnitude and the relative insignificance of race oppression as an impelling force.

The idea received some commentary in the black press as early as 1882, but plans were put on a firm footing in 1890 with the organization of the Oklahoma Immigration Association. Black Topekan Henry Rolfe, president of the association, spent five weeks in Oklahoma in 1890 and found the prospects excellent "in every particular." Edwin P. McCabe, a black and formerly Kansas state auditor, went to Oklahoma in the same year. With political appetite still keen, he nourished ambitions for the governor's chair and hopes for an all-Negro state. That McCabe's plans did not materialize did not stop black Topekans, "many of them well fixed financially," from making the trek. The lure of wealth, race progress, and high politics must have been powerful indeed. St. John A.M.E. was nearly decimated by the departure of Oklahoma-bound parishioners. Even William Eagleson considered the move. By 1895, however, the ballyhoo subsided and migration to Oklahoma, "the land of milk, honey, money, and wine," went the way of most dreams. With increasing frequency the press reported the return of Negro Topekans who, if not wealthier or wiser, were none the worse for their adventure.[58]

In 1894 the black press claimed that Negroes were in accord with the "interests of the average citizen . . . in good schools and good streets" and, to greater and lesser degrees, in the reform concerns common to the period.[59] Reform and the attainment of capital, as well as politics and organized protest, helped shape the black community's social and intellectual character. Both race pride and community responsibility were manifest in the activities and agencies through which black Topekans addressed the problems of social and moral welfare, health, and crime.

As in most areas of Negro life, their efforts at reform emerged under conditions of racial discrimination. It was a factor in black access to ser-

58. *Daily Capital*, April 4, 1890, in *NC*, VI; *Colored Patriot*, May 4, 1882; *American Citizen*, March 22, May 19, June 21, 1889; *Kansas State Ledger*, February 24, 1893, June 5, 1895; *Colored Citizen*, March 10, 1898; Mozell C. Hill, "The All Negro Communities of Oklahoma: The Natural History of a Social Movement," *Journal of Negro History*, XXXI (1946), 260–62; *Colored Citizen*, May 19, 1898.

59. (Black) North Topeka *Blackman*, undated, reprint from New York *Age*.

vices in public welfare. In 1883, blacks could boast of some white endorsement of racial equality in state charitable institutions. A committee of black Topeka citizens awarded James D. Snoddy, speaker of the Kansas House of Representatives, a gold-headed cane for his "manly stand" in support of legislation "granting to colored citizens an equal share" in the benefits from state charity appropriations. The measures were defeated, however, and as black-white relations eroded in the ensuing decade Negroes increasingly experienced discrimination in public-supported agencies of law and social welfare. Blacks had difficulty gaining relief from the Shawnee County Commission for the Poor during the Exodus and they were no better served in 1893. One of the most glaring and publicized cases of race-related problems in state institutions involved black Topekan "Hook Jim" Funston, an epileptic and an amputee, confined to the state insane asylum in 1897. Funston allegedly was beaten to death with a rubber hose by a white attendant. Although the attendant was subsequently dismissed, the courts and the coroner's office saw to it that no charges were brought. To the chagrin of the black Topeka community, the entire issue was swept under the carpet.[60]

Such incidents and conditions caused blacks to develop and share their own social resources. This contributed to a sense of community which defined reciprocal responsibilities between individuals as well as their interaction through institutions. Segregation also permitted a measure of black control over the administration and implementation of reforms, which evolved along lines particularly attuned to the needs of the Negro community.

By 1896, sixteen years after the Exodus, social welfare in black Topeka had become more mature and complex. As was the case with politics, black Topekans subscribed to many of the ideas and concerns for reform that prevailed at the turn of the century. Among these were temperance, the prevention of crime, and women's suffrage.

In the 1880s, temperance merited a qualified endorsement from black Topekans. Among the evils associated with alcohol were rising crime rates and the disintegration of social and moral order. That reform concern, however, never reached a state of high moral outrage or of "absolutist enthusiasm." In fact, from the territorial period forward,

60. *Commonwealth*, March 9, 1893, in *NC*, VII; *Kansas State Ledger*, December 15, 1893, August 7, 1897; *Colored Citizen*, January 4, 1898.

the political fortunes of its adherents were nearly as important as the moral issue—until 1917, when the "bone dry" law passed.[61]

In 1880 the *Kansas Herald* asserted its "right to publish any article either for or against whiskey so long as we receive payment for same." A column entitled "Temperance Reading" regularly appeared in the *American Citizen* in 1889, indicating some interest in the problem. The suggested reforms, however, were benign: "Coffee Houses" offered "one solution to the drinking problem." Facilities at black Topeka's YMCA, established in 1885, also "may be made immensely effective in weaning men from evil association with the dram shop and from the drinking habit."[62] The most strident and publicly indignant, however, were the Negro dramshop owners, who had to run the gauntlet of municipal prohibition laws. If those individuals were not viewed as exemplars of public virtue, they certainly did not receive wholesale censure in the black community. Association with the liquor traffic was a modest venality, and one suspects that the sin was in being caught. The problems of Nick Chiles, a Negro businessman, politician, journalist, and dramshop owner, are a case in point.

In 1893, Chiles and two associates were arrested and charged with selling liquor and running a crap game and a billiards parlor on the first floor of his boardinghouse. In reporting the incident, the *Kansas State Ledger* offered the absolution that "we believe there are quite a number of other secret dives running in violation of prohibition law in this city." In 1898, Chiles was arrested again and a stiff punishment imposed. Reviewing that case, William Eagleson detected race prejudice and political chicanery on the part of the Topeka sheriff, whose candidacy for reelection failed because of a lack of support from black Topekans. Accordingly, "the inequitable use of the prohibition laws of the city required exposure. With joints, barrooms, and drug stores running wide open all over the city, it is rather significant that Nick Chiles should have been selected to take away the sins of the city in that direction."[63] For its part, the *Kansas State Ledger* was disturbed over the rising number of crimes perpetrated by youth under the influence of alcohol: "While we are not

    61. Richard Hofstadter, *The Age of Reform: From Bryan to F.D.R.* (New York, 1955); Zornow, *Kansas*, 190, 224.
    62. *Kansas Herald*, April 23, 1880; *American Citizen*, March 22, 1889.
    63. *Kansas State Ledger*, May 5, June 30, 1893; *Colored Citizen*, May 12, 1898.

crazy for prohibition, we are in favor of a rigid enforcement of the law, especially where it comes in conflict with minors." Liquor also formed an unholy alliance with prostitution. According to one black newspaper, Benjamin Jordan, a black dramshop operator, was a business associate of Etta Bray, "a disreputable Negro woman," whose enterprise included "fourteen white and colored girls." Their establishments, located in Tennesseetown, were billed in the black press as "Popular Resorts for Sports." Despite complaints, police raids, and closings, such businesses mushroomed again in a matter of months at the same location.[64]

The black press spiced its columns with articles giving the names of prostitutes brought before the law as well as "visitors in attendance at the time of arrest." In a curious variation on the theme of discrimination, Fred L. Jeltz of the *Kansas State Ledger* noted that "white men will and are duly able to pay the fines of their wayward and unfortunate women while the defenseless colored women who seek a life of shame are entrapped by this gang."[65] Perhaps the problem would have been alleviated by more black procurers or fewer black prostitutes. Among one group of white Topeka reformers, practical measures to control the problem received more emphasis than strident moralism or a call for the elimination of the profession.

The white Women's Equal Suffrage League was of that mind in their opinion on prostitution, published in the white press under the by-line "A Necessary Evil." The league claimed that "houses of prostitution [were] conducted in the upper part of business buildings . . . located in the heart of the business district downtown and not confined to the lower part of Kansas Avenue," one locale of black business and residence. "The women should be driven to the suburbs, confined to one strip of territory, and examined by a competent physician every two weeks. . . . It would be better to regulate them in a method that all know about than to allow them to run as they do now."[66]

Getting the vote, of course, was the major priority of the league. The Negro women who joined that crusade, albeit on a segregated basis, organized the Colored Women's Suffrage Association in 1887. This sig-

---

64. *Kansas State Ledger*, January 29, 1897; (black) Topeka *People's Friend*, July 7, 1893.
65. *Kansas State Ledger*, June 16, 1893, July 24, 1896.
66. *Daily Capital*, undated, in *Shawnee County Clippings*, XIX.

naled the initial appearance of black women on the public stage. Although the association never achieved much prominence, Negro women were among the active proponents of reform at the turn of the century.

From the numerous articles regarding women's rights that appeared in the black press between 1887 and 1894, it seems the Negro community was aware of the relevant issues. The tone of that commentary, however, remained politely conservative, urging women to enhance their stature as "the natural conservators of decency and morality." After all, politics is a man's domain. How could women "really know what is best for the country in any but a moral sense?"[67]

Social welfare was an area in which black Topeka women exercised influence in public life. Social affairs and community service were fused in the Women's Benevolent Society, Lodge No. 3. That organization believed that a "full and free exercise of mercy and charity" required the joint endeavor of the church and privately organized social welfare. The society, moreover, boasted of being "the largest in the city and with proper management could be made a powerful force for good." There were "500 adult and juvenile members in good standing [and] $650 in the treasury." Gentility and a desire for social service also prevailed among the youth: "A few of us young ladies of Topeka . . . have organized ourselves into . . . the Young Ladies Charitable Union, the object of which is to find homes for orphan children and others who stand in need of help."[68]

Black Topekans' concern for the welfare of their community included homeless and delinquent boys. The Colored Juvenile Benevolent Society was formed to address the causes of crime. Unfortunately, the records of the society's activities and plans are slim. "Whenever the reform school boys parade the streets of Topeka," Eagleson observed, "we feel ashamed and grieved to see so large a number of colored boys, many of them tiny tots who are undergoing punishment for some more or less serious offenses." Proper home training was crucial. One way in which parents could impose a measure of control was "to keep their boys busy

67. *American Citizen,* January 25, 1889; *Daily Capital,* March 10, 1889, in *NC,* VI; *Baptist Headlight,* April 20, May 11, 1894.
68. *American Citizen,* May 31, 1889, June 22, 1888.

at home rather than loafing or running the streets." Children required special vigilance during the summer months: "Schools will be closed ... so parents must provide for them otherwise, reform school, etc."[69]

Delinquency was by no means confined to boys. The problem and solutions were more complex "when young girls inheriting diseased tendencies" left home during adolescence "to follow their natural impulses unrestrained by parental authority." Infant mortality rates also were high and attributable to family inadequacies. Certainly, here were grounds for reform: "The church should engage lady physicians to deliver lectures on the duties of maternity and domesticity to our young women. Sanitation, nutrition, etc. should be included. The establishment of a Negro Young Women's Christian Association also would be in order."[70] In the view of a police matron, economic pressures were an additional reason for black juvenile crime: "Their mothers are working and they have no one to take care of them." No explanation, however, accounted for the "shocking and disgusting behavior of boys and girls in church." Cutting up in Sunday school hardly merited the glaring label "Juvenile Delinquency" used by the black press.[71]

As the evidence of a busy traffic in liquor, gambling, and prostitution among adults attests, black Topeka youth were not the sole perpetrators of crime. Nor were legal transgressions limited solely to the violence and passions of ne'er-do-wells or the indigenous poor. The illegal activities of blacks involved in white-collar crime—mail and real estate fraud, grand larceny, and embezzlement—littered the pages of the black press in the nineties. Professor W. J. Johnson, a black postal employee and formerly an elementary school principal, was convicted of mail fraud in 1895. He received a three-year sentence at Leavenworth Penitentiary, where he parlayed his academic talents into a job as prison librarian. The allegations of race discrimination were mild and Johnson's guilt was not questioned. Rather, the concern was his length of confinement for a theft of ninety-eight dollars, a crime for which many Negroes believed a white man would have received a shorter sentence. Upon his release in 1898, Johnson returned "home to his many friends," seemingly none

69. *Kansas State Ledger*, April 5, 1895, February 5, 1898; *Colored Citizen*, June 17, July 1, 1897.
70. *Colored Citizen*, November 11, 1897, April 21, 1898.
71. *Kansas State Ledger*, January 4, 1898; *Colored Citizen*, May 26, 1898.

the worse for wear. Although Johnson secured a position as a summer school teacher in 1900, his employment is otherwise unknown.[72]

Publicizing reform activities proved to be something of a mixed blessing. In Eagleson's opinion, black Topekans viewed reform "as antagonistic to the race and in the interest of our enemies." He detected, however, more self-serving motives: "The pulpit and press are seemingly afraid to allude to our many short-comings, knowing as they do that it will unfavorably affect the contribution and subscription lists." In addition, "colored men are not given to making martyrs of themselves in the interest of the race."[73] That overstates the case, but for many black Topekans, the issue of reform did have to share place with a desire to make advances in commerce. In part, enthusiasm over the Gilded Age explained that ardent interest. To no less a degree, discrimination made economic development an urgent necessity. Race progress, organized protest, and politics readily accommodated that emphasis on economics and did not depart from the goal of full civil rights.

72. *Kansas State Ledger*, August 19, 1892, October 25, November 11, 1895, March 6, 1896, April 23, 25, 1898; *Colored Citizen*, June 15, 1900.
73. *Colored Citizen*, November 18, 1897.

Chapter 5
Protest Organization and Political Action 1880–1896

"Outer compulsion" and "inner need" began to turn the black community in upon itself in the aftermath of the Compromise of 1877 and the Great Exodus. Discrimination in education, in public accommodations, and in political affairs became increasingly apparent between 1880 and 1896. Racism gained new vigor through the sanction of law in *Plessy* v. *Ferguson* in 1896. In the intervening sixteen years, the battle lines in the campaign against Jim Crow were drawn.[1] In significant ways, that confrontation set the tone for black life. It was a cornerstone of political activity, of protest and community organization, and of associational behavior. Blacks in Topeka and in the nation strengthened the bonds of intraracial communication, largely through organized protest at the local, state, and national levels. Creative stress over political alternatives also helped give definition to organized protest. Adherence to the American ideals of self-help and individual initiative, however, provided no way out of the maze of discrimination encountered on every hand. Segregation in the public schools was a major source of discontent.

All evidence suggests that Topeka Negroes were unstinting in their support and concern for education as a vehicle for race advancement. "Give us good schools; give us good teachers," the black Topeka *Kansas Herald* implored, "and let parents be careful to keep their children in

---

1. W. E. B. Du Bois, *The Souls of Black Folk* (Chicago, 1903), 57; Williamson, *After Slavery*, Chapters 9, 11; C. Vann Woodward, *The Strange Career of Jim Crow* (New York, 1966), 71.

school regularly and our race is safe." E. H. White, Topeka's first black teacher, admonished Negroes to continue to support the goal of education as a fundamental element of race progress. In spite of the liability of discrimination, "let no man or woman stand and fold his or her arms and dream of life, liberty and enjoyment without tendering a helping hand towards educating their race."[2] White established a night school in 1881 where a group of "mothers, fathers, young men and ladies whose opportunities . . . have not been such that they could acquire an education" were given a "regular program of [academic] exercises."[3]

In 1891 the black *Times-Observer* offered the following suggestion to Negro parents: "Purchase books your children need. Children above the third grade should study at home. Encourage children to read aloud at home." In addition to enabling black parents to exercise some control over their child's progress, that prescription helped counteract miseducation in the public schools. In 1896 a black editorial found the syntax and illustrations in texts used for the fourth and fifth grades to be inferior. Moreover, "they are especially objectionable because they excite race prejudice [and] in many places things are said about our people that are untrue. No sensible educator, sane or sound of mind, would recommend it."[4]

The refusal of the Topeka Board of Education to appoint black principals, teachers, or custodians in the city's Negro elementary schools angered Topeka Negroes. That problem triggered increasingly serious disagreements between blacks and the civil authorities.[5] In 1879 the *Colored Citizen* asserted: "We hear of no Irish or German school. All children are at liberty to attend the school closest to them, except the black child." Unity was crucial in combating the problem, and the editorial advocated "a banding together of the black community to put an end to the injustice. A lawyer has been employed and the case tested." Identification of educational conditions at the black Monroe School in 1879, made famous in *Brown* v. *Board of Education of Topeka* in 1954, indicated that segregated schools were inherently unequal: "The management of the Monroe Street School has been such that many children in it are just

2. *Kansas Herald*, April 9, 1880; Tables 7, 8; *Colored Citizen*, October 4, 1879.
3. *Kansas Herald*, May 21, 1881.
4. *Times-Observer*, August 19, 1891; *Kansas State Ledger*, March 13, 1896.
5. See, for example, *Colored Citizen*, December 14, 1878, September 13, 20, 1879.

where they were 2–3 years ago, and it is our deliberate opinion that they are purposely kept back to prevent their entering a mixed school."[6] The comparisons across time are apt and disturbing. In 1881 the Topeka *Tribune* denounced "the un-Republican, un-American, unconstitutional refusal of those in charge of our public schools to admit colored children save into those designated and unlawfully maintained as separate colored schools."[7]

The issue resurfaced with a vengeance in the 1890s. William Reynolds, a black Topekan and the plaintiff in a suit against the Topeka Board of Education in 1890, alleged that the black Lowman-Hill School was "unsanitary, inconvenient, and undesirable." Its location, "a veritable cesspool," further indicated the board's flagrant discrimination against Negroes. In refuting Reynolds' contention and in support of segregation, the board asserted that the separation of black students, "especially in their initial years," was necessary because the Negro children need "a little different discipline from the white pupils [and] have somewhat different intellectual requirements." In its successful defense, the board claimed that facilities and materials were equal: "The supply of school paraphernalia of every kind is the same, both as regards quantity and quality, as in other schools in the city."[8]

If segregation were to prevail, Negroes were steadfast in their insistence that black teachers be retained. There was "a copious supply of black teachers among our people," the *Kansas State Ledger* contended in 1893, and their places in black elementary schools were usurped by white teachers, some of whom were brought in from out of state. In 1893–1894, moreover, there were twenty-two black teachers in Topeka with state certificates, but only eleven had regular appointments.[9] The difficulty was resolved in 1894, when the board of education agreed to appoint only black teachers to Negro schools. In a real sense, however, that reinforced segregation.

---

6. *Colored Citizen*, September 20, June 21, 1879.
7. (Black) Topeka *Tribune* article, undated, reprinted in *Commonwealth*, August 31, 1881, in *NC*, V.
8. William Reynolds, Plaintiff, v. The Board of Education of the City of Topeka, of the State of Kansas, "Brief for the Defendant," *In the Supreme Court of the State of Kansas—1890* (Topeka, 1890).
9. (Black) Topeka *Tribune*, October 7, 1880; *Kansas State Ledger*, June 30, July 28, August 5, 1893, June 8, February 2, 1894.

Some believed that segregated education could be turned to black ends. Without acquiescing in the legal or moral legitimacy of segregation one jot, James Guy, a prominent black Topeka attorney, asserted: "We should not attempt to be in places that we are not wanted. We should recognize our differences and need to establish race pride and confidence." In a series of letters to the *Kansas State Ledger*, W. J. Johnson, a black Topeka educator, concurred with Guy and added: "We are not seeking amalgamation or assimilation . . . we feel that we are justified in insisting that [whites] not obtrude their equally unwelcome presence upon us."[10]

Notably, the first black high school graduate received his diploma from the integrated Topeka High School in 1882.[11] The available statistics for the high school compiled by the state do not reveal race. An incomplete, unpublished listing gave the names of black Topekans who graduated from the high school between 1882 and 1893 and who achieved later prominence. Curiously enough, a black press report revealed that the graduating class of 1894 had only two Negroes.

Clearly black Topekans were aware that education was an important element of race progress. With equal surety, they knew that education alone could not hold back discrimination. The *Colored Citizen* asked in 1879: "What is to become of the many young men who are being educated? . . . They will not be content to follow the pursuits of their fathers." The conclusion of that editorial was prophetic: "This color difficulty is going to outlast many generations, hope and pray, and degrade ourselves as we may" in the search for equality. Fifteen years later, the *Kansas State Ledger* inquired bitterly: "Why do we send our children to high schools and to academies, to earn $1.50/day cleaning the sewers?"[12] Both municipal and state governments remained adamant in their commitment to separate and unequal education. The recalcitrance of the Kansas legislature in not removing discrimination in militia service until 1888, moreover, indicated that the prejudice experienced by black To-

---

10. *Times-Observer*, May 28, 1892; *Kansas State Ledger*, July 28, August 18, 1893.
11. "Retrospective," *Daily Capital*, September 6, 1942 (Topeka High School was integrated from its founding in 1874); *Kansas State Ledger*, May 25, 1894; Topeka Board of Education, "The Colored Schools" (Topeka, 1922), in KSHS.
12. *Colored Citizen*, November 29, 1879; *Kansas State Ledger*, February 9, 1894.

pekans in education was evident in public-supported institutions as a whole.[13]

Discrimination in public employment also was part of the mosaic of race prejudice. In 1878, municipal authorities refused to hire a black policeman and did not do so until 1885.[14] In general, the hiring policy in municipal civil service did not measure up to the aspirations of Negroes for more equitable representation. "We constitute ¼ of the population of the city, we pay taxes . . . we are peaceful and industrious, yet we have only 1 colored official in this city," complained the Topeka *Tribune* in 1880. That single Negro civil servant, a mail carrier, moreover, was unjustly censured in a white newspaper for "incompetency—difficulty in reading the addresses of one or more letters to a citizen in his district." In 1892, Negroes complained that black city employees of the Topeka Railway Company were relegated to the most menial tasks—as the proverbial "Darkey, you must use your shovel while [a white man] steers the car." Conditions had not improved appreciably by 1897, which led the *Kansas State Ledger* to identify municipal civil service as a "damnable farce . . . because it keeps the majority of colored men out of jobs."[15]

There were exceptions to the discriminatory norms in employment in the public and private sectors. On the recommendations of the Reverend William O. Lynch, one of the city's banking concerns hired W. T. Winn, a recent black arrival from Mississippi, as a bank clerk. A black woman, Anne Twyman, was appointed clerk in the office of the speaker of the Kansas House. Discrimination by the Santa Fe Railroad, the city's largest private employer, however, was more characteristic of the experience of blacks in the city's labor market.[16] Even during a protracted railroad strike in 1878, blacks were unable to secure jobs with the Santa Fe, which the *Colored Citizen* accused of "openly . . . manifesting an aversion for colored men."[17] Blacks were more successful in obtaining em-

---

13. *Kansas Historical Collections*, IX (1905–1906), 382–83; Richard Kluger, *Simple Justice* (New York, 1976), 371–72.
14. *Colored Citizen*, September 20, 1879; *Kansas Herald*, August 8, 1885.
15. (Black) Topeka *Tribune*, July 8, 1880; *Colored Citizen*, October 18, 1879; *Kansas State Ledger*, November 25, 1892.
16. *Colored Citizen*, October 18, March 15, July 19, 1879.
17. *Colored Citizen*, October 11, 1879; interview, October 27, 1978, with William D. Fisher, retired black employee of the Santa Fe; *Colored Citizen*, November 29, 1879.

ployment with the smaller Kansas Pacific Railroad: "The noble K.P.R.R. gives employment to a great number of colored laborers, every passenger train has colored porters. The A.T.S.F shows no favor to colored men." Employment discrimination in private industry was particularly onerous because "blacks spend 1000 dollars yearly at local Topeka businesses and the economic importance of the blacks should be recognized by hiring a few of the intelligent of the race."[18]

Endorsing an economic boycott and with a view toward improving newspaper sales, the *Colored Citizen* exhorted Topeka Negroes to "help those who help your race. We ask our colored subscribers to notice particularly the firms that advertise with us, patronize them and thus support your paper." Evidently such protests and threats went unheeded. In 1896 the black press observed that "the large stores do not even hire colored janitors. We know of several large stores in Topeka that have been built up by colored trade, and yet will not employ a member of our race."[19] The Topeka *Tribune* (July 8, 1880) identified the gap between black expectations and the realities of race prejudice: "Is free Kansas after all to prove a snare and a delusion as far as we are concerned? Are all the many sacrifices we have made to secure for ourselves and children a fair chance in the race for life to count for nothing, and are we still to be pursued by that intangible tyrant, caste, even here?"

Race violence, the bane of black life in the South, also generated concern; it was a standard item in the Negro press. A report of a lynching in Fort Scott, Kansas, in 1881 alarmed Topeka blacks.[20] Race violence struck home in 1889, when a black ne'er-do-well, Nat Oliphant, was lynched by a mob in Topeka for killing an unarmed white man and injuring his wife after being caught burglarizing their home.[21] With this exception, there was no overtly racial violence of such magnitude in the city of Topeka in the nineteenth century.

Humiliating personal encounters with discrimination in Topeka began to define a pattern of deliberate race oppression. In 1880, one "Mr. Moody, a colored barber, sat as he has for the last several months at Mr.

18. *Colored Citizen*, October 20, February 1, 1879.
19. *Ibid.*, undated, in *NC*, V; *Kansas State Ledger*, December 11, 1896.
20. (Black) Topeka *Tribune* article, undated, reprinted in *Commonwealth*, August 31, 1881, in *NC*, V.
21. Kansas State Historical Society, *Annals of Kansas, 1886–1925* (2 vols.; Topeka, 1911, 1926), I, 77.

Stern's restaurant in North Topeka." A recently arrived white southerner was also there and "asked Mr. Stern to never allow blacks to eat there at the time that he was dining."[22] There was no follow-up story revealing Stern's response. The ever more strident tone in Topeka race relations suggests that Stern's restaurant became one more locale of discrimination. In 1881 an unnamed writer on the staff of the Topeka *Tribune* in the company of Charles Langston, a prominent black Kansan from Lawrence, was refused ice cream "in the public room kept for that purpose" in a Topeka restaurant. "This insult was given in the presence of several persons, simply and purely because we were colored," the restaurant owner "so avowed." By 1896, evidence of discrimination in "cheap restaurants," elevators, and in nearly every other area of public life frequently appeared in the columns of the local black press.[23]

Pervasive bigotry in public accommodations had become the definitive pattern in the wake of the Supreme Court decision in *Plessy* v. *Ferguson*. After having experienced segregation firsthand on a trip to a political meeting in St. Louis in 1896, Solomon G. Watkins, a black Topekan, had ample reason for asserting that separate facilities were patently unequal: "If Jim Crow cars are perfectly legal, there should be a law passed to prevent bums of all nations from entering these cars and raising a disturbance with colored passengers and making spittoons of the seats and floors. . . . This is a rotten decision handed down by the supreme court of the U.S." Also revealed in Watkins' remarks was a distinct nativist tone: foreigners and new immigrants did not have to run the same gauntlet of discrimination. A black editorial claimed, moreover, that "the savage or red man can walk into our city or cities, and call for lodgings, meals, and the like [with] all the symptoms of a hostile design to the opposite race, yet his demands will be forthcoming."[24]

At all judicial levels, the courts were arrayed against black equality in public accommodations. In 1883 the Supreme Court reviewed five cases of discrimination based on the first and second sections of the Civil Rights Act of 1875. One of those cases was from Hiawatha, Kansas. The Court declared the act unconstitutional, saying Congress had no power

---

22. (Black) Topeka *Tribune*, November 12, 1880.
23. (Black) Topeka *Tribune* article, undated, reprinted in *Commonwealth*, August 31, 1881, in *NC*, V; *Kansas State Ledger*, November 6, 1896, February 7, 1897.
24. *Colored Citizen*, June 12, 1896; *Kansas State Ledger*, March 10, 1893.

to pass the measure under terms of the Thirteenth or the Fourteenth Amendment. In reporting this victory for racial discrimination, the Hiawatha *World* asserted that the abrogation of the act clearly reflected public sentiment. The Court's judgment "will stand and it agrees with the prejudices of every white man, woman and child in the United States." Disregarding that loss of federal protection for black liberty, yet mindful of party politics, Kansas' Republican Senator John J. Ingalls asserted:

> The agitation of Afro-Americans appears to me to be un-necessary. The judgement does not warrant denunciation of the Court, nor abandonment of the Republican party, nor justify the apprehension that Colored people will be denied any of their civil or political rights . . . guaranteed by the Amendments to the Constitution which were placed there by the Republican party. The decision remands the whole subject of civil rights to the states, but does not deprive any person black or white of any of the privileges of citizenship. That Congress has the power, and that it will do its duty to compel justice where it is persistently denied by the Courts of the state, I have no doubt.

With flawed logic and ill-disguised political gamesmanship, Ingalls proclaimed that the Republican party remained a bulwark of the black man's interest and concluded: "The victorious virtues are vigilance, patience, and courage. There is no occasion either for resentment or despair."[25] Such words sounded promising but meant little either in the immediate or the ultimate scheme of things.

State courts, in turn, reflected the prejudice current in the community at large regarding discrimination in public accommodations. In Carbondale, Kansas, in 1888, a black citizen brought suit in the state court. According to Kansas law, discrimination in public facilities or on common carriers that required a municipal license constituted a misdemeanor punishable by "a fine or liability for damage in any court of competent jurisdiction, to the person or persons injured thereby." Affirming the recent decision of the United States Supreme Court in a review of the Carbondale case, the state supreme court held that the Kansas antidiscrimination statute was unconstitutional and "must necessarily be declared void." That decision was reaffirmed in 1892 in a state supreme court case involving a Topeka restaurant. This led one

---

25. (White) Hiawatha *World*, October 25, 1882, in *NC*, V; *Daily Capital*, November 15, 1883, in *NC*, V.

black editorial writer to conclude: "The state court ... scanned the heights of its power to rule the Negro from its clean and complimented lunch counter fare." To the *Kansas State Ledger* in 1896, the implications of race discrimination reenshrined as law were disturbing because "it not only incites the opposite race against us, but it is a growing germ in the race for generations to come. We are still at sea as to our future."[26]

At nearly every turn, *de facto* and *de jure* discrimination defined the order of race relations in Topeka. Relying on techniques forged a generation earlier in the Negro Convention movement, blacks in Topeka and in the nation developed protest organizations through which they measured their alternatives in the face of mounting race prejudice.

The colored convention, a venerable institution in Topeka in the 1860s, remained active and prominent through the 1880s. Before its decline it was the only active protest organization in the city. At its meetings, spokesmen from the Negro community helped arbitrate black Topeka's social, economic, and political fortunes.[27] Topeka Negroes enjoyed a rich exchange of views at conventions with affiliated chapters throughout the state and nation. A network of communications and organized protest augmented by the Negro press, moreover, created a semblance of nationwide black community.

Among the resolutions presented and accepted at the 1883 colored convention, meeting in Lawrence, was a call for a national meeting in Louisville, Kentucky, in September. The 1883 convention resolved: "As long as colored men are discriminated against all over this country in their accommodations at the public schools, hotels, theaters, and other places common to other citizens because of race, it is the sacred duty of intelligent men of the race to meet together in conventions to devise whatever laws they deem best to awaken a public and national sentiment that will make it impossible to continue such discriminations which are as unreasonable in their motives as they are ... pernicious in their operation and results."[28]

    26. *Daily Capital*, August 24, 1888, in *NC*, VI; *Statutes of Kansas* (Topeka, 1889), Chapter XXXI, Section 282; *Kansas State Ledger*, September 23, 30, 1892, November 6, 1896.
    27. *Commonwealth*, March 5, 1880, in *NC*, V; *Colored Citizen*, March 3, 1880, identified those in attendance.
    28. *Commonwealth*, September 6, 1883, in *NC*, V.

In the public notice for the Colored Men's State Convention, scheduled to meet in Topeka in August, 1887, black Kansans were required to select "leading members of the race." This gave the convention a distinct elitist cast and it was one conduit for the distribution of power in the black community in the 1880s. After the turn of the century, membership in organized protest was not so explicitly a function of elite status.[29]

Political action, however, was the prime motive force in the convention. The commentary generated by the convention in black newspapers enhanced familiarity with politics as a mechanism for gaining fuller liberties. Broad political awareness at this level is confirmed by the informed commentary in letters from otherwise unknown Negro Topekans in the black press.

Most blacks knew that political action helped initiate the legal definition of civil rights after emancipation. Race pride and self-determination in alliance with politics provided more tangible rewards than moral suasion or waiting for the courts and the law to realign with justice. Accordingly, a black newspaper editorial identified the black man as "a positive, palpable power in this country. He must be dealt with as such or not at all. His ambition soars higher than being simply the tail of either the Republican or Democratic Kite."[30]

Despite the party and ideological alternatives which developed in the mid-1880s, unity was the watchword in the aftermath of the Compromise of 1877. In "A word to the Colored men of Kansas," the colored convention in 1880 urged political unity. It was at once a mark of defiance and a defense against the Republicans' dimming ardor for an enlightened race policy and refusal to endorse black candidates for municipal and state offices: "The Colored voters of this state compose no insignificant portion of the Republican party, and we think it nothing more than wise and expedient for the Colored State Convention to take some step toward obtaining for the Colored voters more representation than is usually accorded hewers of wood and drawers of water. The Colored voters . . . have allowed others to talk and think for them long enough."[31]

29. *Benevolent Banner*, August 18, 1887.
30. *Colored Citizen*, October 25, 1879.
31. *Kansas Herald*, April 9, 1880.

"Let him maintain an independent front in politics," suggested the *Colored Citizen*, as a means of obtaining redress for grievances short of disaffection from the Republican ranks, "for independence is sure to bring concessions and respect." However, aware of political alternatives, the Republicans retained more than token allegiance in black Topeka. "Both Democrats and Greenbackers try to taunt us with the fact that we have stood solidly for Republicanism since our emancipation and enfranchisement," reported the Topeka *Tribune* in 1880. "We plead guilty, and fear that we will continue until something better comes along, not worse."[32]

In 1880, black Topekans formed the Garfield Club to support the Republican presidential ticket. Republican clubs, organized at the ward level, also were common.[33] Nonetheless, the signs of disaffection with Republicanism were clear in the early 1880s. John L. Buckner, a barber and an active participant in the social and political life of black Topeka, expressed the growing alarm in a letter to the Topeka *Tribune*: "I tell you gentlemen, there must be a sifting. If there is any good in the Republican party, it is time that we are hunting it up. If we are to be deprived of our rights let it be done by those who declare themselves to be our enemies." After enumerating black voting strength, the *Tribune* concurred. Greater political mileage could be obtained if Kansas Negroes "split their vote . . . and did not vote as a bloc." The editorial concluded with a caustic assessment of the Republican party: "These figures are offered gratis to those high-toned, blue blooded milk and H_2O Republicans who think the Negro was created especially to keep him in office and look with supreme scorn upon every colored man who asks that the race be recognized in the distribution of offices."[34] Those issues caused strains in the traditional association of black Topekans with the Republican party.

Exclusion from party councils and an urgent desire for more equitable representation on the Republican slate of elected and appointed officeholders were immediate concerns. Occasionally internal bickering and competition between black politicians dulled their efforts. One such division prevented the election of a black councilman in the Second

32. *Colored Citizen*, October 25, 1879; (black) Topeka *Tribune*, September 16, 1880.
33. (Black) Topeka *Tribune*, June 24, July 1, 8, 1880.
34. (Black) Topeka *Tribune*, July 29, August 26, 1880.

Ward in 1879.[35] In a similar vein, the members of the colored convention quibbled about the merits of sending delegates to the statewide convention to be held in Topeka in April, 1880. One faction considered the convention "inexpedient and uncalled for." A splinter group disagreed and sent delegates anyway. The reason for the impasse was not identified. A display of feints and postures rather than a radical departure from party or political issues characterized this particular type of infighting. Of course, this is not to say that the black political caucus was bereft of ideology and issues. A report of the meeting merely affirmed "a split in the ranks of the colored men that should not exist. We trust that they will see that it is better for them to stand together, and not let petty differences influence their actions."[36]

The quest for elective or appointive office was a powerful lure. Both in its achievement and in the race itself, public office confirmed civic responsibility and conferred status in black political and nonpolitical institutions. One became a decision maker rather than a mere petitioner. Black Topekans filed as candidates for municipal, county, and state offices. Representation in party inner councils and nominating conventions also was a prominent goal. Apparently, infrequent success did not signal a black retreat from politics as an agency of race progress. Defeat and the claim of prejudice, however, went hand in hand. The Reverend Thomas W. Henderson's unsuccessful candidacy for lieutenant governor in 1878 on the Republican ticket indicated that the party "has no use for the Negro except as a voter." While applauding the appointment of the Reverend L. W. Winn, a Negro from Cherokee County, to an unexpired state senate term in 1879, Topeka Negroes did not temper their indictment of Kansas Republicanism.[37] The election of Edwin P. McCabe of Nicodemus as state auditor on the Republican ticket in 1882 was the banner event of the decade for blacks in electoral politics. Nonetheless, blacks immediately resumed the offensive. McCabe's election was no more than a just reward for long allegiance and they pressed for more: "There should be at least three Representatives [in addition to] one auditor."[38]

    35. *Colored Citizen*, April 5, 1879.
    36. *Commonwealth*, March 5, 1880, in *NC*, V.
    37. *Colored Citizen*, September 27, 1878, November 15, 1879.
    38. *Colored Patriot*, May 28, 1882; *Daily Capital*, August 19, 1882, in *NC*, V.

Ironically, a Topeka *Daily Capital* editorial (August 5, 1883) claimed that the desire of black Topekans for an "equal chance in the political arena when stated in plain language" meant that Negroes "propose to demand a portion of the offices because they are colored." This alleged request for special treatment was little more than discrimination in reverse. With lightly veiled sarcasm the newspaper identified itself as "the constant friend of the colored man and as such it protests against the colored people drawing the color line and intensifying race prejudices." The black Topeka press and the colored convention sought the nomination of Alfred Fairfax, a Negro from Chautauqua County, as state congressman-at-large in 1882. The Republican rejection of his candidacy brought the accustomed complaint of discrimination.[39] In 1889, however, Fairfax was elected to the Kansas House, where he made "an eloquent plea for his race" favoring an end to segregated schools.[40] The successes of McCabe and Fairfax in achieving office in state government were the exception and not the rule, leading the *Kansas State Ledger* (June 30, 1893) to complain about the regularity of defeat for "every colored man that keeps his head up for office." Nonetheless, asserted the *Blackman* in 1894, "since spoils are in politics and the Negro is in politics, it will not be out of place for them to get acquainted."[41] The tone and level of black Topekans' aspirations had not changed by 1898, neither had the Republican response. Noting the absence of Negroes on the published list of GOP candidates for state office in that year, William Eagleson, who had by then gravitated to populism, identified the delusion of continued black Republican allegiance in a bit of derisive verse: "'Publican' is my name, 'Publican' till I die, I live and die in the 'Publican' faith, but eat no 'Publican' pie." [42]

Clearly, many of the important decisions affecting the local black community were made at the municipal level. Thus the campaign for municipal elective and appointive office received considerable attention. "John Carter, J. H. Brashears, and A. Kuykendall," reported the *Colored Citizen* in 1879, "are the 3 colored men that are aspiring to positions

39. *Daily Capital*, May 31, 1882; *Commonwealth*, June 1, 1882, in *NC*, V; *Daily Capital*, June 1, 1882, in *NC*, V; *Colored Patriot*, June 22, 1882.
40. (White) Topeka *Capital-Commonwealth*, February 2, 1889, in *NC*, V. In 1889 the formerly separate newspapers were put out by one publisher.
41. *Blackman*, April 20, 1894.
42. *Colored Citizen*, May 26, 1898.

under city government this Spring . . . if we do our duty, they will each be put in the position they seek." William Eagleson, editor of the *Colored Citizen* and candidate for assistant doorkeeper for the Kansas legislature, and Dr. Seth Vernella, candidate for Shawnee County coroner, rounded out the list of black aspirants for public office.[43] Only Kuykendall, elected as constable, was successful. In his bid for reelection in 1880, however, the *Kansas Herald* warned that "a scheme has been inaugurated whereby it is hoped to defeat Mr. Kuykendall." That newspaper called upon black voters "to rally as one man to his support, and see that he is re-elected by a rousing majority."[44] Kuykendall was successful in that campaign and he retained the position of constable through 1887. In the intervening ten years, the appointment and election of black Republicans to municipal office improved. In 1897, five policemen, ten firemen, and one postman were Negro. Fred Stonestreet, a politically active young black man raised in Topeka and employed as a janitor, was nominated and elected constable. Fred Roundtree, a black teacher at Monroe School and an Exoduster, ran successfully for Fifth Ward councilman. John L. Guy, an active politico, secured the Republican nomination for justice of the peace. All were not successful. Solomon G. Watkins, now an ardent Republican and principal of the black Lane School, was defeated for city clerk.[45]

Characteristically, Negroes gauged their support of white municipal officers to fit their race interests. The new Topeka "Mayor David Metsker has done well," announced the *Benevolent Banner* (May 28, 1887). "He has given us more than we expected." A minor appointment of a black man as toll collector at the Kansas River Bridge helped temper the old complaint of discrimination in municipal civil service. "The courteous and gentlemanly manner in which officer R. L. Lewis manages affairs at the bridge is but another demonstration of the fact that all the colored man needs is a chance." In 1888, Metsker helped secure the nomination of Wesley I. Jamison, a black lawyer who came to Topeka during the Exodus, as justice of the peace. Jamison was reelected two times and heralded in the black press as "an honest, impartial, and rep-

---

43. *Colored Citizen*, March 22, January 11, September 20, 1879.
44. *Colored Citizen*, September 20, 1879; *Kansas Herald*, March 19, 1880.
45. *Colored Citizen*, June 17, 1897; *Kansas State Ledger*, April 9, 1897; Kansas 1895 MS census. John L. Guy was not related to the black Topeka attorney, James H. Guy.

resentative Negro."[46] Jamison's defeat in 1894 occurred because the Negro vote split between him and Solomon Watkins. This indicated detrimental competition within Topeka's cohort of black leaders. It also suggests that the number of political positions to which blacks had access was small.

Metsker continued to hold the allegiance of Topeka blacks. In a review of his credentials in the mayoral race in 1889, the *American Citizen* observed that "Metsker's policy in the past has been of extreme friendliness to the race. He has had the backbone to appoint Negroes when it resulted in making his administration unpopular among whites." Notably, black support did not prevent Metsker's loss in the 1889 campaign. In preparation for the coming election, the black press resorted to a technique of political action employed before the halcyon days of Metsker's administration: "Let every Negro who can vote, register." The election had particular importance because of the impending decline in "the representation we now have on the city work force." The best defense remained an adequate offense. The black press and the colored convention trumpeted the candidacy of James Page, "a proper representative of the race," for constable, and G. I. Currin, "a most worthy gentleman and a true Republican," for police judge. Neither man was elected, which led to the usual accusation of racism and a suggestion that black candidates could not rely on "a free ballot and a fair count."[47]

Even the most menial civil service jobs were no longer safe preserves of patronage employment for Topeka blacks in 1889. One black newspaper asserted: "It appears that our white Republican friends are not willing to accord to us the privilege of using the shovels, broom and dustpan. We are told that the Negroes who have been employed at the State House for years as janitors, messengers, and firemen have been summarily dismissed and their places taken by white men. What does this mean? . . . So this is the reward for fidelity to the party," observed the *American Citizen*. Apparently, the single-minded devotion of black Topekans to Republicanism counted for little. "In violation of the recognized custom" of granting patronage "to different elements and nationalities" in return for their voting favors, "every known element ex-

46. *American Citizen*, March 15, 1889; *Kansas State Ledger*, January 19, 1894.
47. *American Citizen*, March 5, 30, 1889.

cept the Negro has been recognized and rewarded." Among the solutions advanced was that "Negroes should think for themselves."[48]

Black expectations for patronage at that level of municipal employment had not changed by 1897. In the view of the *Colored Citizen*, the Republicans "cannot offer a janitor's job or a few days work upon the street and think the Negro will be satisfied. Janitorships no longer fill the ambitions of the Negro." The *Kansas State Ledger* concluded that the then-standard Republican appeal to "the Negro's sentiment and prejudice [and] the old plea of gratitude is no longer potent." The black man should be actively engaged in "selecting for himself his own political company."[49] Indeed, "after giving to the Republican party a solid and continuous support since they were enfranchised in 1869," the *Colored Citizen* asserted, Negroes "have determined in many localities to turn over a new leaf."[50] Black involvement with the Populist and Democratic parties proved to be unstable alliances at best. Nonetheless, those parties made recognizable inroads in the state and in the black Topeka electorate during the 1890s.

The Farmers' Alliance, one element in the coalition of reform interests which culminated in the Populist crusade, received notice but not support in the black Topeka press in 1890. The *American Citizen* disapproved of the proviso in the alliance constitution requiring that a member "must be a white man," thereby making it obvious "to every colored man that this Alliance intends to plot the oppression of colored Farmers." The Colored Alliance, hastily organized the Texas in 1886, was hardly evidence of concern for the economic and political predations against southern blacks. Rather, the separate Colored Alliance reflected continuing segregation and was a ploy to enlist black support in alliance political campaigns.[51] Race violence occurring in the wake of efforts to organize black farmers in the South had not dissipated by 1890. In fact, it brought down "upon the defenseless heads of the colored people swift and sure punishment from . . . marauding midnight assassins." Leonidas L. Polk, a major white figure in the southern alliance, and "his ex-

---

48. *Ibid.*, February 22, April 5, 1889.
49. *Colored Citizen*, August 12, 1897; *Kansas State Ledger*, August 14, 1897.
50. *Colored Citizen*, August 11, 1898.
51. *American Citizen*, August 31, 1888; John D. Hicks, *The Populist Revolt* (Lincoln, Nebr., 1961), 97, 123.

confederate cohorts graciously permitted the Kansas Alliance to admit Negroes into membership," but that did not redeem the organization, particularly in light of continuing political race baiting in the South.[52] The absence of white alliance support for the Lodge federal elections bill, designed to protect black voting rights, also suggested that alliance interest in Negroes was tissue thin.

The collapse of the Colored Alliance after an ill-fated cotton strike in 1891, primarily because of a lack of support from the white alliance, confirmed earlier suspicions that political expediency was the prime directive in its appeal to Negroes.[53] In 1892, however, the white alliance in combination with the Knights of Labor emerged as the Populist party. Given the course of events attendant to its development, one well may ask what drew Topeka blacks to populism.

Populist opposition to lynching and the brutal convict leasing system was sure to attract some black support even though those were not at issue in Kansas. Black Topeka supporters endorsed the tenuous alliance between black and white Populists in southern politics and disapproved of the party's acquiescence in constitutional disfranchisement in the 1890s. There were, however, political and ideological grounds for agreement. Black Populists endorsed the party line exalting the virtues and addressing the problems of labor. They also viewed the coalition of Republicans and monied interest as a revocation of the nation's sacred bargain with freed and common men. Blanche Foster, black Topeka minister and the alliance candidate for state auditor in 1890, believed that Negroes would be well served by the Populists, who validly "proclaim themselves to be friends to the Negro laborers and advocate the cause of the laboring man throughout." Likewise, there was evidence of socialism in Foster's call for black Topeka support: "The drama being rehearsed between the masses and classes" had clear and present relevance for the plight of Negroes. "Thus, after 250 years of slavery and quasi-freedom, we are still laboring to enrich a class." In addition to redressing the economic imbalance, the Populists would "protect the lives of our many helpless [black] brethren even at home." "Currency, Standard Oil, the sugar trust and the railroads" also would be riven asunder when the Populists "storm the citadel behind which the mon-

52. *Daily Capital*, August 15, 1890, in *NC*, VI.
53. Meier and Rudwick, *From Plantation to Ghetto*, 179.

eyed power is entrenched by legislation . . . Republican politicians and their organs."[54] Indeed, asserted William Eagleson, prominent journalist and Populist, enlightened race consciousness required that Negroes be aware of current political and economic crises at their widest range: "As American Citizens we claim that everything that concerns the nation concerns us."[55]

Eagleson conceded that the Republicans of an earlier day, "the men who guided the affairs of state, were giants in their way." That day, however, had passed and "the men posing as leaders of that great old party now, have dwindled into insignificant pygmies, prostituting all the powers of this great government to their benefit." "I will not be used as a tool any longer," asserted John Wright, a Populist and a young man on the rise in black Topeka. Continued allegiance to Republicanism "is a condition, gentlemen, an all fired lowering and mean one at that, that surrounds and confronts us as legal voters, as American Citizens, [and] as men. . . . We have wasted fully enough time and energy in the Republican party establishing our political status." John M. Brown, late of the Kansas Freedmen's Relief Association and an erstwhile Republican, joined forces with black Topeka Populists because of that party's more generous plan for extending black participation in state and municipal politics.[56] Foster, Eagleson, Wright, and Brown were men with impeccable social and political credentials. There was nothing of the prairie rube in their pronouncements regarding the Populist alternative. Through Foster and Eagleson in particular, the Populists had spokesmen for a reasoned appeal to the Negro electorate.

Another important consideration which recommended populism was the party's endorsement of active black involvement in the political process and parity in access to office. By way of illustration, the selection of Blanche Foster as Populist candidate for state auditor in 1890 assured some general support from Negro voters.[57] His defeat neither dispelled the enthusiasm of black Topeka's Populist supporters nor prohibited

---

54. *Kansas State Ledger*, October 28, 1892; (white) Ottawa *Kansas Journal and Telegraph*, September 27, 1894, in *NC*, VI. Foster's views reflected those of socialists and reformers in general in the 1890s.

55. *Colored Citizen*, April 14, 1898.

56. *Ibid.*, and October 28, 1898; *Kansas State Ledger*, June 25, 1898.

57. Meier and Rudwick, *From Plantation to Ghetto*, 181; Zornow, *Kansas*, 198; *Daily Capital*, June 12, August 13, 14, 1890; *Times-Observer*, January 9, 1892.

their subsequent efforts to gain elective or appointive office. John Lytle, a Negro policeman and "a gentleman who is competent and worthy," successfully ran for the position of assistant city jailer in 1896.[58] His daughter, Lutie, moreover, received a patronage position as assistant enrolling clerk for the Populists. Lutie Lytle would achieve later renown as the second black woman lawyer in the nation.[59] Postal appointments, ward committeeships, and judgeships were among the municipal offices for which Negroes ran with considerable success on the Populist ticket.[60]

The mechanics of grass roots political activity took place in the black People's Party Club, organized in 1893. This was not a novel technique: black politicos irrespective of party affiliation established similar forums. Topeka Negroes actively participated in the integrated Populist Flambeau Club, through which Lytle, Brown, and Eagleson achieved support for their nominations and launched their candidacies for municipal office. They and other blacks, moreover, joined a statewide party caucus through the Populist Central Committee.[61]

An important leitmotiv in the Populist appeal to Negroes was not the argument for populism but the case against Republicanism. The quarrel of black Republicans with the party had the bitterness of a breach of faith. Black Topekans had not fared badly under Republicanism. Their actual power and influence, however, fell far short of their just demands. Slim gains merely whetted the appetites of black Topekans for more: they were undergoing a revolution of rising expectations.[62]

By 1896, signs of the impending demise of Kansas populism were apparent, and the state wended its way "back to its easier history" of Republican dominance and to the "conservative politics of prosperity."[63] As a political force, populism went into eclipse in the Kansas elections of 1898 for state and federal offices. The party was victimized by fusion and the major parties' preempting its rhetoric and programs. The debilitating flaw lay in the basic design of populism itself and typified the fate of third parties in general. In addition, the times were changing and the Populist jeremiad was discordant with the realities of the late

58. *Kansas State Ledger*, November 27, 1896; *People's Friend*, December 11, 1896.
59. *Kansas State Ledger*, January 11, 1895; *Colored Citizen*, October 28, 1898.
60. *Kansas State Ledger*, May 28, 1893, March 16, 1894.
61. *Ibid.*, September 1, 1893, March 26, October 15, 1898.
62. Meier and Rudwick, *From Plantation to Ghetto*, 285.
63. *Kansas State Ledger*, August 21, 1896; Zornow, *Kansas*, 204–205, 209.

1890s. Industrialization, which had long since become the cornerstone of the nation's economy, also extended to the mechanization of agriculture in the Midwest if not in the South. Large landholdings consolidated by "frontier real estate builders" and the railroads for at least four decades prior to 1900 further contributed to the decline of populism. For Negroes in particular, moreover, it was not populism itself but its failure that unleashed the race-related political oppression in the South at the turn of the century.[64]

Despite populism's relatively short career, the movement had a considerable impact on Kansas politics. The People's party, moreover, was composed of more than the vestiges of the Farmers' Alliance and the Knights of Labor; there were other influences. Prohibitionists, suffragists, and civil libertarians also endorsed the crusade. Topeka Negroes who joined forces with populism also endorsed one or another of those doctrines and invested their energies in the Progressive movement as the nineteenth century drew to a close.

After 1896, some black Populists rejoined the Republican fold. By 1898 the Reverend William L. Grant, a prominent black Topeka minister and a Populist, had "risen above partisan lines and prejudice . . . and is now urging our people to support the Republican Ticket." Evidently, all did not share Grant's equanimity. "The soreheads in the Peoples Party," reported the *Colored Citizen* in 1899, "are now engaged in digging the party's grave wide and deep by their insensate opposition" to the incoming Republican governor, William Stanley.[65] There would continue to be grounds for black commentary on and opposition to Republicanism. John M. Brown, John Lytle, and William Eagleson remained iconoclasts and looked about for independent or Progressive alternatives. Fusion with populism became the means by which the Democratic party influenced black politics.

"A colored Democrat," proclaimed the *American Citizen* (September 21, 1888), "is as veritable a freak of nature as a white blackbird." Indeed, the traditions of Democratic politics were antithetical to black interests. To all appearances, there was little of substance to recommend the

---

64. Gates, *Landlords and Tenants*, Chapter 9; Paul Glad, *McKinley, Bryan, and the People* (Philadelphia, 1964), 205.

65. *Colored Citizen*, October 28, 1898, May 12, 1899.

Democratic party to black Topekans in the 1880s. Given the increasing discrimination in the city under the aegis of Republicans and the ongoing oppression of southern blacks under the Democratic Redeemers, it seemed as if Jim Crow rode the Republican elephant and the Democratic donkey with equal ease. Kansas Democrats, moreover, could not avoid the party's identification with the political race mongering in the South. To the *American Citizen* the reasons were obvious. The "Ku Klux Democrats" remained "the opponents of the advancing liberality of thought." By these terms, their "past tradition condemns and exposes their double faced attitude toward us." In 1889, however, the *American Citizen* asserted: "Candor compels us to say that Cleveland's policy toward the Negro has been one of even handed justice." The same could not be said of Cleveland's plans for reducing protective tariffs: "Every Afro-American working man should bear in mind that a reduction of the tariff and a consequent reduction of the wages will strike them as well as the white laborer."[66]

In 1897 the liberal race policy of Kansas' Populist-Democratic governor John W. Leedy attracted John M. Brown, William Eagleson, and other thoughtful black Topekans of a reform bent. Leedy actively encouraged black participation in politics. Moreover, Topeka blacks construed Leedy's advocacy of civil service reform as a means by which they would receive greater access to government employment at municipal and state levels.[67] To a relatively greater degree than under the Republicans, those ends were achieved. Blacks boasted that Leedy's administration "gave us ... total, twenty-five places ... while our deceitful, so called Republican friends only gave us eight little places." Thus, with guarded optimism, Leedy's black supporters in Topeka could claim that "the times and issues have changed and that the sentiment of the Democratic party has kept pace with the advanced public sentiment." Leedy's gubernatorial victory in 1897, however, could not restore the Democrats' dissipated influence at the national level. Despite the fusion of Democratic and Populist forces, each was "merely the ally of another

---

66. *American Citizen*, July 13, December 7, 1888, January 18, 1889, September 7, 1888.
67. Zornow, *Kansas*, 204; O. Gene Clanton, *Kansas Populism: Ideas and Men* (Lawrence, 1969), 163; *Kansas State Ledger*, November 13, 1896; *Colored Citizen*, May 12, 1898.

minority party."⁶⁸ Victory for the Democrats or the Populists was a crumb snatched from the Republican table.

Organized Democratic activity in black Topeka did not receive extensive public notice. "The first general conference of Negro Democrats" was held in Topeka in 1893. Representation from the city's Negro population, however, was quite small. In addition, William Eagleson attended the National Democratic Negro League, which met in Indianapolis, Indiana, in 1893. Subsequent reports of that national meeting in the black press contain little of significance for partisan politics in general or for black Topeka politics in particular.⁶⁹

Free silver also generated some interest, and black Topekans organized the Colored Free Silver Club. Newspaper reports in 1898 indicate that the club met weekly "at its own hall and recently purchased a fine piano for the purpose of amusing the young people who come to look on and join." The "Ladies Free Silver Club," moreover, met "every Thursday—6:00" in 1896.⁷⁰

Rather more serious business concerned the sixty-five unnamed delegates to a state convention of the Colored Free Silver League, which met in Topeka in 1897. Resolutions affirmed "the cause of the free and unlimited coinage of silver at the ratio of 16 to 1 [and] other reforms beneficial to the entire people." The convention's hearty endorsement of Governor Leedy and "his administration's economic positions and general care of the people of Kansas" suggests that fusion with populism rather than unqualified support for the Democrats was the major spur to the league's political interests, if not its reason for being.⁷¹

The acuity of political judgment and the variety of options in black Topeka made political independence a viable alternative. On May 3, 1895, the *Kansas State Ledger* warned, "Republicans Beware," as Negro Topekans organized themselves to help unseat the Republican governor

---

68. *Colored Men's Independent State League* (Topeka, n.d.); *Colored Citizen*, July 13, 1898; Zornow, *Kansas*, 204.

69. *Kansas State Ledger*, September 1, 1893, August 17, 1894, March 26, August 27, 1898, November 27, 1900; *Colored Citizen*, June 17, 1897, August 18, 1898. Those newspaper items identified Negro Populist-Democrats by name as well as describing their political activity.

70. *Kansas State Ledger*, December 10, 1898; *People's Friend*, December 11, 1896.

71. *Colored Citizen*, July 8, 1897, January 6, 1898; *Kansas State Ledger*, December 10, 1898.

Edmund Morrill, unpopular because of black exclusion from political patronage under his administration. "There never was a time when the colored voter was more rebellious and independent than at present. . . . The colored independents of Topeka have organized an Independent Voting League, which will come into play in the future." Predictably, John M. Brown and William Eagleson were prominent in Topeka's Colored Independent League. They were joined by John W. Barber, a Negro minister of North Topeka Baptist Church, variously identified as "a well educated, intelligent young colored man" who was also "engaged in the real estate and insurance business." In 1898, moreover, Barber received the support of black Topeka independents in his unsuccessful race for state representative.[72] Likewise, the Independent League endorsed Leedy's gubernatorial candidacy: "We recommend him as deserving of the support of all the members of our local Leagues." In 1898 the league claimed twenty-one chapters throughout Kansas "with a membership of 1834." To its supporters, the existence and growth of the Colored Independent League indicated "the general unrest and disgust of the Black voters of Kansas."[73]

Those political experiments gave Negroes in Topeka a greater awareness of their options. Although Republicanism remained the mainstay of black Topeka politics from 1880 to 1896, the Republican party was not the only agency used in the search for full civil equality. In that regard, George Wellington Gross, a black Topeka journalist and one among many disaffected Republicans, provided a concise summary of "the lesson we have learned from the huge political revolution that took place in Kansas": "It is necessary for the Negro to arouse himself and wield a more potent influence in whatever party he may be identified with." In Eagleson's words: "We are the architects of our own fortunes, politically and otherwise . . . [and will] make the best of our rights and privileges as free, intelligent, and independent American citizens."[74] As black Topeka politics developed in the late 1890s and as racism became increasingly virulent, a host of new organizations of race protest ap-

72. *Colored Citizen*, August 18, October 21, 1898; *Kansas State Ledger*, May 31, 1895, August 17, 1898.
73. *Colored Citizen*, October 28, February 17, April 7, 1898.
74. George Wellington Gross, "The Negro as a Factor in Kansas Politics," *Agora*, II (1893), 166–70; *Colored Citizen*, November 25, 1897.

peared and disappeared. The short-lived Colored League and the Afro-American League, which had longer tenure, helped distill experience into programs for race progress.

The stated purpose of the Colored League, established in Topeka in 1887, was to provide an outlet for the "beneficial-political interests" of its members. Their definitive concern, however, was unstinting opposition to discrimination in any form. It was not merely a rearguard defense of transient civil liberties. Further, integration as an adjunct to reform received considerable attention.[75] As was said in 1887 by T. Thomas Fortune, editor of the New York *Age*, "the necessity and the nature" of the Afro-American League derived from the manifold increase in discrimination indicated "not by a straight color line but an encircling, proscriptive one." Ending race violence and restoring black civil rights immediately were prominent concerns. Toward those ends, "the Leagues in the North and West will serve to create public opinion in those sections and to coerce politicians into taking a broader view of our grievances." The technique of protest proceeded from the thesis that "intelligent sympathy can only be created by intelligent agitation and that politicians can only be secured by compulsion." Forthright black leadership was crucial: "Wherever there are 10 colored men anywhere in this country, let them resolve themselves into a branch of the Afro-American League. Let the work begin now."

The two leagues would have provided attractive fare for William Eagleson, John M. Brown, and company. Curiously enough, their names do not appear on membership lists. The Afro-American League was liberal in the late 1880s, although it took a conservative turn after 1900. The reigning ideas and solutions set forth by the Colored League and the Afro-American League did not reflect an abrupt departure from the program of the colored convention. In 1887 both leagues expressed an integrationist outlook that emerged as a doctrine of organized protest after the turn of the century. A competing ideology surfaced in the proposals offered at the national meeting of the Afro-American League, convened in Pasadena, California, in 1898. Increasing carnage in the South as well as occupational and economic discrimination made black

---

75. *Commonwealth*, August 31, 1887, in *NC*, V.

commercial development, with a moratorium on political action, a potentially effective medium for race progress.[76]

Scattered commentary in the black Topeka press in 1897 foreshadowed the mind and mood of the league convention. Holding its customary activism in check, the *Colored Citizen* conceded that "the long industrial and financial depression of the Negro should suggest the need for change." Prior experience indicated that perhaps "politics is not the route, but possibly through commerce" the larger designs of race progress could be achieved. The *Kansas State Ledger* concurred: "In politics the confrontation from adverse conditions . . . would tend to dishearten any people." The difficulty increased when "the gates of financial prosperity [are] closed against us and, on the outside, we have had to establish industries of our own."[77] The demand for integration and immediate, full, and unequivocal civil rights through political pressure and reform, however, continued unabated.

All things considered, black Topeka handled the last two decades of the nineteenth century with aplomb and saluted the new century with confidence. Through 1915, social and cultural affairs as well as the institutional structure became more sophisticated. Negro Topekans also responded to many of the intellectual currents and socioeconomic experiments that engaged the attention of the nation as a whole. Racism, however, brought the past wrenchingly into the present. The Negro community was well prepared to meet that building crisis. Old and new plans for combating Jim Crow after 1900 developed through intraracial dialogue notable for its substance and rigor. Politics, economics, social affairs, and identity, perforce, were measured in racial terms. Organized protest and political action had firm foundations. The debate over accommodationism and integrationism, as alternative routes to race progress, did not cloud the awareness of Negro Topekans of the common struggle for civil rights; this demanded cooperative endeavor.

---

76. *Benevolent Banner*, September 10, 1887, reprint from New York *Age*; Pasadena, Calif., *Daily News*, August 3, 1898.
77. *Colored Citizen*, July 1, 1897; *Kansas State Ledger*, August 1, 1897.

Chapter 6
Social Order and Social Structure 1896–1915

*T*he number of Negroes in Topeka remained relatively stable between 1895 and 1915, though showing a slight decrease. Citizens of both races pulled up stakes, for many private reasons couched in terms of better economic opportunity, and went to other urban and rural areas, most commonly within the state's borders. Many Negroes returned and invested their energies in community development at home. World War I also did not create significant demographic flux, primarily because Topeka remained an agricultural processing center during and after the war. Neither the city nor the state experienced significant industrial growth brought on by wartime mobilization. Correspondingly, there were no massive increases in urban population.[1] Seemingly out of the sweep of national economic development, there was some grousing in the black press about community decline. Within the larger compass of events through 1920, however, social order and institutional structure in black Topeka were secure.[2]

During the first decade of the twentieth century, social, religious, and economic institutions grew apace, and black Topekans strengthened their ties to other communities. Topekans of both races subscribed to intellectual and social doctrines which developed under the rubric of progressivism. The early tests of the utility of Progressive formulas for social welfare were the result of acts of God and disease epidemics.

    1. Tables 1, 10, 11; Map 2.
    2. *Plaindealer*, December 1, 1916, June 17, 1918; Zornow, *Kansas*, 229–34.

Social Order and Social Structure, 1896–1915

From 1890 through 1900, natural calamities plagued Kansas and adversely affected the citizens' material condition and health. A severe winter in 1895 brought goods and services to a halt and caused many Negro and white Topekans to seek "the refuge of the jail so they could enjoy the warmth of fire and food." Outbreaks of scarlet fever and diphtheria arrived with the spring. Cutbacks in municipal refuse collection on streets adjacent to the Kansas River, one site of Negro residence, further aggravated disease conditions. The summer provided no respite, leaving many black and white citizens displaced by floods. Smallpox also took its toll, and the Negro press was replete with obituaries and reports of the deaths of black citizens.[3] Vaccinations against smallpox became mandatory in Topeka in 1899. The disease, however, reached epidemic proportions the following year, which necessitated a city-wide quarantine.[4]

The 1903 flood of the Kansas River, which separated north and south Topeka, caused widespread hardship, particularly in the black enclave in the First Ward. Public welfare and access to state-sponsored services were vital concerns to Topeka Negroes. Relief under public sponsorship was accomplished through a subscription of $50,000 from state and local sources, although no records indicate the percentage of funds obtained from the Negro community. In any case, relief allotments were made available to all victims, irrespective of race. The administrators of public relief, however, were not imbued with Progressive notions regarding social welfare and they endorsed the traditional puritanical injunctions against unmerited charity. Thus all able-bodied sufferers were required to work on flood control projects.[5]

There is no evidence of a disproportionate amount of chicanery by Topeka blacks in receipt of relief allotments. Nonetheless, the black press observed: "By virtue of a certain number of Negroes who will not work, no more than some lazy people of other races, the relief committee has become somewhat tired of them and hence their rations are practically cut off." There was, however, one humorous anecdote. An elderly Negro woman whose earthly possessions disappeared in the del-

---

3. *Kansas State Ledger*, January 15, April 26, July 26, August 2, September 20, 1895.
4. *Kansas State Ledger*, December 6, 1899, January 6, 13, 1900.
5. J. L. King (ed.), *History of Shawnee County*, 215.

uge was asked if she had not lost faith in the Lord. Her answer: "No honey; I don't go so much now on His mercy, but I have a higher 'preciation' of His powerfulness."[6]

Torrid summers and cold winters continued to plague Topeka in succeeding years, leaving disease epidemics in their wake. Although Negroes were received in Topeka hospitals, they were segregated in a separate wing and treated by white personnel. The Topeka Association for the Study and Prevention of Tuberculosis was integrated and beneficiaries of the association's services paid "very few but trifling amounts for services." There is little information revealing the extent to which the agencies met needs for health care in black Topeka. It must suffice to say that, selectively, some provisions for health services in the larger community were available to the city's Negro citizens.[7] Aggregate statistics in the *Biennial Report* (1899–1900), Kansas State Board of Health, did not report death and disease rates by race. A survey conducted under the auspices of the Russell Sage Foundation in 1914, however, provided the following information regarding comparative black and white mortality in the city in 1912: "Topeka has a Negro element in her population of 10.4% as against 3.2% for the entire state. The crude death rate of these Negroes was, in 1912, 22.9% as against 13.2% for whites."[8]

Even during more temperate periods, unemployment, rising crime rates, and the presence of large numbers of indigenous poor among black and white Topekans provided a focus for social welfare under public and private sponsorship. The Kansas Home for the Friendless, which had Negro and white occupants, sought the "prevention and the cure of crime and the redemption of the criminal through temporary relief." The Board of Trustees of State Charitable Institutions had a similar concern for reform and rehabilitation, evident in its stated desire to provide an intellectual and social environment for wayward youth which would "cultivate their better nature" and break "the cycle of criminality and poverty."[9] That enlightenment did not prevail on poor

---

6. *Kansas State Ledger,* June 27, 1903.
7. *Fourteenth and Sixteenth Biennial Reports of the Board of Trustees of State Charitable Institutions of the State of Kansas* (Topeka, 1916), 10, 27, 7, hereinafter cited as *Biennial Reports—Charity.*
8. Shelby M. Harrison, *Topeka Improvement Survey* (Topeka, 1914), 3–5.
9. *Biennial Reports—Charity,* 27, 3, 5. Although the section on reform schools for boys and girls identifies race, the data are for counties only, and the welter of statistics is not particularly informative regarding relative crime rates for blacks and whites.

farms and in almshouses at the county level. The administrators of those facilities espoused a view common to the period: poverty inspired "repugnance rather than compassion." Frank Blackmar, a chronicler of Kansas history and the state's delegate to the National Conference of Charities and Corrections in 1901, asserted that those institutions did little more than "increase pauperism and encourage crime." The nationally prominent reformer Jacob Riis concurred with Blackmar's assertions regarding the corrosive and debilitating effects of relief through the almshouses.[10] Although race is not explicitly at issue in Blackmar's report, one may generalize that the needs of Topeka Negroes for services were no less adversely affected than the needs of white citizens. Of passing significance, the Kansas legislature in 1913 debated, but did not pass, a bill "providing for the sterilization of habitual criminals, idiots, epileptics, imbeciles, and the insane." It is also worthy of note that Negro Topekans were unsuccessful in their effort in 1909 to secure black representation on the Board of Trustees of State Charitable Institutions.[11]

There were additional problems in the administration of law and order at the municipal level. The black press complained of excessive fines in police court and long sentences imposed on Negroes by "arrogant police judges." Such practices did not reduce crime, but did wreak havoc and impose financial hardships on the families of prisoners. The city jail in 1913 was described as a "bull pen," a school for crime, and a veritable "cesspool." The black community, however, was represented in the city's court system. From the 1880s through 1915, one position as justice of the peace rotated among a succession of black Topeka lawyers. The court of Judge Wesley I. Jamison, who served between 1897 and 1903, for example, was said to exemplify evenhanded justice and concern for the social causes and consequences of crime. His cases, moreover, were not confined solely to Negroes.[12] If state, county, and municipal institutions for social welfare and the prevention of crime did not reveal pat-

---

10. Robert Bremner, *From the Depths: The Discovery of Poverty in the United States* (New York, 1956), 5, 16, 48–49; Frank Blackmar, "Reports from the States—Kansas," in Isabel C. Barrows (ed.), *Proceedings of the National Conference of Charities and Corrections* (Boston, 1901), 315–16; Jacob Riis, "Children of the Poor," *The Poor in Great Cities: Their Problems and What Is Done to Solve Them*, ed. Robert A. Woods and W. T. Elsing (London, 1896), 354; A. B. Paine, *A Kansas Almshouse* (Topeka, 1894).

11. *Kansas Legislative Handbook and Record of the 1913 Session* (Topeka, 1914), 31; *Plaindealer*, June 14, 1909.

12. *Plaindealer*, May 23, 1913; *Kansas State Ledger*, May 21, 1897, May 27, 1903.

ent evidence of racism, it was clear that the development of programs for such services in institutions within the Negro community was an urgent need.

Black newspaper reports of crime and delinquency as well as health-related problems often were accompanied by urgent appeals for reform and self-help through the church, among other institutions. There was a minimum of sensationalism; the keynote was social conscience.[13] One black editorial suggested, however, that scientific social welfare and reform under white sponsorship were not free of the taint of racism: "Sociologists and the society in general feel compelled to study and pursue the deviancy of the black man . . . in accordance with the prevailing prejudice against the Negro." Clearly that view echoed Du Bois' bitter assertion that white sociologists were interested mainly because they could "gleefully count the Negro's bastards."[14]

Topeka had two Florence Crittenden Homes for Unwed Mothers, one white and one black. The "restoration of morals" and "respectability" were counterbalanced by a sophisticated concern for the health of mother and child and programs that sought to make the women self-supporting through industrial education. Mrs. Sarah Malone, a Negro Topekan with a reputation for doing "rescue work among her own people," supervised the black Florence Crittenden Home. "A little group of women," otherwise unidentified, helped Mrs. Malone in the day-to-day operation of the facility and taught "a despised people to build its own institutions without the help of an alien race." The home was supported by private contributions, the Crittenden national office, and the state legislature. Mrs. Malone attended annual conferences on charities and corrections. By this means, techniques in social welfare and reform, current in the state and nation, were brought to bear on problems in the black community.[15]

Topeka Negroes were well aware of the arguments of Progressives

---

13. See, for example, *Kansas State Ledger*, September 16, 1899, November 27, 1900; *Plaindealer*, June 5, 1914.
14. *Colored Citizen*, April 7, 1898; Du Bois, *The Souls of Black Folk*, 8.
15. "Benevolent and Charitable Work in Kansas and Classification and Reports of Private Associations and Institutions," *First Annual and Biennial Reports of the Kansas State Board of Control, 1906–1916* (Topeka, 1916), 5–24, 48–54; *State Journal*, July 18, 1914; *Daily Capital*, April 11, 1915, January 10, 1947; *Plaindealer*, December 15, 1916, January 12, 1917.

regarding the insidious effects of racism on social order. In 1913 the black Topeka press reported the proceedings of a symposium on the Negro question, meeting in Chicago. The name or number of Topeka representatives is unknown. Among those in the vanguard of the social justice movement who attended were Jane Addams, W. E. B. Du Bois, and Ida Wells Barnett. References made by white spokesmen to the "exercise of moral force in the eradication of prejudice" and the need to "reform our social attitude toward them" were interspersed with racial stereotypes: the Negro's "love of rhythm, bright colors, and carefree gaiety."[16]

As was characteristic of philanthropic activity during the Great Exodus, however, blacks and whites were not united in their efforts. In effect, if not by design, programs for social welfare were separate because they evolved in segregated institutions, such as the church and fraternal orders. Additional social and economic factors influenced welfare and reform within the black community.

Most commonly, Negro women initiated charity and reform in black Topeka. Negro men tended to invest their reform energy in politics and the law. In the main, black Topeka reformers constituted a middle-class cohort whose households were clustered in integrated neighborhoods; most, moreover, were property owners. Many husbands of charity workers were professionals or otherwise gainfully employed in occupations that conferred stability and status, such as civil service or business. Characteristically, women reformers were not employed and therefore had the leisure to pursue charitable activities. Their names often appeared in published reports of black leadership in church and in fraternal activity.[17]

In significant ways, Negro reformers were victimized by a variant of what Richard Hofstadter identified as "status anxiety."[18] Relations with the larger community revealed the blanket indictments of racism and confirmed their long-standing fear that whites made no distinction between reputable and disreputable Negroes. By exercising social responsibility and moral probity, and by regarding poverty as a cause for social

16. *Plaindealer*, February 7, 1913.
17. A selection of names of twenty women associated with charity was cross-checked with the Kansas 1885, 1895 MS census.
18. Hofstadter, *The Age of Reform*, 135–66.

disorder, black reformers hoped to temper the view that all Negroes were profligate and lazy. Crime and delinquency as well as charity and self-help, therefore, received ardent attention. Thus, black reform in Topeka was not solely an expression of unqualified altruism; for blacks as well as whites, it reflected a desire for social control. In this context, race progress and vested class interests were correlative. This same "status anxiety" determined the equivocal response of the established Negro community in Topeka to the Exodusters in 1879.

The Alpha Assisi Charity Club and the Kansas Hospital Aid Association were examples of concern for social change and community betterment, as well as the enlightened black self-awareness evident in the ongoing debate over alternative routes to race progress, after the turn of the century. Alpha Assisi philanthropy covered a broad spectrum, from medicines for charity patients to food supplies and household goods for indigent families. Private subscriptions from black churches and fraternal orders financed the club. The social influence and prestige enjoyed by Alpha Assisi members doubtless helped gain community support for their philanthropy.

In 1916 the eight Negro women who founded the club posed for a photograph, which appeared in the *Paul Jones Magazine*, a black Topeka journal of current events and social activity. Each of the founders was fair of complexion and, without exception, appeared to be a model of middle-class decorum. All were prominent in other spheres of social activity and the church; four were founding members of St. Simon's and four were pillars of St. John A.M.E.[19] Exemplifying techniques that guided the charity-organization movement in general, Alpha Assisi coordinated its activity with other agencies devoted to public and private charity. This practice helped prevent duplication of services and assured communication of ideas and current practices in the administration of health and welfare services.

The Kansas Hospital Aid Association, organized under the auspices of the Kansas Industrial and Educational Institute in 1919, was another agency for charity and reform under black sponsorship. The institute itself, black Topeka's "Western Tuskegee," will be discussed subsequently

19. *Paul Jones Magazine* (April, 1916), 24–25; *Plaindealer*, December 17, 1915, April 17, 1916; *State Journal*, July 24, 1915, January 20, 1932, in *Protestant Episcopal Church Clippings*, I; "For a New Church," *St. John Souvenir Program*.

in the context of the Negro community's response to the Booker T. Washington philosophy.

Black Topeka women dominated the association's administrative board, which consisted of eight Negroes representing other counties in Kansas. The representatives from Topeka conformed to the social and economic profile of Alpha Assisi members, although there was no overlap of membership between the two organizations.

The association came into being following the injunction from Principal George Bridgeforth of the institute to "serve our state and our people in a needy time" and had the endorsement of the government, the legislature, and the Kansas State Board of Health. The association obtained support from black churches, fraternities, and businesses. In 1914, George Hodges, the Democratic, Progressive governor of Kansas, improved his standing with the black Topeka electorate by placing Negro women in "responsible positions" as attendants in state hospitals. The black press identified that action as a long-overdue "square deal" and as an "open door of hope." However enlightened, Hodges' actions did not fulfill the need for black, professionally trained nurses. The hospital facilities planned for the institute also would provide operating room facilities for black physicians.[20] Although the white Jane C. Stormont Hospital and Training School for Nurses admitted Negro patients, the school did not train blacks as nurses.[21] The association launched a subscription drive for $25,000, the estimated cost of constructing a hospital and school for black nurses.

Prominent in the publicity used to get the hospital and association campaign under way was the following statement: "Twenty-one colored persons die out of every 1,000 population. The death rate is too high. Let us reduce it. Sick people spread disease and are very costly to society." The appeal was supported further by the observation that there were no nurse training facilities for Negroes in the state. Accordingly, "we can change this by every colored woman in Kansas putting her shoulder to the wheel and pushing."[22] By 1922, the hospital and school facilities were built at a cost of $15,000 and became a permanent part of the Kansas Industrial and Educational Institute. The complex was

20. *Plaindealer*, May 18, September 8, 1914.
21. *First Annual and Biennial Reports of the Kansas State Board of Control*, 57.
22. *Kansas Hospital Aid Association* (Topeka, 1919), 3.

named for one Nellie Johns, a white Topekan, who willed $1,000 to the cause. The state legislature appropriated $10,000 and Negroes contributed the balance of $4,000 for the completion of the facility.[23]

Black Topeka churches, during periods of severe economic hardship, extended charity to their parishioners and to the unchurched. Such efforts could not have prevailed without the supervision of unknown "genial and benevolent, motherly old ladies" who were stalwart if not "untrammelled by denominational bickerings." St. John A.M.E. and its numerous auxiliaries collected food, clothing, and coal which were given to the poor without regard to denomination. No need was too small nor was residence in the city proper prerequisite for the church's benevolence. Second Baptist Church was no less unstinting in social welfare. In addition to providing a free Christmas dinner for over three hundred people, the Baptists stated their commitment "to continue in their relief work."[24] Special collections of food and money for indigents at holiday seasons were standard practice in all denominations. Black activists in social welfare and reform, moreover, were church members and they readily enlisted church financial support for their endeavors. Formal, ongoing programs and agencies for social service within black churches, however, were not common. Thus, the institutional church, among other social Christianity experiments at the turn of the century, did not develop in black Topeka. Under the sponsorship of the Reverend Charles M. Sheldon, an ardent proponent of the Social Gospel and pastor of the white Central Congregational Church, however, the institutional church did leave an imprint on black Topeka.

Central Congregational Church, founded in 1889, served a white residential area contiguous to Tennesseetown, a Negro enclave settled by Exodusters. Black and white settlement adjacent to Tennesseetown in the Third Ward increased as a result of the city's westward growth.[25] The Third Ward also was the site of Shiloh Baptist Church, which the Reverend William L. Grant made one of the more prominent black

---

23. *Daily Capital*, October 18, 1922; *Plaindealer*, October 19, 1922.
24. *Colored Citizen*, November 11, 25, 1897, January 6, 1898.
25. "Lifting Up the Lowly," Kansas City *Star*, October 30, 1898; Robert Swan, *The Ethnic Heritage of Topeka, Kansas: Immigrant Beginnings* (Topeka, 1974), 67–83, provides an excellent general account of Sheldon, Central Congregational Church, and its social service programs.

churches in the city at the turn of the century. Negroes in the Third Ward were members of city and state black political caucuses and garnered their share of opportunities for municipal offices. Sundry black businesses also developed in that section of the city.

In contrast, the social and economic fortunes of Tennesseetown residents had not improved since the Exodus period. Although the Negro press identified other Negro enclaves in Topeka similarly afflicted by poverty, living conditions in Tennesseetown were substandard by any criteria. Unemployment created serious economic dislocations. Juvenile crime was rampant, as was vice, and there was a lively traffic in liquor.[26]

The Reverend Charles Sheldon accurately observed that the influence of Negro churches in the area had not been manifest in Christian stewardship. Tennesseetown lay within the boundaries of his parish and, in 1892, was one of several areas he investigated "in order to study the problems of the different classes of people of the city."[27] In an 1896 retrospective on that investigation, Sheldon asserted: "I determined to live in the district myself for two weeks and study [it] in my own way." This sojourn confirmed his suspicions regarding the severity of social and economic problems. Race prejudice, a contributing factor in the cycle of poverty which infected the district, when properly viewed, was a "human problem ... capable of being resolved into simple terms which apply equally to every race and condition." Sheldon, however, recognized the danger of oversimplification: "The caste prejudice which lies at the bottom of all this is a thing which I, in my Puritan, Anglo-Saxon stupidity, have never been able to analyze."[28]

In 1899, Sheldon visited institutional churches in eastern cities and obtained additional information about implementing social welfare through the church. Political and social regeneration in the larger community also lay within the scope of Sheldon's concerns. Ultimately he sought what the historian Allen Davis describes as "the spiritual awakening of society at all levels." Without doubt Sheldon concurred with Graham Taylor, a fellow Congregationalist minister and a nationally

---

26. *Plaindealer*, October 24, 1899; Halbert and Sherman (comps.), "Tennesseetown Census, 1898."
27. Leroy A. Halbert, *A History of the Work of Central Church for the Redemption of Tennesseetown* (Topeka, 1892), 1.
28. Charles M. Sheldon, "A Local Negro Problem," *The Kingdom*, Vol. VIII, No. 52 (April, 1896), 28.

prominent exponent of social justice, in the view that "the church must stay in the forefront of social reform."[29] In all of his endeavors to "christianize the social order," Sheldon displayed the "moral, ethical, optimistic, and fundamentally religious strain" which the historians Charles Hopkins and Henry May find characteristic of Progressive reform and of the Social Gospel movement.[30]

In accordance with the tenets of progressivism, Sheldon believed that poverty was not solely the evidence of sin but was a result of social and economic imbalances created by society. Responsible Christian stewardship, moreover, required that "the preacher should preach less and the congregation work more to gain the best results."[31] Between 1896 and 1901, Sheldon inaugurated an extensive program of social services in Tennesseetown.

Convinced that "the great hope for the Negro or for any man lies in the children of the races," Sheldon was determined to establish a kindergarten in Tennesseetown. Then, he asserted, "I can revolutionize the manners and morals of the whole district."[32] Influential members of Central Congregational Church initiated a successful subscription for funds from white charity organizations. No record indicates that black individuals or institutions were enlisted in the campaign. The kindergarten opened in 1893 in a building rented for that purpose in Tennesseetown. In 1895 the school moved to facilities in Central Congregational Church. At that date the kindergarten served 210 children, with an average daily attendance of 28. The auxiliary, forty Negro women residents, instructed black mothers in child care, health, and hygiene. The kindergarten enjoyed success and popularity with the families of the district.[33] Among its successful alumnae was Ruby McKnight, a

29. "A Power for Good," *Daily Capital*, February 5, 1899, in *NC*, VII; Sheldon, *The Kingdom*, 28; Charles M. Sheldon, *In His Steps* (New York, 1972); Allen Davis, *Spearheads for Reform: The Social Settlement and the Progressive Movement, 1890–1914* (New York, 1967), 7, 13.

30. Charles Hopkins, *The Rise of the Social Gospel in American Protestantism* (New Haven, 1940), 224; Henry May, *Protestant Churches in Industrial America* (New York, 1949), 229.

31. "A Power for Good," *Daily Capital*, February 5, 1899, in *NC*, VII. On Sheldon's later career, see "To Better the Cities," (white) Topeka *Daily Herald*, November 1, 1901; *New York Times Magazine*, December 3, 1939; Kansas City *Star*, May 29, 1912; Sheldon, Introduction, *In His Steps*.

32. "A Power for Good," *Daily Capital*, February 5, 1899, in *NC*, VII.

33. Leroy A. Halbert, *Across the Way* (Topeka, 1900), 3–6; "He Made a Hit," (white) North Topeka *Mail and Breeze*, December 2, 1898.

member of the first class in 1893. She eventually graduated from Washburn College and was a teacher in training at the kindergarten in 1914. In 1908, however, the kindergarten became part of the public school system.[34]

The Library and Literary Society, the Christian Endeavor Society, to encourage Sunday school attendance, and the Mothers' Club were among the expanding social services instituted by Central Church. In Sheldon's view, if "[you] interest the child you have interested the parent." Such activities also engendered community-wide participation. In fact, Sheldon secured the cooperation of Andrew Jordan, black owner of a notorious Tennesseetown tavern, which he made available to house the library.[35] B. C. Duke, a Negro who came to Topeka from Tennessee in 1887, served as the first librarian. He was one of the small contingent of black Congregationalists living in Tennesseetown before Sheldon's program began. Subsequently, Duke joined Second Christian Church and entered the ministry. After a successful pastorate at the black St. Mark's Christian Church, Duke became state supervisor of his denomination "in the colored brotherhood," and was a member in 1905 of the governing board of black and white Kansas Christian churches.[36]

Sewing and manual training classes for young adults, in Sheldon's opinion, were useful because "people will employ Negroes to do" those sorts of jobs. In addition, "it is cheaper to teach these people to be self-respecting and help themselves than to spend large sums of money to keep the worst of them in jail." Indeed, Sheldon's program did cause a drop in crime rates in the region, according to a report from the city jail. Sheldon was aware that unemployment was a critical factor in Tennesseetown's problems. After diligent though unsuccessful efforts to obtain employment for a black man, Sheldon found unemployment widespread. Its alleviation was the responsibility of private citizens as well as government officials.[37] It was in this area that he encountered considerable frustration.

 34. *Daily Capital*, April 2, 1914.
 35. Halbert, *Across the Way*, 6–16, 19–21, 35–36; "Sheldon's Congress of Mothers," *Brochure of Parents' Meeting at Sheldon Kindergarten* (Topeka, 1906).
 36. Howard Berret, *Who's Who in Topeka* (Topeka, 1905), 32.
 37. "The Sheldon Uplift of the Old and Young," *Daily Capital*, September 9, 1906; "Lifting Up the Lowly," Kansas City *Star*, October 30, 1898; "No Work Was Found," *State Journal*, January 11, 1897.

The library, the Sunday school work, the training programs, and the Mothers' Club were part of home missions; this conformed to patterns in evidence in institutional churches throughout the nation. Calvinist denominations had long prior experience with home missions, designed to bring spiritual renewal and social control to the unregenerate frontiersmen as the nation expanded west. When Congregationalists and Presbyterians confronted the urban crises at the turn of the century, they were guided by similar motives, and home missions were regarded as proven means of achieving those ends. Satellite congregations of established churches were the agents of home missions and an adjunct to the institutional church.[38] In this respect, Central Congregational Church at once adhered to and departed from that pattern.

The black Congregational church, organized as Freedmen's Church in 1863 in the region that became Tennesseetown and renamed Second Colored Congregational Church in 1866, predated the founding of Central Congregational Church. The white First Presbyterian Church, which was established in 1859 and located in the First Ward, organized Second Church as a mission for runaway slaves. Through the turn of the century, when Sheldon's institutional church work was at its height, Second Congregational had only eighteen members and no regular pastor. "Although the spirit pervading them is excellent," according to one report, the black parishioners requested mission status "under the care of Central Church."[39]

Central Church's activity in behalf of the mission consisted primarily of financial support for repair of the parsonage. Expanding the roster of black Congregationalists through the mission, however, was not the intent of Central's institutional programs. Sheldon believed that "the work must be so planned as to be in reach of all regardless of their denominational preference." Sheldon did not subscribe to the view that "the way to a man's stomach was through his soul." Thus evangelism was not concealed beneath the cloak of social service. Enlightenment and the absence of competing institutional programs helped prevent the "unacknowledged hypocrisy" of denominationalism, which, in the opin-

38. Griffin, *Their Brothers' Keepers*, 201–205; Aaron Abell, *The Urban Impact on American Protestantism, 1865–1900* (Cambridge, 1943), 177.
39. Russell K. Hickman, "Founding a Pioneer Church," *Shawnee County Historical Society Bulletin*, No. 3 (March, 1905), 4–5; Kansas 1865 MS census; *Radges' Topeka Directory*, 1870–71; Halbert, *Across the Way*, 3.

ion of the theologians Richard Niebuhr and Walter Rauschenbusch, precluded a unity of interests in social salvation.⁴⁰ Even if not part of Sheldon's view, possibly race prejudice also intervened. Central Church did not have black members. Moreover, there was no evidence of significant growth in black Congregationalism through the 1900s. Black Baptists and Methodists remained predominant in Tennesseetown and in the black community as a whole. Perhaps for this reason, there were no published reports of resentment on the part of pastors of the four Negro churches in the Third Ward over members lost to Central's Negro mission.

In Sheldon's opinion, "a man who lives in an unpainted, squalid, gardenless place will naturally get from his surroundings a shiftless disposition." Correspondingly, "as his surroundings and his body and house become clean, his daily work begins to conform to it." Sheldon thus inaugurated the Village Improvement Society in Tennesseetown in 1898. Supervised by white parishioners, the program was to encourage residents to clean up the physical environment. Many Tennesseetown residents raised hogs, which formed a large part of their winter food supply. This contributed to the general odiousness of the district. In response to pressure from the community at large, the city passed an ordinance preventing livestock raising in Topeka proper.⁴¹ Prizes were awarded to encourage the residents to extend their best efforts in the campaign. The project also had the endorsement of the Reverend William L. Grant of Shiloh Baptist, among other black pastors in the Third Ward.⁴² According to published reports and pictures of the district in the black and in the white press, before and after the campaign, there was considerable improvement in the physical appearance of Tennesseetown. In keeping with Sheldon's view that the Village Improvement Society "should be left in the hands of the colored people themselves," in 1901 the society elected a slate of black officers.⁴³

  40. Halbert, *Across the Way*, 27–29; Griffin, *Their Brothers' Keepers*, 253; H. Richard Niebuhr, *Social Sources of Denominationalism* (Hamden, Conn., 1954), 6, 21; Benson Y. Landes (ed.), *Rauschenbusch Reader* (New York, 1957), 19, 9, 62.
  41. Sheldon, *The Kingdom*; Halbert, *Central Church*, 28; *Plaindealer*, November 7, 1897.
  42. *Colored Citizen*, September 16, 1897; Halbert, *Central Church*, 33; "He Made a Hit," *Mail and Breeze*, December 2, 1898.
  43. Halbert, *Central Church*, 30–34; "Lifting Up the Lowly," Kansas City *Star*, October 30, 1898; *Colored Citizen*, March 10, 1898.

Progressive reform and scientific social welfare were evident in the 1899 census of Tennesseetown conducted by Leroy A. Halbert, assistant pastor of Central Church and chronicler of the church's social services in the district. Taken to evaluate living conditions as a basis for planning social services, the census contained a wide range of entries, from the number of fruit trees to the type of reading materials in the homes of the respondents. It is interesting that the 585 residents enumerated in the district owned 5,306 books and 147 subscribed to newspapers. Purportedly, 87 percent could read and write, a higher literacy rate than that in the black Topeka community at large in 1895. Indicative of the social and economic contour of the district, the census identified age range, household size, home ownership, public welfare recipiency, as well as income and employment rates. As an example, of the 145 laborers and their families in Tennesseetown, 52 percent owned their homes. In contrast, figures compiled by the Kansas Bureau of Labor and Industrial Statistics for the state as a whole in 1898 indicated that only 33 percent of black laborers were homeowners. The average family consisted of four members, mother, father, and siblings, living in a single family household. Children did not work, as a rule. The male head of household usually was a common laborer, although a few practiced a skilled trade such as carpentry. Men's wages averaged $1.43 per day or $33.31 per month. In a separate report on city government in which race was not identified, Sheldon described the prevailing wage rate for manual laborers employed by the city as $1.50 per day for street workers and as $1.70 per day for a driver with a team. Approximately 58.8 percent of the adult females worked and were employed as domestics at an average wage rate of $1 per day. The household had an annual median income of $399, with real and personal property valued at $92. Notably, only 11 percent received aid from the city or the county.[44]

Although there is no precise correlation among variables employed in the Halbert census, the Kansas Bureau of Labor and Industrial Statistics compilation, and the Kansas 1895 manuscript census, the figures from

---

44. Halbert and Sherman (comps.), "Tennesseetown Census, 1898"; "Tennesseetown," *Daily Capital*, undated, reprinted in *Plaindealer*, April 27, 1899; "Tennesseetown Surveyed," *Daily Capital-Journal*, March 3, 1883; Charles M. Sheldon, *Some Facts Regarding City Government Together with a Catechism on Good Citizenship* (Topeka, 1902), 19; *Kansas State Bureau of Industrial Statistics, 1895–1915* (Topeka, 1916), 273; Kansas 1895 MS census.

each source do not reveal marked disparities in the general social and economic profile of Tennesseetown and the Negro community in Topeka. The most decisive difference between Tennesseetown and other Negro enclaves was the absence of any community-based organizations, other than Sheldon's institutional church program. In addition, there were relatively fewer individuals identified with the black Topeka middle class or elites. The Negro press, however, suggested that Redmonsville, a black enclave in North Topeka, was no less in need of social welfare and reform programs than was Tennesseetown.[45]

The social services instituted by the Reverend Charles Sheldon and Central Congregational Church represented an efficient balance of Christian stewardship and Progressive reform. Whatever the paternalistic undertone, the goal was the application of spiritual energies and values directly to human affairs. If there were no measurable changes in the economic fortunes of Tennesseetown, Sheldon's programs enhanced community participation and self-awareness to a noticeable degree. Of more enduring significance, Central Congregational Church established such agencies as the Village Improvement Society and the kindergarten in a community formerly lacking such organizations.

The response of the Negro press and black teachers to Sheldon's programs was positive. Sheldon reciprocated, keeping open the lines of communication to the city's black institutions and taking care to avoid the appearance of rivaling or dominating them. For instance, in a speech presented at the Kansas Industrial and Educational Institute in 1901, Sheldon asserted: "Whatever is done in Tennesseetown does not in any way conflict with the splendid work . . . at the Industrial Institute. All that is done by us in Tennesseetown indirectly and directly helps the Institute." Sheldon also proclaimed his willingness to "do everything in my power to help the school as both endeavors are being done for the same purpose."[46] Central Church also used other means to maintain harmonious relations with the Topeka black community. The Fisk University Jubilee Singers were invited to appear in a series of church-sponsored musicales in 1913. The concerts were well received by an inte-

---

45. "Self Help and Our Environment—Let Us Work," *Plaindealer*, October 24, 1899; "Reverend Sheldon and Tennesseetown," *Colored Citizen*, February 25, 1899.
46. See, for example, *Colored Citizen*, September 16, 1897; *Western Correlator* (May, 1901), 1 (the official newsletter of the institute).

grated audience. Church auxiliaries saw to it that the black visitors were housed, fed, and entertained "in some of the best and leading houses in Topeka." The *Plaindealer* (November 7, 1913) observed further: "The devil and Jim Crow were not visible. We are glad to know that there is in Topeka one congregation of white Christians which practices what it teaches and preaches."

The failure of blacks themselves to be active in reform under the aegis of the institutional church did not signify a lack of concern for social welfare and race progress. One manifestation of that concern was black Topeka's enthusiastic support of the Kansas Industrial and Educational Institute. Billed as "the Western Tuskegee," the institute was modeled after Booker T. Washington's school in Alabama. The institute, however, enjoyed community-wide support irrespective of predisposition on the contending philosophies of accommodation and integration as represented by Booker T. Washington and W. E. B. Du Bois, respectively. It remained an emblem of race pride and identity for the black community as a whole throughout its history.

The Kansas Industrial and Educational Institute had an inauspicious beginning in 1895 as a kindergarten, sewing school, and reading room. It was a small, one-room house located in a heavily settled black enclave in the southeastern section of the Fifth Ward called Mud Town because the unpaved streets became a quagmire after a rain. That the institute and Sheldon's institutional church established similar programs at similar times may be attributed to the general intellectual and moral climate of the period. Sheldon also acknowledged the existence of an unnamed black kindergarten in Topeka in 1896.[47]

The Negro founders, Edward Stephens and Lizzie Reddick, for all their spirit and enterprise in establishing the institute, were not in the published records of the socially prominent, nor did they have any ascertainable credentials as Progressive reformers. Stephens was an elementary school teacher and a resident of Topeka since 1885. He claimed to have traveled widely, had some flair, and, one suspects, the gift of gab. Reddick, too, was an elementary teacher and a member of St. Simon's. Little else is known of her social life. With funds secured from

47. Sheldon, *The Kingdom*.

friends of the institute, Stephens purchased in 1898 a small building on Second Street and Kansas Avenue, in the heart of the black business district, to expand the school's services. By 1899, through an unknown agency, the institute received an appropriation of $1,500 from the state.

Stephens incurred the wrath of the black community in 1900, however, for his allegation to the Topeka Board of Education that "the colored people of Topeka are the most corrupt set of people I ever saw." There were no specifics regarding the basis of Stephens' claim or complaint. In any case, attorney James Guy and the Reverend George Shaffer of St. John A.M.E., among other black Topeka notables who emerged as institute supporters, formed a committee, which met with the board of education to protest Stephens' charge. At a subsequent meeting, the committee condemned Stephens for placing Topeka Negroes "in the most odious light possible before the white community." His penchant for identifying Negroes by ethnic slurs in front of whites was equally offensive. Furthermore, Stephens' reputation in the black community as "a drunkard, a wastrel and a braggart destroyed his usefulness (if he ever had any) among us." Stephens' alleged chicanery in the use of funds, moreover, provided sufficient grounds for the legislature's cutting off the appropriation for the institute. The committee urged the board of managers to find a new director "whose Christian deportment, intelligence and manly bearing will insure a success of the school in our midst." In the absence of any response by the board of managers and the legislature to their complaint, the committee threatened to withdraw the black community's support of the institute.[48] Whatever the validity of the case against Stephens, his name was not associated with the institute after 1900. There were no subsequent reports of complaints or of the committee's having met.

In 1900 the board of managers reorganized the institute. They were aided by Booker T. Washington, who sent advice for developing the school and a Tuskegee graduate, William Carter, to superintend operations. The institute enjoyed considerable success under Carter's administration, and the legislature restored the $1,500 appropriation.

In 1899 a committee of prominent Negro Topekans organized an auxiliary to support the institute. The committee was not a conduit for

---

48. "A Colored Meeting," *Plaindealer*, July 20, 1900.

financial support for the school; it served to strengthen the bond between the institute and the black community.[49] As the uproar over Edward Stephens in 1900 attests, relations between the principals of the institute and the black community were not always models of cordiality and confidence. In 1916, Principal William Carter also received the censure of the black community, allegedly for being on "too friendly terms with some women members of the faculty." James Guy and John Wright were among the Negroes who conducted the investigation. Although no formal charges were proffered, Carter's name disappeared from the roster of institute officials. George Bridgeforth, formerly director of the agricultural department at Tuskegee, became principal in 1917 and thereafter the administration of the school was unsullied by public controversy.[50]

For the school's administrators, the affairs of the institute, relations with the black community, and the influence of state political leaders were closely correlated. Carter, for example, supported black involvement in city, state, and national politics. His own political preferences and customary one-party dominance dictated his support for Republicans. Between 1912 and 1914, however, the efforts of Governor George Hodges, in behalf of Negro rights, merited nonpartisan praise from Carter.[51] Bridgeforth also employed political contacts to advance the school's interests.

In 1919, Bridgeforth effectively coordinated the institute's relations with the Republican administration of Governor Arthur Capper in order to establish a hospital and a school for nurses at the institute. The activity and fund raising of the Kansas Hospital Aid Association also strengthened the mutual interests of the Negro community and the school. That Governor Capper was a founding member of Topeka's NAACP chapter further indicates that the contending ideologies of race progress did not disturb the working relationship of the institute, the black community, and the state government. Doubtless, the increasing investment of state money in the institute between 1900 and 1919 did

---

49. *Daily Capital*, November 14, 1899.
50. *Daily Capital*, April 30, 1916; *State Journal*, March 1, 1917, in *Kansas Legislative Clippings*, XIV.
51. *State Journal*, August 16, 1909; *Plaindealer*, August 18, 1909, May 8, September 8, 1914.

exercise some control over the administrators' public posture and partisan orientation.[52]

In 1903, expanding services required and financial stability permitted the institute to purchase a farm costing $10,000 and consisting of 105 acres one and one-half miles east of Topeka. The new location was on one of the few elevations in the county. With its growing complement of buildings and its bustling activity, the institute was "a city on a hill," in the phrase Booker T. Washington used to describe his school at Tuskegee. State reports proudly asserted that from this vantage, the institute had "one of the most commanding views in the state."[53]

A committee appointed by the legislature made annual visits to the institute. In response to their consistently favorable reports, the legislature granted increasing appropriations. In 1908 and in 1911, Andrew Carnegie gave $5,000 and $10,000 to aid in the educational and building programs. Improvement of the facilities for teaching industrial arts and the addition of an extension service to provide training in scientific agriculture for Negro farmers throughout the state were evidence of the institute's expansion and progress.[54] Prior to 1907, the institute was an independent charity, partially supported by appropriations from the Kansas legislature. By 1919 the major part of its funding came from the state, and in that year the legislature assumed full control and renamed the facility the Kansas Vocational Institute.[55]

The financial support of the institute by the Kansas legislature provides one measure of approval by the white community. The popular currency of Booker T. Washington's philosophy of race progress and interracial relations contributed substantially to the legislature's consistent endorsement. The report of a visit in 1901 of a committee from white Topeka's Ministerial Union to the institute provides additional evidence of white community attitudes. In registering their approval, the

52. *Kansas Hospital Aid Association*, 1–9; *Western Correlator* (May, 1919); Kansas Industrial and Educational Institute, *Annual Catalogue* (Topeka, 1919), 7–10.
53. Harlan, *Booker T. Washington*, 142; "Historical Sketch," *Annual Catalogue*, 6; *Nineteenth Biennial Report*, Kansas Superintendent of Public Instruction (Topeka, 1914), 77; *Colored Citizen*, November 16, 1900; J. L. King (ed.), *History of Shawnee County*, 195.
54. *Annual Catalogue*, 7–8, and *Nineteenth Report*, 77–79, identified Carnegie's first gift; *Daily Capital*, May 3, 1911, identified the second; Theodore E. McCord, "The KIEL of Topeka," *Paul Jones Magazine* (October, 1919), 20–21.
55. *Nineteenth Report*, 77–79; *Annual Catalogue*, 5–15; "Industrial and Educational Institute of Topeka," *Kansas Session Laws, 1919* (Topeka, 1919), Chapter LXIII; *State Journal*, February 14, 1917.

Ministerial Union identified the school as an institution that made "our colored population safe, happy, and desirable citizens." The ministers also applauded the school's emphasis on religious and moral training. The enrollment of local Negro youth at the institute would "lessen the numbers of the street vagrant class, so conspicuous in this town, by putting them in schools and teaching them trades so that they can become useful and respectable citizens instead of a menace and disgrace to the race and the community."[56]

The above evidence of white Christians' stewardship and endorsement indicated prevailing race stereotypes and revealed a perception of the institute as an agency for the control of black youth. There also was a disparity in the way in which black and white Topekans viewed Negro advancement. The institute, however, inculcated values subscribed to by Topekans of both races, self-reliance as well as moral and circumspect social behavior.

Thrift, enterprise, self-help, and economic development, basic to the philosophy of Booker T. Washington and the institute, were not novel solutions to the continuing problem of Jim Crow. For black Topekans, those pragmatic values had long tenure, having found expression in some form since the Exodus period. Race progress as a generic concept also encompassed civil and political equality. The school, moreover, centered black community interests, regardless of one's philosophy of race progress. The administrators of the institute made that liaison more secure by participating in local churches, fraternal orders, and political organizations.

Between 1900 and 1919 the principals of the institute often were invited to speak at black church, social, and civic functions. In 1909, as an example, Principal William Carter addressed the Kansas A.M.E. Conference meeting in Topeka. On this and other occasions, Carter's remarks contained standard anthems of race progress: education of the head, the heart, and the hand—with politic reference to the accomplishments of prominent Negro Topekans and of the black community as a whole. The injunction to self-help, economic development, and morality set the tone in the speeches but did not reflect a monolithic adherence to the tenets of accommodationism.

56. *Daily Capital,* May 12, November 10, 1901.

Soon after it began operation the institute established close working relations with other institutions in the black community. In 1896 a bazaar at St. John A.M.E. featured items from the institute sewing class. Mrs. Seth Vernella, wife of the prominent Negro physician, and Mrs. J. C. C. Owens, wife of the pastor, assisted with instruction in sewing at the institute.[57]

Through 1918 the institute's administrators and faculty were Negroes. Black Topekans secured teaching positions in manual arts, music, and dressmaking. James Guy and John Wright, black Topeka leaders, served on the board of managers in 1916.[58] The decisive importance of the institute for organized black interest groups was not its educational function. Instead, the institute was the locale of many community services and became a significant element in the social life of black Topeka. The Sunflower State Agricultural Association is an outstanding example.

The association, part of the institute's extension service, provided an important tie to the black Topeka community and to other Negro communities throughout the state. The organization held annual conferences at the institute. However distant the issues of crop rotation and scientific agriculture were from the immediate economic interests of Negro Topekans, the conferences were testimony to the race's progress. John M. Brown, black Topeka's own gentleman farmer and a man otherwise prominent in the community, as well as other successful black farmers from Shawnee County, were active participants. The conferences had the atmosphere of a county fair and a chautauqua, with exhibits, prizes, and speeches. Tours of the exhibits by black elementary schools were common, and the conferences enjoyed considerable popularity in the black community as a whole. Extensive coverage of the Sunflower Association in the Negro and the white press suggests that Topekans irrespective of color joined in celebrating the state's abundance and the black man's enterprise.[59]

As for the students' background, since there are no rosters, one must

---

57. *Kansas State Ledger*, June 26, 1896.
58. *Daily Capital*, March 13, 1901, identified Topeka Negroes who taught at the institute, but no complete list has been compiled at this time; McCord, "The KIEL of Topeka," 21; "Will Hear Charges," *Daily Capital*, April 30, 1916.
59. On the Sunflower Association, see *Plaindealer*, December 19, 1910, November 17, 1913, December 22, 1916; "Black Farmers Meet," *Daily Capital*, December 9, 1914; *State Journal*, December 8, 1915.

rely on newspaper reports. The *Daily Capital* (March 12, 1901), for example, says the students represented Cherokee, Doniphan, Douglas, and Wyandotte counties, in which there was a sizable black population, as well as several midwestern states. Occasionally the Negro press identified Topeka Negroes attending the institute. Without exception, however, those articles concern socially prominent young women. Mabel Jeltz (daughter of Fred Jeltz, the editor-publisher of the *Kansas State Ledger*) was enrolled in a stenography class. Elizabeth Cooper (daughter of William Damascus Cooper, black small businessman and sometime associate of Nick Chiles, editor of the *Plaindealer*) attended the sewing class. Enrollment in such classes cannot be regarded as preparation for employment. Rather, the tone of the news reports suggests that for those individuals, their course of study resembled a finishing school or was an enrichment of high school training.[60] Thus, attendance at the institute was by no means a precise indicator of social class or economic position. In the view of the *Plaindealer*, nevertheless, parents whose employment did not permit proper care of their children were urged to place these youth at the institute. The large number of households with small children and with both parents working and the popularity of Sheldon's programs in Tennesseetown suggest that the institute may have helped fulfill the educational needs of the Negroes at several economic levels.

Both the scope and implementation of services at the institute adhered closely to the Booker T. Washington design at Tuskegee and reflected his dictum that self-help, industry, and thrift prescribed the route to race progress. "A consecrated heart, a trained mind, and a skilled hand" was the sustaining rationale for the institute's goal: to train Kansas Negroes in agriculture, domestic arts, and the trades. As will be seen, however, black Topeka's support for the institute did not mean unequivocal endorsement of Washington's philosophy. Their ideological alternatives were governed by concerns broader than industrial education and the economics of accommodationism.

Western University, located in Quindaro, a black suburb of Kansas City, Kansas, was another institution devoted primarily to Negro education. The Reverend Eben Blatchley, a white Presbyterian minister,

---

60. *Kansas State Ledger*, January 10, 1903; *Plaindealer*, May 23, 1913.

founded and christened the school Freedmen's University in 1863. Blatchley's warrant as a reformer is unknown. Nevertheless, like abolitionists who founded schools for southern blacks after the Civil War, Blatchley conceived of Negro education as a means of securing a tangible hold on freedom.[61]

After Blatchley's death in 1877 the Kansas A.M.E. Conference took over the school and its property and rechartered it as Western University. Under the supervision of A.M.E. bishops the university almost closed its doors in 1899, having no endowment and inadequate financial support. In the same year, however, the Kansas legislature granted an appropriation of $10,000, with the proviso that industrial education supplement the school's academic program. Between 1899 and 1914 the legislature granted over $300,000 for the maintenance of the school's expanding programs and physical plant. Through 1914, however, private financial support remained negligible. Although legislative appropriations helped, the state did not take over the management of the school.[62]

Despite the later addition of an industrial department, teacher training was the mainstay of education at Western University. State reports concerning the institution indicate that it also numbered lawyers and physicians as well as stenographers, musicians, and tradesmen among its three hundred graduates through 1914. Evidence of the academic emphasis at Western University is reinforced by the absence of reference to training of the hand (a euphemism for industrial education); rather, cultivation of "the heart and mind," "self-government," and "self-control" were virtues which "should adorn every Christian man and woman."[63]

Other than occasional references to Topekans attending A.M.E. conferences at Western University, there is little mention of the activity of that school in Topeka's black press.[64] News accounts did focus on Chancellor William Tecumseh Vernon and his selection, under the sponsor-

61. Rose, *Rehearsal for Reconstruction*, 229–31, 233; McPherson, *The Abolitionist Legacy*, 143–44, 184–85; Harlan, *Booker T. Washington*, 58–62.
62. *Nineteenth Report*, 80; "Uplifting the Negro at Quindaro," *Daily Capital*, March 13, 1902.
63. *Nineteenth Report*, 79–80.
64. "Western University," *Plaindealer*, March 13, 1914; "The Colored School at Quindaro," *Plaindealer*, April 20, 1910.

ship of Booker T. Washington, as registrar of the treasury during the administration of Theodore Roosevelt. Kansas City, Kansas, was the city in which Vernon rose to prominence. He spoke at political functions in Topeka, but had no intimate association with black affairs in that city.[65]

There is no indication that Topeka Negroes obtained their higher education at Western University. In contrast, the attendance of black Topekans at the University of Kansas, the local Washburn College, and Emporia State Teachers College received a disproportionate share of publicity in the city's Negro press. The popularity of professional training at state and private institutions of higher learning suggests a preference for integrated schools. This generalization is supported further by the unrelenting pressure against segregated education in any form, a sentiment shared by most Negro Topekans. Perforce, many of the city's black professionals received training in medicine or the law in southern black institutions as well as in integrated state and private universities in the North.[66] Advocacy of higher education and training for the professions, undiminished by support of the institute, was abundantly clear in the social behavior of Negro Topekans.

Social organizations upheld the standard of race progress, with an added concern for cultural and intellectual life. At a statewide black political meeting in Topeka in 1900, chaired by the Reverend William L. Grant, the conferees asserted that the evaluation of political alternatives presupposed development in other spheres of social and institutional life. Accordingly, "the Negroes of Kansas, like all persons in this and every other civilized country, are aspirants for higher literary and educational qualifications commensurate with the spirit of the age."[67] Negro newspapers, moreover, identified black graduates of Topeka High School and pointed to any sign of increase in their numbers over the

65. See "Chancellor Vernon Talks," *Daily Capital*, January 17, 1901; "Political Gossip," *State Journal*, May 28, 1906; "Wm. T. Vernon, Noted Negro Educator of Kansas, Is Named as Registrar of the Treasury," news article of unknown source, January 13, 1906, in *NC*, VI.
66. Clifford S. Griffin, *History of the University of Kansas* (Lawrence, 1973), 18, 209–210; *Plaindealer*, May 18, 1900, June 13, 1904; "Colored Students and Graduates of the University of Kansas," *Graduate Magazine of the University of Kansas*, VII (May, 1909), 294–303, contains statistics regarding courses taken, along with passing reference to living conditions; *Plaindealer*, October 10, 1913, identifies cases of discrimination at the university.
67. *Plaindealer*, May 18, 1900.

previous year. Black baccalaureates in whatever field also received plaudits from the Negro press. However, countervailing views existed on the uses of education. "There is an undeniable tendency among our young men to seek the professions rather than the trades and thereby hangs a tale of woe," asserted Robert Buckner, a socially prominent, politically active, and successful contractor, in an address to fellow members of the Ivy Club. The ambitions of young men seeking to become "head push" at a hotel or studying for the bar are "laudable insofar as they seek to earn an honest living and do their duty in their various positions." Nonetheless, a Negro youth would do well to consider the skilled trades and thereby "prepare himself for a life of usefulness in a new field," Buckner concluded.[68]

The Interstate Literary Association, organized in 1892 in Topeka, provided an outlet for cultural interests of black Topekans primarily, with modest representation from other cities in the state as well as from Missouri and Nebraska. Educators and other professionals predominated in its membership. In addition to readings from Shakespeare and Tennyson, the association sponsored lectures, art exhibitions, and musicales, all of which were carried off with some sophistication. Social consciousness and endorsement of race progress were evident in the association's active support of quality public education and in strident opposition to segregated schools.[69]

The Topeka affiliate of the National Federation of Colored Women's Clubs was organized in 1893 and by 1917, consisted of eight separate organizations. Mrs. John Wright, Mrs. James H. Guy, and Mrs. J. M. Jamison, prominent in the social life of black Topeka, were active in the federation. A full calendar of local and state conferences and meetings helped coordinate cultural and philanthropic endeavors amid a swirl of social activity. In the parlance of the times, "the work" of the Oriental Club, Alpha Assisi, the Oak Leaf Club, and members of the Topeka federation resulted by 1916 in the collection of "2,207.07 dollars." However the sum was arrived at, it was an impressive figure that was matched the following year.[70]

68. *Plaindealer*, April 13, 1900.
69. *Ibid.*, January 5, 12, 1900.
70. *Ibid.*, June 16, 23, 1916, June 29, 1917; *Daily Capital*, June 25, 1906, June 28, 1914.

Indeed, the federation chapters at Topeka and Kansas City, Kansas, were in a veritable race to be first in beneficence and fund raising. In addition, Topeka, Kansas City, and Wichita competed for preeminence in women's affairs, and Topeka garnered more than its share of elective and appointive offices. As an example, Lulu Harris of Topeka was president of the federation's state convention in 1906 and in 1916. Topeka Negro women also held the vice-presidency, among other offices, in the intervening years.[71] In tribute to the Kansas federation and its Topeka affiliate for their social consciousness and concern for race progress, the *Plaindealer* (June 15, 1900) identified the group as a "band of earnest, intelligent colored women who have given and are giving much of their lives to lift the race to a higher plane."

At a statewide convention at Wichita in 1916, the Kansas federation joined with chapters in other states in sending a memorandum to Congress to enact laws making lynching a federal offense. The clubwomen also recommended national women's suffrage. The noted reformer Jane Addams addressed the federation's 1913 national convention in Chicago and spoke for women's suffrage in particular and civil rights for Negroes in general.[72] Although the goal of race progress took precedence, the organization and activity of the federation reflected trends in the women's movement in general. While influence and power in black men's social organizations were more widely distributed throughout the state, Topekans enjoyed parity in representation and successfully fielded candidates for elective office.

The black Topeka federation, as well as other organized forums for economic development and for political action, recited the beatitudes of race progress and articulated them to the community at large. The members' public posture indicates that they formed a cohort of black leadership. They also comprised the "social register," governed its membership, and presided over an elaborate social season.

Presently available sources do not make possible a comprehensive, formal group biography of black leaders. For one thing, no absolute or clearly defined criteria exist for identifying them. For another, membership lists are incomplete. Newspaper articles and obituaries do not provide precise indicators of the economic and occupational characteristics

71. *Daily Capital*, June 28, 1914.
72. *Plaindealer*, June 16, 1916, February 7, 1913.

of black Topeka leaders. Nonetheless, in aggregate, they were an impressive lot. Many were professionals, businessmen, or civil servants of varying status—from custodial work at the Kansas State House to a municipal or county clerkship. High occupational status among blacks generally, of course, was not inconsistent with work as caterers and headwaiters.[73] Without significant exception, the wife in the household of a leader did not work. Indeed, as an indicator of leadership status, the wife's use of leisure in social and philanthropic affairs was as important a criterion for status as her husband's activities. Neither census materials nor newspaper photographs of leaders give a reliable indication of skin color, so it cannot be correlated reliably with status; the picture of Alpha Assisi, previously described, is one of the few exceptions. Locale of residence also does not provide a key to one's position as a leader. Leaders could be found in clusters randomly distributed in one or another of the city's Negro enclaves. A greater percentage of them, however, lived in integrated or contiguous black and white neighborhoods. Most leaders came to Topeka during or following the Great Exodus (1879–1880). That was a bench mark for tenure in the city, to the limited degree that such was a qualification for leadership status after the turn of the century.

With few exceptions, Exodusters and later immigrants had preempted most positions of authority and responsibility before the 1880s were over. After 1900, individuals who were part of the pre-Exodus population received only occasional public notice, as faithful servants of the church or upon retirement from employment of long duration. Most churches had representatives in the leadership cohort and had equal claim to whatever institutional prestige accrued from sponsoring social activities or from providing facilities for the many meetings.

All black Topeka leaders exercised political and social responsibility and displayed a high degree of race consciousness. Relative affluence along with prominence in political and nonpolitical institutions at once conferred power in the black community and confirmed their role as decision makers. The criteria for black leadership did not differ in other Kansas cities or in American urban communities in general, from the

---

73. Table 16; for the occupational patterns among black leaders in other urban areas, see Katzman, *Before the Ghetto*, 115–17, 126–34, Appendix B; Spear, *Black Chicago*, 71–89; Kusmer, *A Ghetto Takes Shape*, 113–54.

1850s through 1900. In addition, the energy invested by black leaders in organization for reform or for social and economic advancement, as well as their thirst for success, reflected values current in the nation as a whole.[74] Within that general framework, the dislocations of discrimination created differences between Negroes and whites in the social and economic configuration defining elite status. A relatively larger percentage of blacks were at the bottom of the economic, prestige, and power hierarchy.

Studies of the social structure in black urban communities support the assertion that economic and social status is a factor in both the definition and distribution of power and in the roles of black and white decision makers.[75] Further, race has an impact on the definition of the social structure and leadership patterns. In this context, David Katzman's discussion of caste, and its influence on social stratification, intraracial class antagonisms, and definition of elites, is particularly informative. Negroes in Topeka, however, had relatively greater access to elective and appointive office than did Negroes in Detroit, so the boundaries of caste were not so impermeable. Correspondingly, Topeka blacks were less proscribed by caste in their dealings with whites.[76] In no sense did the dialogue between whites and blacks in Topeka politics indicate a radical redistribution of power. The contacts, however, were

---

74. Rischin, *The Promised City*, 95–111, and Milton Gordon, *Assimilation in American Life* (New York, 1964), 71–83, 107–114, 127–31, discuss the development of intraracial antagonisms among other ethnic groups; on values then current, see David Potter, *People of Plenty* (Chicago, 1954), 84–90, 95, 98; Samuel P. Hays, *The Response to Industrialism, 1885–1914* (Chicago, 1957), 22–27; Robin Williams, *American Society: A Sociological Interpretation* (New York, 1965), 417–26.

75. Kahl, *The American Class Structure*, 221–50; Aaron Antovsky, "Aspirations, Class, and Racial-Ethnic Membership," *Journal of Negro Education*, XXXVI (1967), 385–93; Stanley Liberson, "Stratification and Ethnic Groups," *Sociological Inquiry*, XL (1970), 172–87; Martin Katzman, "Opportunity, Subculture, and the Economic Performance of Urban Ethnic Groups," *American Journal of Economics and Sociology*, XXVIII (1969), 351–66; E. Franklin Frazier, "The Negro American Community and Class Realities: The Ordeal of Change," in Celia Heller (ed.), *Structured Social Inequality* (New York, 1969), 387–96; Donald Noel, "Theory of the Origins of Ethnic Stratification," *Social Problems*, XVI (1968–69), 157–71; T. B. Bottomore, *Elites and Society* (London, 1964), 11–14.

76. August Meier, *Negro Thought in America, 1880–1915* (Ann Arbor, 1963), 161–89; Kusmer, *A Ghetto Takes Shape*, 66–90, 113–56; Spear, *Black Chicago*, 111–18, 147–66, 181–200; St. Clair Drake and Horace Cayton, *Black Metropolis: A Study of Negro Life in a Northern City* (2 vols.; New York, 1945, 1962), I, 214–312; Katzman, *Before the Ghetto*, 81–85.

relatively more numerous and were spread with fair uniformity over a broad spectrum of class. This makes Topeka significant.

High literacy rates for the black population as a whole strongly suggest that Topeka Negroes at most class levels were cognizant of events and issues that affected the community at large. Three thriving Negro newspapers, in which appear letters about race relations and current events from otherwise undistinguished Negro citizens, confirm black awareness of a wide range of issues. Conforming to well-established patterns, Negro Topekans at the turn of the century actively engaged in politics. Although there would be some political advancement, through 1912, Negroes were not completely successful in shaping public policy to fit race interests. Combating discrimination through organized protest, however, was their dominant concern. The social and intellectual life of black Topeka was enlivened by the resultant debate over alternative philosophies of race protest and progress.

Chapter 7
Protest Organization and Political Action
1896–1915

Since the 1880s the struggle for equality had undergone periods of advance and retreat. By 1900, however, increasing racism posed an imminent threat to American Negroes regardless of region. Black Topekans concurred with W. E. B. Du Bois: "The problem of the twentieth century is the problem of the color line."[1] If the most virulent manifestations of Jim Crow occurred in the South, the random racial violence in the urban North was no less serious. Topeka lay in the wake rather than in the eye of that storm. Discrimination in Topeka and in other Kansas cities, however, forced Negroes to summon all of their intellectual and social resources to combat the problem. Correspondingly, black Topeka's social, political, and religious institutions became a home guard against the advance of Jim Crow. Their unstinting fight against discrimination was part of the sustaining rationale for reform and self-help, educational endeavor, and political action. Behind every injunction to progress, however defined, racism was a goad to organized protest.

Ever aware of the violence against southern Negroes, increasingly severe since the 1890s, the black Topeka press chronicled the "beastly and dastardly crimes committed by the rebel populace of Dixie." Race violence in the North was no less disturbing. Having been in New York City during its bloody race riot in 1900, a black Topeka minister, upon returning home, devoted an entire sermon to that issue: "Innocent men and women ... cruelly assaulted" and police brutality were among the

---

1. Du Bois, *The Souls of Black Folk*, xxvii, 33.

horrors "perpetrated upon our defenseless people."[2] The dedication of a Jim Crow YMCA in Chicago in 1913, a "magnificent monument to race prejudice, intolerance, inhumanity, and white American hypocrisy," was an event decried in the black Topeka press despite segregation in the city's own YMCA. "Oklahoma's disgrace" for attempting to disfranchise Negroes in 1916 further indicated that Jim Crow was spreading.[3]

The alarm in the black Topeka press became increasingly strident as the wave of discrimination swept across Kansas. Black Kansans protested and witnessed the defeat of efforts to institute segregated schools in cities of the second class between 1900 and 1917. Theretofore, because of the relatively smaller size of the student population, in second-class cities the schools were unsegregated. In 1900, however, whites and blacks were bitterly split over that issue in Fort Scott, a second-class city in southeastern Kansas. "A race war is on at Fort Scott," asserted the Topeka *Colored Citizen* (September 21, 1900), in its report of "a vast amount of trouble in this city over the race question in the schools." The issue was not resolved at the local level and it resurfaced in a series of bills before the Kansas legislature between 1900 and 1917. Bills favoring segregated schools in second-class cities in 1900 and 1912–1913 went down to defeat in the Kansas legislature. Building new segregated facilities was said to cause a drain on municipal and state educational budgets. In 1916–1917, whites in Galena, Kansas, a second-class city on the Missouri border, favored segregated schools. Introduced as a bill before the Kansas legislature in 1917, the measure was defeated for the same reasons in force in 1913. Financial considerations rather than thoroughgoing liberalism in race matters dictated the rejection of segregation. A bill prohibiting interracial marriage also was defeated in 1913, if for less apparent reasons.[4]

In the school segregation cases in 1913 and in 1917, the black Topeka

---

2. *Kansas State Ledger*, August 20, 1900, and *Plaindealer*, December 15, 1916, describe lynchings and race brutality in New Orleans and in South Carolina; *Plaindealer*, January 31, 1913, reported conditions in the South in general; "On New York Riots," *Colored Citizen*, August 31, 1900, reprint of *State Journal* interview of the Reverend William Brooks, pastor of black Topeka's St. Mark A.M.E. Church.
3. *Plaindealer*, July 11, 1913, January 14, 1916; Kusmer, *A Ghetto Takes Shape*, 50, 58–59, asserts that discrimination in the YMCA also was a source of rancor between blacks and whites in Cleveland.
4. *Colored Citizen*, September 21, 1900; *Plaindealer*, December 27, 1912, February 9, 17, 1917.

press argued that the insidious influence of southern bigotry was the source of the trouble. In 1913 the *Plaindealer* admonished the legislature, "that dignified body of educated and refined men," not to be "bathed in the infamy of southern prejudiced ideas and whims." Of the same mind in 1917, the *Plaindealer* asked the state to defeat resoundingly legislation "patterned after [that] fostered by [southern] murderers, lynchers, and riff-raff."[5]

Attempts to introduce segregation into new areas of public education in Topeka were particularly disturbing to the city's Negro citizens. Primary schools were segregated in Topeka as in other first-class cities. The seventh and eighth grades as well as the high school, however, were integrated. In 1908, white parents of seventh and eighth graders boycotted a Topeka school because of what they conceived to be an unfavorable balance of Negro and white students: thirty blacks in a student population of ninety. The black Topeka press immediately entered the fray, proclaiming that segregation at any level of education was wrong, "but since we have it, segregation should not be extended further and if anything it must be repealed." Although Topeka Negroes were powerless to remove that blight from public education in general, they were successful in preventing the incursion of segregation into the seventh and eighth grades in 1908. The superintendent of the public schools took the matter in stride, asserting: "The river will run dry." In a more guarded mood, however, he expressed "regret that the thing has occurred as it will stir up prejudice."[6]

If Jim Crow did not make new inroads in public education, discrimination assaulted Topeka Negroes in other areas of public life between 1900 and 1917. In 1900 the Reverend George Shaffer of St. John A.M.E. observed: "There is not a restaurant or lunch counter . . . in this city where a Negro can obtain a meal . . . or a cup of coffee." A black visitor to Topeka, who subsequently made Shaffer's acquaintance, alleged that upon arrival and without friends, he was "compelled to stop at the city jail overnight because no hotel or lodging house would furnish him accommodations." Shaffer's complaint somewhat overstates the case. Occasionally Negroes alone or, more commonly, accompanied by

5. *Plaindealer,* January 31, 1913, January 26, 1917.
6. *Public Schools—General Clippings,* I; *State Journal,* September 24, 25, 1908; *Plaindealer,* September 24, 1908.

whites were accorded equal treatment in Topeka restaurants.[7] Not knowing when one would or would not encounter discrimination created black insecurity and distrust regarding that aspect of interracial relations in Topeka.

The absence of a consistent pattern in discrimination created peculiar variations on the theme of Jim Crow. For example, Topeka Negroes protested the showing of the film *Birth of a Nation*, presented at a theater with segregated seating. Thus, even within an established domain of prejudice, blacks protested further denigration of the race, invidious depictions of Negroes on the screen. Significantly, black efforts to stop the showing of the film were accomplished largely through the aid of whites. The Kansas Board of Censors found the film "immoral . . . slanderous, and . . . untrue to history." In a further refinement on that judgment, the state attorney general, speaking for the board, declared that the film was little more than a patent effort to "slander and vilify the Negro race and the Union soldier . . . to create race prejudice, engender passion, [and] strife." The Reverend Charles Sheldon, among other white Topeka ministers, concurred with the board and registered his disapproval.[8] An aroused public caused the film to be banned. The response of whites was not solely a testament to racial liberalism, since there was no collateral move to end Jim Crow seating in Topeka theaters. By the same token, it would be a distortion to view their action exclusively as an effort to protect the sanctity of John Brown's legacy and the Union cause, independent of Negro freedom.

Discrimination in the job market was one of Jim Crow's most troublesome manifestations. That problem undermined the economic structure of the black community. To a greater degree than for professionals and businessmen, however, Negro workers were subject to the prejudicial whims of white employers and unions. Because Topeka Negroes were predominantly unskilled laborers, the results of discrimination in employment were most pronounced at that occupational level.[9]

    7. *Colored Citizen*, September 28, 1900; Sheldon, *The Kingdom.*
    8. *Plaindealer*, January 28, March 8, 1916.
    9. On discrimination in the workplace, with particular reference to black skilled and unskilled workers and unions in national perspective, see Philip Foner, *Organized Labor and the Black Worker, 1619–1973* (New York, 1974), 130–35; Bernard Mandell, "Samuel Gompers and the Negro Workers, 1886–1914," *Journal of Negro History*, XL (1955), 40–46, argues that Gompers' advocacy of integrated unions reflected not racial liberalism but his

"The Board of Education seems to discriminate against black workmen," observed the *Colored Citizen* in 1900. For instance, the board's refusal to allow Negro workers to do the repair work on black schools raised the hackles of Negroes. "Since we must have separate schools," the editorial concluded, "we think it nothing more than just that colored mechanics be given an opportunity to do the repair work on the colored school buildings." The comment was to no avail, and the black press reported similar complaints in the ensuing decade.[10]

The Negro press was equivocal on the question of labor unions in 1898. Segregated unions jealously guarded the routes to success in the labor market and further limited economic opportunity for black Topeka workers. On the other hand, labor unions could "compel employers to pay a standard scale of wages." Most commonly, however, organized labor "is manipulated only for the benefit of a favored few, and draws the color line on the black man and debars him from membership; it is a falsehood on its face."[11] That was the case in a confrontation between Negro flagmen and yard workers with the railway union in 1913.

A committee of Negro railroad workers, with the local chapter of the National Negro Business League, acting as friend of the court, petitioned the Kansas legislature against a bill that would grant the union exclusive representation of all line crews and yard workers. In view of the union's excluding Negroes, passage of that legislation was tantamount to firing black railroad workers. Through the petition and an influential lobbying effort against the measure by the Santa Fe Railroad, the legislation was defeated. According to a Santa Fe spokesman, the bill would "absolutely put out of business thousands of capable, industrious and thrifty railroad men for no other reason than the cruel and unjust rule of the railroad unions." What passed as equalitarian sentiment also promoted self-serving ends: it proscribed both union interference and legislative meddling. The Santa Fe was somewhat more than a fair-weather ally, having earned a reputation in the 1890s for an en-

---

wanting to prevent the use of Negroes as strikebreakers; Sidney Kessler, "The Organization of Negroes in the Knights of Labor," *Journal of Negro History*, XXXVII (1952), 253–55, believes that the Knights endorsed integration for equally pragmatic reasons—they were more imbued with politics and reformation than was Gompers.

10. *Colored Citizen*, July 6, 1900; *Plaindealer*, September 24, 1908.
11. *Colored Citizen*, October 21, 1898.

lightened hiring policy.¹² Nonetheless, discrimination in the workplace and exclusion from the unions remained major stumbling blocks for black skilled and unskilled laborers.

Discrimination in the job market and in public accommodations had reciprocal effects on the economic and occupational structure. The development of black businesses and professional services to a Negro market was among the consequences of segregation. The ever more strident and pervasive influence of Jim Crow at the turn of the century provided the immediate preconditions for the pattern. As a general phenomenon, however, economic discrimination as a factor in the black occupational structure had antebellum origins. Long familiarity with the problem aided blacks, irrespective of region, in formulating resolutions to current crises.¹³

Occasionally Negro businessmen complained that they did not have enough black customers. Advertisements for black enterprises, however, were prominent in the Negro press, as were innumerable articles which chronicled the entrepreneurial success of individual Negroes. The Commercial Club and the NNBL, moreover, provided forums wherein Negro businessmen worked out economic designs for race progress and techniques for gaining a larger share of the market. Among the popular topics for debate at the meetings were how to improve merchandising, the use of advertising, and the value of joint financial ventures.

Black professionals also enjoyed the ancillary benefits of segregation. The eight physicians and two pharmacists in Topeka in 1913 did not lack for clients, since such services were usually if not uniformly segregated. Topeka Negroes were a litigious people, and black lawyers were kept busy. Most professionals advertised their services, specialties, and credentials in black newspapers or municipal business directories. The relative affluence of these individuals, moreover, helped propel Negro professionals and businessmen into positions as community leaders.¹⁴

    12. C. W. Kaimas, *A Statement to the Senate and the House of Representatives Against the "Full Crew Bill"* (Topeka, 1913), 1, 4–6; *Plaindealer*, February 21, 1913, on Santa Fe hiring policy in 1880 and 1895; on union discrimination, see *Colored Citizen*, July 27, 1900, October 21, 1898, and *State Journal*, January 21, 1915.
    13. Ira Berlin, *Slaves Without Masters: The Free Negro in the Antebellum South* (New York, 1976), 217–49; Litwack, *North of Slavery*, 153–86.
    14. For a brief biographical sketch of four black Topeka lawyers, see *Plaindealer*, May 18, 1900.

Negro Topekans took stock of the reigning arguments for accommodation and integration and gravitated toward organizations which provided outlets for those alternatives. The role of leaders and decision makers in the organization and activities of race protest received extensive public notice. While less often documented, the alignment of blacks at lower social and economic levels may be inferred.

The National Association for the Advancement of Colored People and the National Negro Business League were principal forums for debate over the direction and thrust of organized protest. Removing impediments to race progress also generated much discussion. A profile of the socioeconomic position and the associational behavior of the two organizations' membership can help identify the underlying social significance of the protest alternatives: full and immediate integration into American society or accommodation to the *status quo* in race relations while consolidating black community resources. The issues, of course, were not cut and dried. Topeka Negroes were more pragmatic than doctrinaire in their assessment of protest alternatives. Common cause also was a viable option.

The NNBL was the most prominent agency for expanding black Topeka's commercial interests and for expressing the doctrine of accommodationism. Between 1913 and 1917, Topeka's chapter of the NAACP grew but was relatively smaller. As was the case in the NAACP at the national level, the chief administrative officers of the Topeka chapter were white, although the rank and file was Negro. The NNBL and organized white business interests in Topeka occasionally engaged in joint ventures, although there were no explicit organizational ties.[15] Further, interracial cooperation was an important adjunct to the programs at the Kansas Industrial and Educational Institute.

In terms of sheer numbers of members and affiliated organizations, the accommodationist genre of race protest carried the day in black Topeka. The disparity in size of the Topeka NNBL and NAACP, however, cannot be used as an exclusive indicator of the ideological temper of black citizens. The accommodationists' repeated injunction to thrift, self-help, and economic development in the 1900s, for example, had been part of the race's common store for decades. In the main, black

---

15. *Kansas State Ledger*, April 30, 1897; *Colored Citizen*, June 17, 1897; *Daily Capital*, August 31, 1906.

Topekans rejected a gradualist, acquiescent approach to race progress, irrespective of affiliation with the NNBL or the NAACP. In fact, membership in both organizations was not uncommon. For all the gamesmanship and rancor generated in discussion of the relative merits of accommodation and integration at the national level, unity remained an important leitmotiv of organized race protest in Topeka during the 1900s.

However circumscribed by discrimination, Topeka blacks in 1900 were imbued with the acquisitive spirit common to the period and kept their eyes on the main chance. Most blacks conceded that the professions and higher education were important for community development and race progress. Many also endorsed business success as the mark of the man and of the race in ascendancy. "Let us jump into the commercial world with as much zeal and vigor as we do into the political, educational, or religious," asserted James Guy, lawyer and businessman, in support of organizing the Commercial Club in 1900. "Race cooperation is the great desideratum," Guy continued, and growth "along business and commercial lines will change permanently our financial condition as nothing else will." Therein lay the "only true solution to what has been erroneously called a race problem."[16]

At a meeting convened to discuss employment discrimination in 1872, William Brooks, a laborer, advised Topeka Negroes to "stand and work together" for better economic conditions and "to build up the race." In 1879, C. L. de Randamie, black Topeka's first real estate agent, tried to encourage Negroes in a cooperative business venture. The black *Kansas Herald* concurred, in "A Word to Colored Capitalists" (February 27, 1880). With a little money judiciously invested in a joint-stock company, "we can derive some of the benefits now reaped by whites." The editorial concluded: "If we let these chances go by we ought not to complain if we remain . . . the hewers of wood and the drawers of water." As early as 1893, before the influence of Booker T. Washington grew strong in black Topeka, the *Evening Call* summarized ideas that had been articles of faith for twenty years: "Industry, education, commerce, and wealth [will] enable us to stand side by side on equal terms with whites."[17] Thus,

16. *Plaindealer,* June 15, 1900.
17. *Commonwealth,* August 9, 1872; *Colored Citizen,* October 28, November 29, 1879; *Evening Call,* June 19, 1893.

a confluence of traditional and current values and the harsh realities of Jim Crow gave shape to the economic order of the Negro community. This prefigured black Topekans' favorable reception of Booker T. Washington's philosophy and their enthusiasm at the prospect of his visit to the city in 1897.

In his Topeka lecture Washington proclaimed that "the spirit of the Age" required commercial development and organization to promote success in business, the best guarantor of Negro progress. The merits of industrial education also received emphasis, and he saluted the industrial training program in Topeka initiated by Edward Stephens at the Kansas Industrial and Educational Institute two years earlier.[18]

The *Colored Citizen* endorsed the theme of Washington's lecture and impressed upon "parents and guardians of the young, the absolute necessity [for] educating the hand as well as the heart in the struggle for existence and preferment." Business organization also was an urgent requirement, "excluded as we are from the shops and factories by the labor unions." The *Plaindealer* applauded his call for the organization of the NNBL in 1900. Accordingly, Negro businessmen should "organize and prosperity will follow."[19] In fact, black Topekans already had seized the initiative. The founding of the black Commercial Club predated publication of Washington's call for the NNBL national meeting in August. By no mere coincidence, the ideas made current by Washington had a direct influence on the development of the club even though it was patterned on the white Topeka organization of the same name.[20] This was not, however, patent imitation of a white model because the impetus to such activity had long tenure in the black community. The black Commercial Club changed its name to the NNBL and sent James Guy, president of the local chapter, as its representative to the first national meeting in Boston in August, 1900.

There were fifteen charter members in 1900, and forty by 1906. According to the white Topeka *Daily Capital*, they were men "who have attained the highest success in their respective vocations and . . . are setting an example for their race to follow."[21] Although no list of those

18. *Kansas State Ledger*, April 30, 1897; *Colored Citizen*, November 16, 1900.
19. *Colored Citizen*, June 17, 1897; *Plaindealer*, June 22, 1900.
20. *Plaindealer*, June 15, 1900; J. L. King (ed.), *History of Shawnee County*, 158; *Plaindealer*, July 2, 1900.
21. *Daily Capital*, August 31, 1906, in *NC*, VI.

who joined the NNBL between 1900 and 1906 is presently available, the charter members were an illustrious group and fit the *Daily Capital*'s glowing assessment. Numbered among them were civil servants, lawyers, judges, and educators. Individuals engaged in trade or business were a minority. Neither business directories nor newspapers, moreover, revealed an appreciable increase in Negro businesses between 1900 and 1906. Nonetheless, black Topeka could boast approximately thirty businesses, including a theater, two newspapers, three restaurants, two catering businesses, two mortuaries, and two builder-contractor concerns, as well as grocery stores, coal dealerships, and barbershops.[22]

Black news reports of NNBL activities from 1900 to 1906 repeated the standard injunction to commercial development. Perhaps because the institute was prospering under the state's financial management and because the interest in higher education was traditional, there was less emphasis on industrial training associated with NNBL activities. The organization also had some of the trappings of a social club. Business success stories as well as lectures on race progress were common at the meetings, often concluded with a fancy repast and entertainment. Excursions to meetings with NNBL chapters in other Kansas cities also were popular.

The Topeka NNBL regularly sent a representative to national meetings. At the 1906 national conclave in Atlanta, Georgia, Topeka's representative Ira Guy, a successful barber and James Guy's younger brother, was selected as first vice-president of the national organization. Perhaps on the strength of that coup and the presence of the institute in the city, the local chapter entered a successful bid to have the 1907 NNBL national meeting in Topeka. Such a banner event and Washington's national prestige merited special protocol. Accordingly, Ira Guy enlisted the cooperation of the white Commercial Club, the mayor of Topeka, and the governor of Kansas, who issued a formal invitation to Washington. That cooperative endeavor was in accordance with Washington's stated interest in establishing close working relations with white chambers of commerce and with white public officials. The conclave, held August 14–16, was a rousing success, increasing the civic pride of black and white Topekans alike. Welcoming speeches by the governor

22. *Plaindealer*, June 15, 1900; *Radges' Topeka Directory*, 1900–1907.

and the mayor and a keynote address by Booker T. Washington began a round of meetings conducted at the municipal auditorium and at the institute.[23]

On the basis of the NNBL's increasing representation throughout Kansas, in 1912 the Topeka chapter initiated plans for a state organization. John Wright, deputy county clerk and long prominent in the affairs of black Topeka, presided over the meeting held at St. John A.M.E. The election of Fred Roundtree, principal of Monroe Elementary School, as auditor and the election of two Topekans to the six-man executive committee were indicators of the city's prominence in that state caucus.[24]

The local chapter itself increased dramatically. By 1913 it claimed 106 members, among whom tradesmen and businessmen were in the majority. Their new preponderance, a reversal of patterns evident in 1900 and in 1906, did not reflect a decline in the number of professionals in the NNBL. Rather, it indicated a veritable explosion of affiliates in the commercial and business categories. The welter of new representatives included a booking agent, a huckster, and an inventor, as well as those in occupations customarily associated with black commercial endeavors, such as barbers, contractors, tailors, and grocers. In addition, four women—a dressmaker, a teacher, a chiropodist, and a baker—rounded out the expanding Topeka NNBL membership list. Significantly, the overwhelming majority claimed both real and personal property. With the exception of one Negro insurance man, however, there were no real estate agents or other financial managers in the local chapter.[25] Perhaps for that reason, the Topeka NNBL did not establish satellite organizations, such as the Colored Merchants' Association or a branch of the Negro Chamber of Commerce.[26] Be that as it may, the Topeka NNBL had ample reason for confidence in 1913.

Black Topekans listened with pride to the assessment of their com-

23. *Daily Capital*, August 31, 1906, in *NC*, VI; Booker T. Washington, *The Negro in Business* (Reprint; Chicago, 1969), 274; *Eighth Annual Session of the NNBL* (Topeka, 1907).
24. *Plaindealer*, July 12, 1912.
25. *Ibid.*, August 15, November 14, 1913; *Radges' Topeka Directory*, 1912–13.
26. Washington, *The Negro in Business*, 274; on the Colored Merchants' Association, the Negro Chamber of Commerce, and the National Negro Bankers' Association, see J. L. Nichols and William H. Crogman, *Progress of a Race or the Remarkable Advancement of the American Negro* (Chicago, 1920), 227–29; J. H. Harmon, Arnett G. Lindsay, and Carter G. Woodson, *The Negro as a Businessman* (College Park, Md., 1929), 53; Joseph A. Pierce, *Negro*

mercial and economic development up to 1914 made by Ralph Tyler, former auditor of the United States Navy and a national organizer for the NNBL. A guest speaker at a meeting held at St. John A.M.E. to commemorate the fourteenth anniversary of the local chapter, Tyler asserted: "Although Topeka has a Negro population of but 5,000, the race here has $155,000 invested in business and owns $700,000 worth of real estate." Tyler also took due note of the accomplishments of professionals and offered paeans to the community's black leaders by name.[27]

News of Washington's death in 1915 marred a year otherwise made auspicious by the selection of Topeka's own John Wright as first vice-president of the national organization. The NNBL's efforts to spur commercial development in Topeka continued through the early 1900s, although there was no evidence of the dramatic increase in Negro business apparent between 1907 and 1913. A social profile of a selection of NNBL members through 1915 reveals that they were heterogeneous in economic interests and demographic background as well as in ideology.[28]

Martin Oglesvie, a Tennessee Exoduster, came to Topeka in 1878, leading an early contingent of migrants who settled the enclave Tennesseetown. Oglesvie was of a breed of leaders who, with no recognizable prior claim, surfaced in response to the exigencies of the long migration and to the requirements of frontier settlement. He remained a gardener and a common laborer throughout his life. Nevertheless, Oglesvie had savings as well as a good eye for investment and acquired one-third interest in the black Apex Theatre in 1916.

Oglesvie was described as substantial in spirit and in girth: "a leading man" and a pillar of St. John A.M.E., "with heart as large as his body and tempered sweet as a child." A charter member of the NNBL, Oglesvie had a quiet influence, manifest in committee activity rather than in speechmaking. The products of his truck garden and orchards in Tennesseetown were the pride of the Sunflower Association Fair at the institute. In his leisure, Oglesvie went pheasant hunting in the western counties. As he posed for a news photograph on one such occasion Og-

---

Business and Business Education: Their Present and Prospective Development (New York, 1947), 206–210.

27. *Plaindealer*, June 19, 1914.

28. *Ibid.*, August 25, November 17, 1916, April 20, 1917; *Radges' Topeka Directory*, 1914–17.

lesvie had the appearance of a country gentleman, every inch a "Popular Topeka Sportsman . . . Planning a Big Trip."[29]

John Wright, born in Michigan, arrived in Topeka in 1882 as a youth of fifteen. Wright graduated from Topeka High School and presented as additional credentials for his job as a postal clerk: "a head for figures" and, purportedly, "attendance at a business college." For one as "competent . . . tidy," "polite and obliging" as Wright, public service and politics seemed tailor made, and in 1897 he was appointed deputy county clerk. Maintaining that post under Democratic and Republican administrations, from 1897 to 1901, suggests considerable political acumen. Such skill is underscored by his Populist and independent leanings in Republican Kansas.[30] Apparently Wright had no difficulty reconciling political activism and holding national office in the NNBL in 1914. He and his wife were members of St. Simon's as well as many social and service organizations.[31]

Spencer and Lucinda Hawkins, with six children in tow, came to Topeka in 1880, Exodusters from Tennessee. Hawkins settled in an integrated neighborhood in the Third Ward, where he plied his trade as a carpenter, supplementing that with income as a trash collector. By 1892, just before Mrs. Hawkins' death, there were eleven children in the family. Necessity created initiative and in 1895 Hawkins parlayed part-time trash collection into more stable and lucrative municipal jobs as a garbage collector and street cleaner as well as watchman for the city dump. Between 1895 and 1900, Hawkins held both jobs and worked as a carpenter, leaving little time for ascertainable social activity other than membership in the NNBL and in St. John A.M.E.[32]

Hawkins, however, looked with pride upon the success of his eleven children, all of whom were high school graduates. His five daughters received normal school or college training and taught elementary school in Topeka and in Oklahoma. One son was "Director of the Western Porters Association" in Edmonton, Alberta.[33]

29. *Plaindealer*, February 21, 1943.
30. *Ibid.*, September 22, 1913; *Colored Citizen*, February 28, 1897.
31. *Plaindealer*, June 19, 1914.
32. *Kansas State Ledger*, April 19, 1895; Kansas 1895 MS census; *Plaindealer*, August 15, 1913.
33. *Plaindealer*, January 16, 1914.

Wesley Jamison, affectionately known as the Squire, came to Topeka in 1885 from Tennessee. He began but did not complete legal training at Central College in Nashville. Quickly finding his bearings in the Midwest, Jamison got a job teaching at a school in Shawnee County. With money saved from sundry odd jobs, he finished his education and, after showing "a natural aptitude for politics," served three terms as a Topeka justice of the peace between 1894 and 1897. Subsequently out of politics, the Squire was a criminal lawyer of whom it was said: "Jamison can fix things if anybody can." Of impeccable reputation, he also was a charter member of the NNBL and held a number of local offices in that organization.[34]

Robert Buckner was born in Canada and came to Topeka as a youth between 1875 and 1880. His family was one of a small contingent who returned to the United States after the Civil War and emigrated to Kansas during the Exodus. As the *Plaindealer* (April 13) described him in 1900, Buckner was "a poor unlettered colored boy who has developed by his own efforts into one of the most prominent and successful Afro-American mechanics and contractors in this city." Buckner made his mark in 1895, when he and his nephews, partners in the carpentry business, secured a contract with the Santa Fe to build housing for railroad crews in Illinois. He also profited from home improvements, popular with affluent Topeka Negroes in the 1890s. By 1912, Buckner was acclaimed "one of the wealthiest blacks in the state." In addition to the NNBL, Buckner was a member of St. John A.M.E. Both Mr. and Mrs. Buckner were active socially, she "a leader of society" in the late 1890s.[35]

These NNBL members exemplified self-help and initiative as organizing principles of life and, by implication, as emblems of race progress. The NNBL and the economic accommodation it embodied provided an outlet for commercial interests otherwise stunted by Jim Crow. The men's various interests in education and radical politics, however, suggest they were drawn to a more liberal, integrationist course. The ultimate goal of race progress was a matter somewhat apart from the

---

34. *Kansas State Ledger*, January 19, 1894; *Colored Citizen*, July 29, 1897; *Plaindealer*, May 18, 1900.

35. *Kansas State Ledger*, August 30, 1895; *Plaindealer*, December 27, 1912; *Colored Citizen*, April 7, Jue 9, 1898.

pragmatic adjustments to Jim Crow in the marketplace. Granted, economic discrimination required that Negroes husband their resources and look to their own commercial development. By no means, however, was that accommodation regarded as a *sine qua non* of race progress. Thus, Oliver A. Taylor, a physician and a charter member of the NNBL, as well as other NNBL activists, joined fellow Topeka Negroes in 1914 who called for "civil and political" equality and for the full restitution of their "natural and constitutional rights."[36] As part of a black community familiar with the intellectual dilemmas associated with race progress, they listened to the alternatives proposed by new leaders of the vanguard that founded the Topeka NAACP.

Black Topekans long had organized to exchange ideas about the present and future course of race progress. To Julia D. Roundtree, an elementary school teacher, and to the Reverend C. G. Fishback, pastor of Shiloh Baptist Church, along with Negro representatives from other Kansas cities, the crisis in race relations in 1914 required "uniting the blacks into a body to fight Jim Crow laws, and . . . building up the race individually and collectively."[37]

W. E. B. Du Bois repeated that anthem in his speech "The World Problem and the Color Line" in Kansas City, Missouri, in May, 1913, one year before the black Topeka protest meeting. The number and identity of black Topekans in Du Bois' "large and appreciative audience" is not known. Without doubt, however, Roundtree and Fishback applauded Du Bois' assertion that ending racial discrimination and promoting black civil and political liberty were critical problems, the resolution of which demanded immediate attention.[38]

Appropriate to its lineage, the NAACP arrived in Topeka in 1914, heralded by reference to the antislavery pantheon. The names of William Lloyd Garrison and Oswald Garrison Villard, prominently mentioned in a newspaper article entitled "An Appeal for Justice to the Colored People," were sure to garner support for the fledgling protest organization. The "Appeal" invited the public to consider "the seriously humane question" of the systematic encroachments on Negro civil and constitutional rights and the denial of equal opportunity. The magni-

36. *An Appeal for Justice to the Colored People* (Topeka, 1914).
37. *Plaindealer*, March 14, 1913.
38. *Ibid.*, April 7, 1913.

tude of the problem required nothing less than "the vigilant action of the patriotic Christian people" of Topeka.[39]

The momentum for radical protest against racial discrimination gathered strength locally in 1915. In January, William Monroe Trotter, "the colored editor from Boston . . . who was ordered from the White House by the president several months ago" for an alleged discourtesy, spoke to an integrated audience of fifteen hundred at Second Baptist Church. Trotter's invective against segregation and Woodrow Wilson as well as his prediction of a Republican victory in 1916, however, had to share the agenda with more immediate local concerns. The full crew bill and a prohibition of intermarriage were pending in the Kansas legislature. Those measures were contested and defeated in the ensuing months.

Soon after the Topeka NAACP took root, another agency for radical protest developed. The Young Men's Educational Organization of Kansas, founded in 1915, concentrated on segregated education, a major front in the NAACP's assault on discrimination. That most members of the organization also joined the NAACP suggests mutual interest if not affiliate status. The focus of the Educational Organization, interestingly enough, was to prevent the legislature's appropriations to the Kansas Industrial and Educational Institute and to Western University at Quindaro: "Every thinking and intelligent colored citizen of this state" should be aware that support of and attendance at those two schools "means ultimately an attempt to impose Jim Crow and to segregate the colored people of this state."[40] Whatever the legitimacy of that complaint as a measure of white attitudes, the continuing endorsement of the institute by black Topekans more accurately reflected their acceptance of the facility as an agency for community services rather than as a bastion of segregated education. Perhaps because its single-issue campaign offered no meaningful solutions, the Educational Organization faded from public notice.

Through 1916 the NAACP held regular monthly meetings at the segregated white YMCA, another instance of the peculiar inversions of enlightenment and discrimination in Topeka race relations. The infre-

---

39. *Daily Capital*, December 27, 1914, in *NC*, VI; on the continuity of theme in the antislavery crusade and the founding of the NAACP, see McPherson, *The Abolitionist Legacy*, 368–93.

40. *Daily Capital*, February 2, 1915, in *NC*, VI.

quent reports of NAACP activity in the black and in the white press between 1915 and 1917 indicate neither an expanding membership nor major inroads against discrimination.[41]

Arthur Capper, editor of the Topeka *Daily Capital* and governor of the state from 1916 to 1920, was president of the NAACP through 1917. His prior credentials as an advocate of race liberalism are unknown. The *Plaindealer*, however, had misgivings about the depth and quality of Capper's allegiance to the cause of Negro equality in 1914. Allegedly, "old Jim Crow flapped his wings with glee every time a black face appeared at the famous Capper Cafe," which was adjacent to the *Daily Capital* printing plant and owned by the governor. That the *Daily Capital* "rejoiced in using the term 'Darky'" in reporting the news of the black community was an additional indignity. In view of that evidence, the *Plaindealer* concluded: "Either Mr. Capper is mistaken in the aim and object of the NAACP or he is the wrong man in a righteous cause." It is worthy of note that the *Daily Capital* gave favorable or unbiased accounts of NAACP activity. The relative weight of Capper's influence and enlightenment in racial matters is difficult to determine. Be that as it may, in 1914 the NAACP had seventeen Negro members, one of whom, Julia D. Roundtree, was secretary of the organization and a member of the board of directors.[42] A résumé of the associational behavior and the demographic characteristics of a selection of NAACP members is an informative if not definitive indicator of social patterns in black Topeka protest thought and action after the turn of the century.

Solomon G. Watkins, Topeka's second Negro teacher, arrived in 1871 from Tennessee. Protest against segregated schools in 1880 and affiliation with the Anti-Taft League in 1906 were part of his long career as a civil rights activist prior to joining the NAACP. Membership in the Colored Republicans' Club and in St. John A.M.E. secured Watkins' reputation for community service.

Julia D. Roundtree was a teacher at Douglass Elementary School as well as a member of Alpha Assisi Charity Club and St. John A.M.E. Often speaking for integration and civil rights in the 1890s, Roundtree readily subscribed to the philosophy of the NAACP. She was a charter

41. *Plaindealer*, December 8, 1916.
42. *Ibid.*, June 13, 1913, June 5, 1914; *Daily Capital*, December 27, 1914, in *NC*, VI.

member of that organization, served as its first secretary, and sat on the executive committee.

Nathaniel Sawyer, a teacher, was an Exoduster from Tennessee. He found an outlet for his intellectual interests in the Interstate Literary Association. Sawyer frequently contributed articles to the black press, expressing his views on the state of the race or describing in romantic detail his sojourns in the Colorado mountains.

James Guy, a prominent attorney, came from Ohio and established residence in Topeka in 1885. A charter member of St. Simon's, Guy was active in many social, protest, and political organizations. In addition, Guy served as deputy county attorney in 1896.

William McKnight came to Topeka in 1895 from Tennessee. Perhaps because of his late arrival, he appeared infrequently in chronicles of black public life. As a custodian at the Kansas State House, however, McKnight enjoyed an occupational status recognized locally as above that of a journeyman laborer. Benjamin Perkins, a laborer from Kentucky, and George Hagan, a stonemason from Missouri, were literate and claimed residence in the city since 1885. Other than membership in the NAACP and in the Populist party, indicators of their associational activity are scant. Oliver A. Taylor, a physician, was one among several NAACP members for whom no demographic information or extensive record of associational behavior is available.[43]

Whatever their influence on the black community in matters of race protest, the Negro members of the Topeka NAACP cannot be defined as a distinct social and economic cohort. Of decisive significance, they displayed no fine consistency in their orientation to organized protest. Roundtree, Sawyer, Guy, Taylor, McKnight, and Hagan were among the many who were active in both the NAACP and the NNBL. Those affiliations confirm that the common goal of race progress was of greater importance than adherence to a single ideology.

The social profile reveals that tenure in the city and educational attainment did not govern membership or election to office in either the

43. Information on the eight NAACP members was compiled from U.S. 1880 census; Kansas 1875, 1885, 1895 MS census; *Kansas State Ledger*, 1885–1905; *Colored Citizen*, 1878–1903; *Plaindealer*, 1900–1917; *Daily Capital* and *State Journal*, 1906–1915, in *NC*, IV, V, VI; *Eighth Annual Session of the NNBL*. In general, protest behavior in Topeka did not conform to the pattern identified by Meier, *Negro Thought in America*, 169, and by Meier and Rudwick, *From Plantation to Ghetto*, 212.

NAACP or the NNBL. Nor were occupation and associational behavior, as indicators of economic and social status, reliable determinants of affiliation with organized protest. Although NNBL members helped set the quickening pace of commercial development in black Topeka, they did not constitute a newly emergent elite; they had been there all along.[44] The NAACP, with equal seniority, shared but did not dominate the ranks of decision makers. Most individuals who attained that status were members of either or, commonly, both of the organizations.

Indeed, the NAACP and the NNBL represented the black social and economic order in its broadest aspect, and members held similar views on the immediate and long-term goal of Negro advancement. That mutuality at once affirmed the validity of traditional mechanisms for achieving race progress and encouraged NAACP and NNBL members to support with equal verve contrasting ideologies. Of course, contentious partisans proclaimed the singular benefits of their own protest alternative: Robert Buckner's single-minded advocacy of education for the trades rather than for the professions and the Young Men's Educational Organization's rejection of industrial training are examples.[45] Nevertheless, reasoned pragmatism rather than doctrinal purity determined the thrust of black Topeka's assault on discrimination. As an ideological and an institutional force, organized protest reflected a desire to strengthen "inner cultural and geographical bonds, both for intrinsic progress and for offensive power against caste" as well as ardent support for integration "wherever and however possible into the surrounding American culture."[46]

The biracial membership of the NAACP and the collateral, if separate, interests of the NNBL and the white Commercial Club did not necessarily indicate rejection of all-black protest organization as a viable alternative. The more pervasive political and economic influence of whites was the definitive factor. Topeka Negroes had considerable ex-

44. August Meier and David Lewis, "History of the Negro Upper Class in Atlanta, Georgia, 1890–1958," *Journal of Negro Education*, XXVIII (1959), 135–38. In Topeka and in Atlanta, black entrepreneurship developed in response to economic discrimination. In Topeka, however, black businessmen did not emerge as a new elite whose social, economic, and ideological profile differed materially from that of other leaders. The ages of the communities do not account for that disparity. Moreover, Meier and Lewis do not precisely define elite or class in either sociological or economic terms.
45. *Daily Capital*, February 2, 1915, in *NC*, VI; *Plaindealer*, April 13, 1900.
46. Du Bois, *The Souls of Black Folk*, 41–46.

perience with all-black protest organization, in evidence as early as 1870 in the campaigns against segregated schools. The planned migrations of blacks to Kansas, between 1875 and 1880, organized and directed exclusively by Negroes, offer additional, compelling testimony to the fact that the black community at the turn of the century was not "short on organizational experience."[47] The intramural squabbles of black Topekans over the means of achieving race progress, moreover, were not different in kind from the abrasive dialogue and countervailing opinions common among white reformers, politicians, and businessmen regarding progressivism versus the unrestrained growth of capitalism. Those divisive and constructive crosscurrents were symptomatic of the period; they were not peculiar to Negro leadership or to all-black protest.

Enumerating the oppressor's wrongs was not the sole preoccupation of the Topeka NAACP and NNBL. Like most informed Americans, those black Topekans bore the imprint of political, social, and economic ideas in force in the 1900s. Political activity, organized protest, and social service agencies reflected the trend toward organization that was then typical in reform and in business endeavors. More decisively, organization enhanced communication between successively larger units of community throughout the state and nation. Some historians suggest that the Progressives tried to preserve a "scheme of individualistic values," that their movement was "the complaint of the unorganized against the consequence of organization." Quite probably, however, the unorganized required some level of organization to air their complaints.[48]

Members of protest organizations and politicians in black Topeka had a common social lineage. They also addressed similar concerns: race progress and civil liberty. Politics, however, provided a touchstone for influence in the decision making process and, potentially, a more equitable distribution of power. Political consciousness in black Topeka was made acute by a high literacy rate, an informed press, and a zest for political action. Thus, they relied on the ballot, elective office, and patronage to hold Jim Crow at bay.

Political activism in black Topeka had long tenure and exhibited consid-

47. Weiss, "From Black Separatism to Interracial Cooperation," 65.
48. Hays, *The Response to Industrialism*, 48; Robert H. Wiebe, *The Search for Order, 1877–1920* (New York, 1967), 173–75; Hofstadter, *The Age of Reform*, 216–17.

erable vitality at the turn of the century. Political organizations at the local and state levels, enhanced by a national network of black protest and political groups, further augmented their experience in public affairs. Most informed sources confirm the significance of politics as an agency for race progress.[49] Impressionistic evidence suggests, moreover, that black Topekans were less victimized by Republican partisanship and more successful in achieving elective office. Through groups and other political agencies, Topeka Negroes tried to define their place as a race and as citizens in the cat's cradle of domestic and international issues which delineated American development between the late 1890s and 1912.

In the opinion of the Topeka *Colored Citizen* in 1900, a full-blown political revolution was taking place: "The colored man now believes he is working from the standpoint of principle when he supports those issues, the success of which will result in the greater benefit of his race." To an equal degree, Negroes "no longer believe their interests and welfare differ from the white man's but think all political and economic conditions beneficial to one are beneficial to the other."[50] This, of course, was illusory, and therein lay a perennial dilemma: Topeka blacks could establish no firm party alliances in the welter of political alternatives bearing the stain of racism. Progressivism, for example, was a contrasting but parallel theme in the Republican and Democratic parties. Lacking precise definition, however, it masked manifold contradictions. Progressivism was in the vanguard of political and urban reform, although some Progressives endorsed racism as a dictum of science and of social order.[51]

Republicanism received mixed reviews from blacks in Topeka and

49. Katzman, *Before the Ghetto*, 195–97, 205–206, 83; Kusmer, *A Ghetto Takes Shape*, 143–49, 153–54; Spear, *Black Chicago*, 125–26, 192; Drake and Cayton, *Black Metropolis*, I, 342–46; Osofsky, *Harlem*, 168–78.
50. *Colored Citizen*, August 31, 1900.
51. Peter G. Filene, "An Obituary for the Progressive Movement," in Barton J. Bernstein and Allen Matusow (eds.), *Twentieth-Century America: Recent Interpretations* (New York, 1972), 44, cogently argues that progressivism had neither a clear-cut program nor a definite set of values and therefore resists precise definition as a coherent political or social movement; Arthur S. Link and William B. Catton, *American Epoch: A History of the United States Since the 1890s* (New York, 1967), 68, confirm the substance if not the sweep of Filene's generalization; Woodward, *The Strange Career of Jim Crow*, identifies the undertone of racism in the Progressive movement.

throughout the nation. Despite the legacy of Lincoln and the neoabolitionist crusade, Negroes perceived themselves to be little more than pawns in that party. The lily-white Republicans in the South did not help restrain increasing race violence, and that also provided grounds for censure. Although the Republican party retained Negroes' allegiance in the 1900s, the moorings loosened considerably as they entertained Progressive alternatives in both major parties.

Antebellum tradition and political behavior during Reconstruction gave the Democratic party an enduring reputation for resistance to the cause of Negro liberty. Although Topeka blacks enjoyed some success under Democratic state administrations, they were not often successful in threatening to vote for Democrats in order to wring concessions from the Republicans, whose hegemony defined Kansas' political tradition.[52] Nonetheless, Negroes continued to press their claim for civil rights. Issues and events at the municipal level signaled the political maturation of the black Topeka community.

Political clubs were particularly active during state and national elections. McKinley Clubs vied with Bryan and Colored Free Silver clubs in 1897 and in 1900, proclaiming the merits of their respective candidates in the black Topeka press. That pattern was repeated in succeeding elections. The debate, in which race interests were central, also focused on national issues and their implication for local and state affairs.[53] Political organization and race protest alignment were combined effectively in the Afro-American League, organized in Topeka in 1898. The Washingtonian refrain was unmistakable in their pamphlet, *To the Colored Voters of Kansas*. The political fortunes as well as the "moral and financial conditions of the race" would be best assured with "our business and professional" men in the vanguard. The league, ardently Republican, was justified in supporting Governor Hodges' reelection in 1912, his first term having been notable for enlightenment in racial matters. As events would prove, however, the league's distrust of William Howard Taft and dislike of Theodore Roosevelt presented a problem in 1912. Political clubs also served an educational function. The stated purpose of the

---

52. See August Meier, "The Negro and the Democratic Party, 1875–1915," *Phylon*, XVII (1956), 173–91.

53. *Colored Citizen*, June 22, 29, 1900; *Kansas State Ledger*, February 22, 1902.

First Voters' Club, organized in Topeka in 1913, was to "investigate all candidates prior to endorsement" and to "assume responsibility for researching their credentials."[54]

The Colored Republicans' Club, founded in 1875, was a venerable institution which organized political activity, provided an entrée to political caucuses at local and county levels, and served as a watchdog for race interests in the party. In order to secure better black representation at a statewide Republican convention in 1900, the Colored Republicans' Club of Topeka met to "consider means of garnering greater responsibility and recognition." Most commonly, however, Topeka blacks attended Republican conventions as a matter of course. By these means, as David Katzman observed in Detroit, blacks became involved in the political process "without first having to submit themselves to the party electorate."[55] In the public arena, racism and the vagaries of the ballot often stunted black political aspirations. By 1908, moreover, Kansas adopted the primary system, which imposed additional limits but did not completely short-circuit black participation in the political process.[56]

In the 1890s, black Democrats, Populists, and Progressives established similar organizations to gain supporters for their partisan persuasions. A well-organized minority, those political parties had a common interest against Republicans and, in concert, made successful appeals to the black electorate. The liberal race policy of the Populist-Democratic governor John W. Leedy, for example, was a spur to black Democratic activity in Topeka. Under Leedy's aegis, from 1897 to 1899, Topeka Negroes also received patronage and ran successfully for elective office. Thus, the threat that blacks would bolt the Republican ranks was real and ever present. Though not consistently effective, it was a reasoned, pragmatic exercise in pressure group politics.

Numbered among black Progressives were erstwhile Republicans, independents, and Democrats. In conformity with established patterns of political behavior, they organized the Progressive League in 1910. The

---

54. *To the Colored Voters of Kansas* (Topeka, 1898); *The Afro-American State League* (Topeka, 1912); *Plaindealer*, March 14, 1913.

55. *Plaindealer*, April 27, 1900; Katzman, *Before the Ghetto*, 180–81.

56. *State Journal*, December 28, 1907, in *Republican Party Clippings*, VI; *Kansas Session Laws, 1908* (Topeka, 1908), Chapter LIV. Notably, the Republican state committee voted twenty-one to thirteen to continue to hold nominating conventions.

members of the league made pronouncements regarding the elimination of corruption in government and decried the venality of politics as a whole, all of which was presented under the rubric of nonpartisan reform. The league membership included Solomon Watkins, long a political independent, and James Guy, theretofore a staunch Republican.[57] Of decisive importance, William Eagleson, a political iconoclast of the first order and editor of the *Colored Citizen*, was a leader of black Topeka independents before his death in 1901. Under his control and until it ceased publication in 1905, the *Colored Citizen* reflected an independent or nonpartisan course in politics. Between 1890 and 1905 the *Colored Citizen*'s varied crusades for reform incisively articulated Progressive interests, with some overtones of muckraking journalism.[58]

Black Topeka also had publicists whose opinions were blatantly partisan, however well informed. A pamphlet entitled *Thoughts for Careful Consideration*, written and published independently by black Topekan John M. Dorsey in 1906, was an example. Voicing his opposition to black allegiance to Republicanism, Dorsey asserted: "Get out of the old rut and travel in a path of enlightenment and let common judgement rule. Do not forever remain the servile tool of a gang of office seekers under a banner with the name, but without the principle of Republicanism. Be men, not dogs!"[59]

The ward was the geographical and political level at which blacks gained entrance to municipal politics and access to patronage. Topeka Negroes secured positions as ward councilmen, among other appointments, with regular success from the 1880s through 1912. Topeka blacks also were well represented in county government in such influential positions as county attorney. Notably, there was no marked increase in the actual numbers of blacks in municipal or county government between 1900 and 1912. Rather, Negroes succeeded or competed with other Negroes for available positions, which were not, however, specifically earmarked for blacks. Significantly, there had been no confrontations between Negroes and whites over employment on municipal

57. *Daily Capital*, April 11, 1910, in *NC*, VI; Zornow, *Kansas*, 203–204, notes that John Leedy was "a member of all three parties at one time or another."
58. See "Government Ownership of Railroads," *Colored Citizen*, September 22, 1898. It is an editorial and not a reprint from another news source.
59. John M. Dorsey, *Thoughts for Careful Consideration* (Topeka, 1906).

construction projects since the 1880s.[60] Although the largest concentration of Negroes was in the Second and Third wards after 1900, there were black enclaves throughout the city. Some Negro ward councilmen, moreover, served biracial constituencies. If the Second and Third wards enjoyed a proportionately larger share of patronage positions, black populations in each of the wards were represented at some level of municipal government.

There was no counterpart of the ward boss in black Topeka. Nonetheless, personal ambition and the intraracial competition for office bred some rancor. Nick Chiles, resident of the Third Ward, editor of the *Plaindealer*, and a party to sundry legal and illegal business ventures, also exercised considerable influence in city and state Republican councils. Throughout the 1900s, Chiles had a reputation as a ward heeler, as one through whom elections could be bought and who meted out patronage, primarily to the Third Ward. Such accusations, reflecting the sound and fury of competing black newspapers and politicos, were undocumented.[61] For all Chiles's derring-do, moreover, the *Plaindealer* was a responsible if venturesome conservative organ in political matters and dependably Republican. The newspaper also could be counted on in the campaign for racial and social progress. Chicanery and corruption were not the norm for black Topeka politicians, who were sensitive to the particular interests of their black constituency. Negro officials who represented the community at large also earned reputations as competent public servants.

Topeka Negroes were elected or appointed to a wide range of positions in municipal government and civil service, regardless of shifts in partisan control of local and state government. Whatever the differentials in training, prestige, and remuneration, Negroes at all socioeconomic levels enjoyed a piece of the "partisan pie," to borrow a term from the black press. John Wright was an accountant who served as city treasurer and county clerk at various times between 1900 and 1916. Wesley Jamison was a lawyer and nearly a permanent fixture as a justice of the peace during the 1890s and early 1900s. Socially prominent and economically well off, both men exercised political influence beyond that

60. *Kansas State Ledger*, April 8, 1899, October 19, 1900; *Plaindealer*, November 22, 1912, January 18, 1916.
61. *Colored Citizen*, October 18, 1900.

defined by their municipal offices. However, Wright and Jamison represented only one dimension of black political involvement. William B. Townsend, municipal coal inspector, William Sharp, messenger at the mayor's office, and James Boyd, overseer of the rock pile at the Topeka jail, were among the many Negroes who held appointive positions in civil service.[62] Although Townsend, Sharp, and Boyd were remote from the decision making process and their names were not included on black Topeka's social register, they did not obtain their municipal appointments through the agency of Negroes at higher levels of civil service. Having made a separate peace with the power structure, a middle-grade civil servant could claim to be his own man. By no terms was control over political patronage the exclusive bailiwick of the black elite. One may generalize, moreover, that Negroes in service positions gained more than passing familiarity with the doings of influential white officials, and this increased their prestige in the black community. There was, for example, a moment of silence in the legislature, official mourning for black service employees of long tenure. Of greater importance, contacts between white public officials and civil servants in menial occupations well may have provided a conduit for the dissemination of information about public affairs to the working class. Characteristically, moreover, black political involvement in official as well as in service occupations allowed some interracial dialogue, thereby giving a measure of permeability to the barrier of caste.

Kansas blacks did not attain elective or appointive office in state government to a notable degree between 1896 and 1912. The election of the Republican Edwin P. McCabe of Nicodemus, as state auditor in 1882, represented the high point of black politics at the state level. Nonetheless, in the interim, black Topekans enjoyed auxiliary benefits of residing in the capital city. They held most of the service jobs at the State House. Negro Topekans also had more than proportionate representation in the state power structure than did blacks in other Kansas cities.

Black Topekans were concerned about the larger domain of national politics. As was the case at the local level, race concerns provided the definitive frame of reference for political consciousness and action. Wil-

62. *Kansas State Ledger*, March 21, 1903, November 27, 1900, January 22, 1901; *Plaindealer*, December 20, 1912, March 31, 1916.

liam McKinley's election as president in 1896 received the endorsement of blacks in Topeka. Even for the Negro Democrats and independents, who doggedly supported William Jennings Bryan and reform, the election came as no surprise. Without doubt, many Negroes who were engaged in new commercial ventures opted for McKinley, gold, and stability.[63] For the black community as a whole, however, there was little to celebrate. Neither the race problem nor the region had McKinley's full attention. During his administration, the Spanish-American War, and the domestic and international problems it exposed, served to underscore black Topekans' interest in national political affairs.

For Topeka Negroes and for most other Americans, economic interests and cultural chauvinism did not prevent their joining a democratic crusade to rescue Cuba from the clutches of Spanish autocracy. Although Negro aspirations for equal treatment and pay were not realized during the course of the war, the nation's sense of mission and international adventure seemed consonant with the interests of the race. As the *Kansas State Ledger* (April 16, 1898) pointedly asserted: "We are for saving the Cubans because they are black." In the opinion of the *Colored Citizen*, race advancement and the nation's economic interests were reconcilable: "At the prospect of building the Nicaraguan Canal, several young Negro Topekans ... fully aware of the business openings which the close of the war will create ... have begun studying Spanish. Certainly the absence of color prejudice in Central and in South America [also] recommends these areas." In view of Negroes' having contributed to the freedom of Cuba, the *Colored Citizen* queried: "Will the Cuban government offer an inducement to settle to the American blacks?"[64] Reflecting interest in the race and a desire to be among the first in the nation's service, Topeka Negroes enthusiastically responded to the call for two battalions of black troops, which comprised the 23rd Kansas Colored Volunteers. Had it ever been otherwise? One should not "lose

---

63. Meier, *Negro Thought in America*, 168, asserts that opponents of Booker T. Washington and accommodationism "tend to lean toward economic radicalism—toward Bryanism, trade unionism and socialism." Glad, *McKinley, Bryan, and the People*, 199, 205, indicates that, particularly in the East, farmers and urban workers rejected Bryan's Populist overtures despite the Democratic appeal to their class interests. Voting patterns in the Midwest also were revealing. In Kansas, for example, Bryan carried the state as a whole but not the cities.

64. *Colored Citizen*, April 21, May 26, September 15, 1898.

sight of the history of the United States," William Eagleson asserted, and in time of war, "the colored race always showed its devotion to the stars and stripes."[65]

As the 23rd Kansas Colored paraded through Topeka in full regalia on their way to training camp, "thousands flocked to the depot to do them honor, and there was great danger at one time of the men being disrobed on the spot, owing to the importunities of the women for buttons." Representing "the best element of their race," young Negro women in Topeka formed a corps of cadets who "drill nightly . . . and will perform shortly in their uniforms." All were not so enthusiastic. Black Topeka males who remained at home, jealous of the attention received by soldiers, picked fights with men in uniform on leave. In the main, however, Topeka Negroes gave their unqualified support and organized the Friends of the 23rd Kansas Volunteers as well as the Ladies Relief Committee to furnish hospital bedding and other material for troops at the training camp and in the field.[66]

Discrimination, however, dogged the Negro soldier at every turn. Jim Crow accommodations on troop trains and in southern towns along the route to the front were particularly onerous because "a citizen good enough to wear the uniform of the American army is good enough to ride in any car with anybody: there should be no color line in patriotism." The refusal of state and federal authorities to recruit and train black officers, as well as the government's unfulfilled commitment to grant one year's pay after enlistment, added to black Topeka's discontent.[67] The Sulu treaty, acceded to by President McKinley, was additional evidence of racism. By its terms, a slave in the Sulu Archipelago, one of Spain's former imperial possessions, could obtain freedom only by paying his master full market value. Symbolically, the treaty dashed whatever hopes Negroes had for racial justice in the postwar international order.[68]

For many Topeka Negroes, the crowning insult was Colonel Theo-

---

65. *Kansas State Ledger*, June 18, 1898; *Colored Citizen*, May 5, 1898. For a partial listing of Topeka Negroes who fought in the Spanish-American War, see J. L. King (ed.), *History of Shawnee County*, 98–100.
66. *Colored Citizen*, April 28, October 28, August 18, September 8, November 4, 1898.
67. *Ibid.*, May 5, 26, June 2, 1898.
68. *Colored Citizen*, August 3, September 21, 1900.

dore Roosevelt's denigrating remark about the fighting capacity of black troops under his command at San Juan Hill and his refusal to accord them due honor. This left a residue of bitterness that did not dissipate in the ensuing years. As Roosevelt's war record and rising political fortunes propelled him into the vice-presidency in 1900, the *Colored Citizen* (November 2) promised to make him pay at the polls: "A vote for McKinley is, of course, a vote for Roosevelt. Is there a self-respecting Negro anywhere who wants to see that cowardly blowhard in the vice-presidential chair?" Prophetically, that newspaper threatened to redouble its opposition "if by any mischance Mr. Roosevelt should ever slip into the president's chair." McKinley's assassination in 1901 and Roosevelt's becoming president, however, neither advanced nor retarded race oppression.

South Carolina Senator "Pitchfork Ben" Tillman, among other rabid southern segregationist Democrats, set the high mark for virulent racism. This tainted the party beyond redemption, despite the efforts of Bryan, the Democratic presidential nominee, to recall the halcyon days of populism and fusion. Tillman, of course, had solid Populist credentials, which suggests that both populism and progressivism reflected extremes on the race question. The result was that Negroes had no viable alternative to Republicanism in the national election of 1900.[69]

The case against Roosevelt, however, remained in force. The riot in Brownsville, Texas, in 1906, after which Negro troops were summarily given dishonorable discharges by President Roosevelt for alleged complicity, represented one more perversion of justice. Roosevelt's ballyhooed dinner at the White House with Booker T. Washington in 1901 and patronage appointments for blacks in federal civil service, such as that of Kansas' own William Tecumseh Vernon, were not fit recompense. Thus racism at home and abroad, in war and in peace, defined black Topeka's experience with national politics in the 1900s. Negroes' fortunes did not improve markedly during the decade, and the presidential election of 1912 offered few prospects for racial justice.

In 1912 the Republican party, headed by President William Howard Taft, made no pretense of supporting Negro rights. During his administration, the lily-white Republicans cemented their control over the

69. *Kansas State Ledger*, September 15, 1900; *Colored Citizen*, July 13, August 24, September 14, 15, 1900.

party in the South. Taft further reduced black political opportunity by supporting ballot restriction and disfranchisement. The erosion of federal patronage for Negroes also confirmed the increasingly conservative turn in the GOP since 1908 regarding the race question.[70] When the apostate Roosevelt defected from the Republican ranks to form the Progressive party in 1912, many black Topeka Republicans, still bitter about San Juan Hill and Brownsville, bid him good riddance.[71]

The nomination of Woodrow Wilson as the Democratic standard-bearer in 1912 did not foreordain racial enlightenment in that party. Wilson's Progressive program, geared primarily to the interests of the middle class, paid little attention to the particular needs of poor whites and Negroes. He considered their vote insignificant. In the opinion of Arthur S. Link, Wilson's biographer, "the Negro question was one of those ticklish problems, like the liquor question and women's suffrage, that Wilson would have preferred to ignore." Wilson chose to frame his appeal to blacks in the nebulous terms of "gradualism and fair dealing." Nonetheless, "according to Mr. Wilson's explicit pledge," a black Topeka journal asserted, his administration heralded "a New Freedom to all ... peoples, the colored people definitely included."[72] Many Topeka Negroes concurred and interpreted the New Freedom in literal terms. If Wilson's tepid pronouncements on race did not eliminate past or current animosity, they did provide a mild catharsis for many blacks, irrespective of party, who could not stomach either Roosevelt or Taft. Black Democrats in Topeka identified Wilson as "a learned, high class, Christian gentleman. The Negroes in Kansas and in the nation will make no mistake in voting for Governor Wilson." Wilson, therefore, received a larger plurality from the black electorate than had any previous Democratic presidential nominee.[73]

70. Meier, *Negro Thought in America*, 163–65; P. C. Thomas, *A Few Facts for Your Careful Consideration* (Topeka, 1908). P. C. Thomas, a Negro Topekan, was executive secretary of the Negro National Anti-Taft League.
71. George Mowry, *The Era of Theodore Roosevelt and the Birth of Modern America, 1900–1912* (New York, 1958), 295; Arthur S. Link, "The Negro as a Factor in the Campaign of 1912," *Journal of Negro History*, XXXII (1947), 84, 94, 96, 99; *The Afro-American State League*.
72. Link, "The Negro as a Factor in the Campaign of 1912," 93; Henry Blumenthal, "Woodrow Wilson and the Race Question," *Journal of Negro History*, XLVIII (1963), 1–8.
73. *Plaindealer*, November 1, 1912; Arthur S. Link, *Wilson: The New Freedom* (Princeton, 1956), 244.

Before Wilson's administration was a year old, however, it was apparent that his concept of gradualism was synonymous with racism. The entrenchment of segregation in federal facilities in Washington in 1913, with his acquiescence if not outright complicity, and the loss of federal patronage positions, such as registrar of the treasury and ambassador to Haiti, were compelling evidence of Democratic duplicity. As Wilson's behavior regarding blacks attested, one could espouse progressivism "without any over-riding concern for social justice" or for Negro rights. Likewise, the reelection of Wilson in 1916 did not forecast an enlightened race policy. His declaration of a fair deal and his promise to act in the interest of Negroes, therefore, fell on deaf ears. During the 1916 campaign, letters and editorials in the black press indicated wide support for Charles Evans Hughes, the Republican standard-bearer: both the man and the party seemed more attuned to Negroes' interests.[74]

Black Topekans did not hold the reins of power in politics at any level in 1916. In gaining elective and appointive office, nevertheless, they fared as well or better than most in other urban Negro communities. The interracial dialogue in politics, evident at all class levels, made black Topekans aware of and part of public affairs. Politics as well as organized protest provided efficient instruments for formulating and articulating the exigent demand of Negroes for full equality. Those agencies also were forums for a debate on the social, economic, and philosophical dimensions of race progress, thereby enriching an intellectual tradition nearly a century old.

Neither the government nor the law had secured civil liberty for Negroes by 1916. For decades they would be denied an equal share of the covenant. The social fabric and the institutional structure in black Topeka, however, were strong. Thus, the Negro community withstood the rude shocks of discrimination and transmitted to subsequent generations the many lessons learned in the struggle for equality.

---

74. Link, *Wilson*, 243; *Paul Jones Magazine* (April, 1916), 4–6; *Plaindealer*, June 16, 30, October 10, November 10, 1916.

Epilogue

The development and maturation of black Topeka, between 1865 and 1915, indicated the collateral influence of race oppression and the promise of American life. Decisively, racism dictated the terms for interracial relations and the access of Negroes to institutions in society at large. Yet the quest for full civil liberty did not abate, and the redemption of the deferred promise became a powerful social and intellectual force that helped mold black Topeka into a viable community.

The early emergence of organized protest and the evolution of doctrines of race progress provided a matrix for institutional development and enhanced cohesion in the community. Social and economic class as determinants of stratification and of intraracial relations, moreover, did not separate the black community into competing interest groups on matters related to race advancement. Although there was active debate over the means, unity was the watchword in most considerations of the ultimate goal. Of additional importance, the black Topeka press facilitated communication and a rich exchange of ideas within the community and apprised Negroes in the city of the condition of the race in other locales. Also through the press, Negro Topekans became aware of the compass of issues that dictated the pace and the condition of national life. In cumulative effect, the institutional, social, economic, and political development of black Topeka, as well as media for internal and external communication, gave the community effective means of exercising some control over its own destiny. By these terms, the black experience in Topeka was not a case study in urban pathology. Rather more compelling is the evidence that Negro Topekans in 1915 could depend on institutions and ideas, forged over the previous fifty years, to chart their course into an uncertain future.

Appendix
Tables and Maps

Table 1 Population of Topeka, 1860–1920

Year	Negro	White	Total
1860	0	759	759
1865	83	1,227	1,310
1870	473	5,317	5,790
1875	724	6,548	7,272
1880	3,648	11,880	15,528
1885	4,411	19,088	23,499
1890	5,024	25,983	31,007
1895	4,500	25,651	30,151
1900	4,807	28,801	33,608
1905	4,111	34,875	38,986
1910	4,538	39,146	43,684
1915	3,874	42,273	46,147
1920	4,272	45,750	50,022

SOURCES: 1860–1900, J. L. King (ed.), *History of Shawnee County*, 167; 1875, *Fourth Agricultural Report and Census*, 407; 1885, *Fifth Biennial Report of the Kansas Board of Agriculture*, 36; 1905, Kansas MS census; 1910, U.S. Department of Commerce, *Negro Population*, 694; 1915, *Quarterly Reports, Kansas State Board of Agriculture*, 56.
NOTE: White population includes other races.

Table 2 Origin of Topeka's Negro Population

	1865 (%)	1870 (%)	1875 (%)	1880 (%)	1885 (%)	1895 (%)
Northeast	2.5	0.7	0.8	0.4	0.0	0.4
Deep South	19.3	24.4	17.9	23.4	15.7	15.3
Border South	59.0	52.3	47.5	61.9	63.1	45.6
Great Plains	13.2	17.3	26.4	10.7	17.7	36.3
Old Northwest	1.2	4.0	5.0	1.7	1.4	1.9
West	0.0	0.0	0.0	0.0	0.1	0.1
Foreign	2.4	0.9	1.4	0.6	0.2	0.1
Not known	2.4	0.4	1.0	1.2	1.9	0.3
Total	100.0	100.0	100.0	99.9	100.1	100.0
Population size	83	451	724	3,628	1,077	1,084

SOURCES: Kansas 1865, 1875, 1885, 1895 MS census; U.S. 1870, 1880 census.
NOTES: Data for 1885 and 1895 populations are based on a stratified random sample of recorded dwelling units.
  Northeast = Conn., Maine, Mass., N.H., N.J., N.Y., Pa., R.I., Vt.
  Deep South = Ala., D.C., Del., Fla., Ga., La., Md., Miss., N.C., S.C., Tex., Va., W.Va.
  Border South = Ark., Ky., Mo., Okla., Tenn.
  Great Plains = Iowa, Kans., N.Dak., Nebr., S.Dak.
  Old Northwest = Ill., Ind., Mich., Minn., Ohio, Wis.
  West = Ariz., Calif., Colo., Idaho, Mont., N.Mex., Nev., Oreg., Utah, Wash.
  Foreign = Africa, Asia, Canada, Europe, Mexico, West Indies.
  Not known = not given, not legible.

Table 3 Dwellings of Topeka's Negro Population

	1865 (%)	1870 (%)	1875 (%)	1880 (%)	1885 (%)	1895 (%)
Single family	75.9	80.3	86.4	55.3	85.4	87.2
Multifamily	10.8	4.7	0.0	33.8	8.2	6.6
Boardinghouse(s)/ Hotel(s)	0.0	0.0	0.0	0.9	0.3	2.7
Public/private institutions	0.0	0.7	0.0	3.5	0.1	0.0
White	13.3	14.4	13.5	6.5	6.1	3.6
Total	100.0	100.1	99.9	100.0	100.1	100.1
Population size	83	451	724	3,628	1,077	1,084
Residents/dwelling (median)	6.5	5.5	5.1	8.4	6.1	5.3

SOURCES: Kansas 1865, 1875, 1885, 1895 MS census; U.S. 1870, 1880 census.
NOTES: Data for 1885 and 1895 are based on a stratified random sample of recorded dwelling units.
The public institution (1870) was the city jail.
Dwelling unit classifications presented for 1875 are speculative at best; specific identification of dwellings and households did not occur on a regular basis. Referral to classifications of previous and subsequent census periods aided in dwelling unit delineation for most of the 1875 population.
The public institution (1880) was the Barracks.

Table 4 Households of Topeka's Negro Population

	1865 (%)	1870 (%)	1875 (%)	1880 (%)	1885 (%)	1895 (%)
Primary	34.9	32.8	46.2	48.0	48.7	51.3
Subfamily	0.0	0.0	0.0	2.3	1.3	0.2
Male head	0.0	0.7	4.0	2.1	2.6	1.8
Female head	3.6	3.3	6.3	3.7	5.7	8.9
Male primary	0.0	0.7	0.3	0.6	0.2	1.1
Female primary	0.0	0.2	0.0	0.4	0.1	0.3
Extended/augmented	48.1	47.2	29.6	35.6	33.4	30.1
Not known	13.3	15.1	13.5	7.3	8.0	6.3
Total	99.9	100.0	99.9	100.0	100.0	100.0
Population size	83	451	724	3,628	1,077	1,084
Residents/household (median)	5.6	5.2	5.2	5.6	5.7	5.0

SOURCES: Kansas 1865, 1875, 1885, 1895 MS census; U.S. 1870, 1880 census.
NOTES: Data for 1875 are based on examination of earlier and later census records, since classification was irregular, and are therefore approximate.
Data for 1885 and 1895 are based on a stratified random sample of recorded household units.
Augmented households represented about one half of the extended household population in each census.
Not known = most individuals lived in white dwellings.

Table 5   Occupations of Adult Negro Males in Topeka

	1865 (%)	1870 (%)	1875 (%)	1880 (%)	1885 (%)	1895 (%)
Professional	0.0	0.7	0.6	4.9	5.9	6.1
Service entrepreneurial	5.5	5.1	8.4	5.4	4.4	5.0
Skilled	11.1	10.1	8.4	12.5	7.7	3.6
Semiskilled	0.0	5.8	1.7	4.0	4.1	2.2
Unskilled	38.9	67.4	62.9	67.0	62.0	69.7
Agricultural	5.5	1.4	6.2	4.9	3.0	2.2
Other	0.0	6.5	0.0	1.3	4.4	2.9
Not known	38.9	2.9	11.8	0.0	8.5	8.3
Total	99.9	99.9	100.0	100.0	100.0	100.0
Population size	18	138	178	224	271	277

SOURCES: Kansas 1865, 1875, 1885, 1895 MS census; U.S. 1870, 1880 census.
NOTES: Adult males are twenty-one and older.
Data for 1880, 1885, and 1895 are based on a stratified random sample from population records.
Unskilled (1865) includes a male whose age was not given, since he did not know the time or place of birth. This suggests that he was older than twenty-one. However, omitted from the adult population were the five in the sample (three in 1880; two in 1885) whose age was not shown.

Table 6   Occupations of Adult Negro Females in Topeka

	1865 (%)	1870 (%)	1875 (%)	1880 (%)	1885 (%)	1895 (%)
Professional	0.0	0.0	0.0	0.0	0.4	2.3
Service entrepreneurial	0.0	0.8	0.0	0.9	0.4	0.0
Skilled	0.0	0.0	0.0	0.0	0.0	0.0
Semiskilled	0.0	0.8	0.0	3.2	1.5	2.3
Unskilled	5.5	35.9	17.1	25.4	21.8	23.8
Agricultural	0.0	0.0	0.0	0.0	0.0	0.0
Other	55.5	53.0	58.6	69.1	64.5	67.0
Not known	38.9	9.4	24.3	1.4	11.4	4.6
Total	99.9	99.9	100.0	100.0	100.0	100.0
Population size	18	117	169	220	262	303

SOURCES: Kansas 1865, 1875, 1885, 1895 MS census; U.S. 1870, 1880 census.
NOTES: Adult females are twenty-one and older.
Data for 1880, 1885, and 1895 are based on a stratified random sample from population records.

Table 7   Literacy of Adult Negroes in Topeka

	1865 (%)	1870 (%)	1875 (%)	1880 (%)	1885 (%)	1895 (%)
Literate	25.0	39.6	60.8	48.2	63.6	80.7
Reads only	0.0	5.1	3.2	12.4	0.0	0.0
Writes only	0.0	0.0	0.0	0.4	0.4	0.5
Illiterate	75.0	48.2	35.7	39.0	34.9	18.6
Not known	0.0	7.1	0.3	0.0	1.1	0.2
Total	100.0	100.0	100.0	100.0	100.0	100.0
Population size	36	255	347	444	533	580

SOURCES: Kansas 1865, 1875, 1885, 1895 MS census; U.S. 1870, 1880 census.
NOTES: Adults are twenty-one and older.
   Data for 1880, 1885, and 1895 are based on a stratified random sample from the population records.
   Illiterate (1865) includes a male head of household whose age was not given. Although such omissions frequently indicated that the individual did not know the time or place of birth and thus suggested the person was over twenty-one, in this case the enumerator did state the man was illiterate and thus older than twenty-one.
   The five individuals (three in 1880; two in 1885) in the sample whose ages were not given were omitted from the adult population.

Table 8   School Attendance Among Negro Children in Topeka

	Male (%)	Female (%)	Total Attendance (%)	Total School-Age Population
1865	46.4	35.7	82.1	28
1870	14.4	20.4	34.8	132
1875	11.6	17.3	28.9	249
1880	25.7	22.1	47.8	303
1885	23.8	24.3	48.1	378
1895	30.9	34.3	65.2	359

SOURCES: Kansas 1865, 1875, 1885, 1895 MS census; U.S. 1870, 1880 census.
NOTES: School-age children are between six and twenty years old.
   Data for 1880, 1885, and 1895 are based on a stratified random sample from the population records.
   These data do not suggest that each child attended school for the entire year; in fact, only the U.S. 1880 census enumerated attendance, and that varied with the enumerator.

Table 9   Persistence of Topeka's Negro Population

	1870 (%)	1875 (%)	1880 (%)	1885 (%)	1895 (%)
Census periods					
One	56.6	56.7	90.2	83.6	81.2
Two	14.5	26.3	5.5	13.6	4.5
Three	22.9	14.6	3.8	1.4	6.0
Four	6.0	1.9	0.5	1.1	6.5
Five	0.0	0.4	0.0	0.1	0.6
Six	0.0	0.0	0.0	0.2	0.9
Total	100.0	99.9	100.0	100.0	99.7

SOURCES: Kansas 1865, 1875, 1885, 1895 MS census; U.S. 1860, 1870, 1880 census.
NOTES: Persistence values were determined by cross-checking names of black Topekans from 1865 through 1885 and 1895, recording the number of times each individual was found (the frequency), and summing the frequencies of each for the year enumerated.
  Some families who resided in townships adjoining Topeka were monitored. Frequently, those areas were annexed to the city, so some demographic profiles indicated long tenure in Topeka.
  The U.S. census of 1860 was applied to three persons through 1875, two through 1880, and one through 1885 and 1895.
  Persistence values are based on census records from 1860 through the particular year.
  Data for 1880, 1885, and 1895 are based on a stratified random sample from the population records.
  Three tenths of the 1895 sample population had resided in Topeka longer than six census periods.

Table 10   Negro Residence in Topeka's Wards

	1870 (%)	1880 (%)	1885 (%)	1890 (%)	1895 (%)	1905 (%)
First	64.1	21.4	28.7	24.5	28.0	18.1
Second	4.7	29.0	24.1	16.4	42.6	30.2
Third	31.3	32.2	26.2	23.9	11.3	20.3
Fourth	0.0	17.4	21.0	15.2	7.6	10.9
Fifth	0.0	0.0	0.0	20.0	10.5	17.9
Sixth	0.0	0.0	0.0	0.0	0.0	2.6
Total	100.1	100.0	100.0	100.0	100.0	100.0

SOURCES: Kansas 1865, 1875, 1885, 1895, 1905 MS census; U.S. 1870, 1880, 1890 census.
NOTES: Kansas 1865, 1875 MS census did not provide geopolitical information for Topeka residents.
  Geopolitical distribution 1885 and 1895 is based on a stratified random sample of the records.
  The relatively high concentration of Negroes in the Second Ward in 1895 is an anomaly; however, it might be explained by the return of Negroes from Oklahoma after the 1890 migration, thereby indicating the general state of flux in the black population. Most hotels and other businesses as well as the homes of influential whites were in this ward, and many Negroes lived on the premises.

Table 11 Topeka Population by Ward

	1880			1885			1890		
	Black (%)	White (%)	Total (%)	Black (%)	White (%)	Total (%)	Black (%)	White (%)	Total (%)
First	27.7	72.3	19.8	26.2	73.8	20.4	21.3	78.6	18.7
Second	22.3	77.7	33.5	12.4	87.6	36.8	9.8	90.2	27.2
Third	39.1	60.9	21.3	27.9	72.1	17.7	17.1	82.9	22.6
Fourth	17.7	82.2	25.3	15.6	84.4	25.1	11.7	88.3	21.1
Fifth	0.0	0.0	0.0	0.0	0.0	0.0	30.9	69.0	10.5
Total			99.9			100.0			100.1

SOURCES: U.S. 1880 census; Kansas 1885 MS census; U.S. 1890 census.
NOTES: These values represent the racial composition of the particular ward, not the total city population.

The total count of whites enumerated in the U.S. 1880 census is 9 percent lower than the value found in other sources.

The three Total columns show values based on the total population of the city of Topeka and give population distribution as a function of total ward size.

Table 12 Profile of Negro Elites in Topeka, 1880–1895

A. *Residence by Ward*

	1880 (%)	1885 (%)	1895 (%)
First	14.1	14.4	12.8
Second	41.0	30.4	38.3
Third	21.8	22.4	20.6
Fourth	23.1	32.8	11.3
Fifth	0.0	0.0	17.0
Total	100.0	100.0	100.0
Population size	78	125	141

Table 12 (cont.)

B. Neighborhoods' Racial Composition

Negro (%)	1880 (%)	1885 (%)	1895 (%)
100–76	9.0	17.6	11.3
75–51	28.2	24.0	19.1
50–26	19.2	14.4	9.9
25–13	17.9	29.6	21.3
12–0	25.6	14.4	38.3
Total	99.9	100.0	99.9

C. Dwellings

	1880 (%)	1885 (%)	1895 (%)
Single family	83.4	85.6	88.6
Multifamily	14.1	8.8	5.7
Hotels	1.3	0.0	1.4
White	1.3	2.4	2.8
Public service	0.0	3.2	1.4
Total	100.1	100.0	99.9
Population/dwelling unit (median)	5.4	5.0	4.6

NOTE: Public service includes individuals enumerated at their place of employment, fire station or offices, but not their place of residence. Newspapers and/or clippings identified these individuals as Topekans. Most frequently census enumeration indicated an individual at his place of employment as well as his residence.

D. Households

	1880 (%)	1885 (%)	1895 (%)
Primary	53.8	60.8	57.4
Subfamily	1.3	0.0	0.0
Male head	1.3	0.0	4.3
Female head	0.0	0.0	1.4
Male primary	2.6	1.6	3.5
Female primary	1.3	0.0	0.0
Extended	37.2	36.0	29.1
Not known	2.6	1.6	4.3
Total	100.1	100.0	100.0
Household size (median)	4.8	4.7	4.6

Table 12 (cont.)

E. *Employment*

	1880 (%)	1885 (%)	1895 (%)
Male (head)	96.2	97.6	97.2
Female (wife or head)	10.3	4.0	10.6
Children	0.0	0.0	1.4

F. *Color, Sex, and Age*

	1880 (%)	1885 (%)	1895 (%)
Color			
Black	74.4	82.4	67.4
Mulatto	24.4	17.6	32.6
Not given	1.3	0.0	0.0
Total	100.1	100.0	100.0
Sex			
Male	92.3	98.4	89.4
Female	7.7	1.6	10.6
Total	100.0	100.0	100.0
Median age	37.3	38.7	39.8

NOTE: Not given (1880) = the enumerator did not indicate the color of this individual; likewise, newspapers only indicated that the person was Negro.

G. *Areas of Origin*

	1880 (%)	1885 (%)	1895 (%)
Northeast	1.3	2.4	1.4
Deep South	35.9	32.8	28.4
Border South	52.6	52.0	58.9
Old Northwest	5.1	5.6	5.0
Midwest	0.0	1.6	2.1
Foreign	5.1	4.8	4.3
Not known	0.0	0.8	0.0
Total	100.0	100.0	100.1

NOTE: See Table 2 for states in each category.

Table 12   (cont.)

H. *Occupations*

	1880 (%)	1885 (%)	1895 (%)
Professional	25.0	34.7	58.6
Service entrepreneurial	10.5	11.3	14.3
Skilled	15.8	13.7	10.7
Semiskilled	2.6	4.0	0.7
Unskilled	34.2	33.1	12.1
Agricultural	3.9	0.8	0.0
Other	7.9	0.8	3.6
Not known	0.0	1.6	0.0
Total	99.9	100.0	100.0

I. *Literacy*

	1880 (%)	1885 (%)	1895 (%)
Literate	66.7	88.0	90.0
Reads only	9.0	0.0	0.0
Writes only	0.0	0.0	1.4
Illiterate	24.4	12.0	8.5
Total	100.1	100.0	99.9

J. *Persistence in Topeka*

	1880 (%)	1885 (%)	1895 (%)
Census periods			
One	71.8	51.2	53.2
Two	11.5	16.0	7.8
Three	10.3	8.0	4.2
Four	1.3	14.4	22.7
Five	5.2	7.2	5.0
Six	0.0	3.2	5.0
Seven	0.0	0.0	2.1
Total	100.1	100.0	100.0

Table 13   Profile of Exodusters in Topeka, 1880

A. *Residence by Ward*

	Sample (%)	Barracks (%)
First	18.1	100.0
Second	24.1	0.0
Third	38.8	0.0
Fourth	19.0	0.0
Total	100.0	100.0
Population size	116	127

NOTE: The sample Exoduster population represents those identified as Exodusters who fell within the sample studied. Exodusters lodged in the Barracks did not fall within this group; the tenure of those individuals in the Barracks or Topeka is not known.

B. *Neighborhoods' Racial Composition*

Negro (%)	Sample (%)	Barracks (%)
100–76	10.3	100.0
75–51	42.2	0.0
50–26	29.3	0.0
25–13	8.6	0.0
12–0	9.5	0.0
Total	99.9	100.0

C. *Dwellings*

	Sample (%)	Barracks (%)
Single family	38.8	0.0
Multifamily	58.6	100.0
Boardinghouses/Hotels	2.6	0.0
Total	100.0	100.0
Households/dwelling unit (median)	2.1	31.0
Population/dwelling unit (median)	12.8	127.0

Table 13 (cont.)

D. *Households*

	Sample (%)	Barracks (%)
Primary	59.5	52.8
Subfamily	8.6	0.0
Male head	0.0	11.8
Female head	0.0	13.4
Male primary	0.0	3.1
Female primary	0.0	2.4
Extended	31.9	16.5
Total	100.0	100.0
Household size (median)	7.6	6.6

E. *Employment*

	Sample (%)	Barracks (%)
Male (head)	97.4	50.4
Female (wife or head)	15.5	11.8
Children	0.0	5.5

F. *Color, Sex, and Age*

	Sample (%)	Barracks (%)
Color		
Black	72.4	76.4
Mulatto	25.9	23.6
White	1.7	0.0
Total	100.0	100.0
Sex		
Male	54.3	56.7
Female	45.7	43.3
Total	100.0	100.0
Median age	10.5	14.8
Median age of household head	48.0	61.0

Table 13 (cont.)

G. *States of Origin*

	Sample (%)	Barracks (%)
Delaware	0.0	0.8
Alabama	0.9	7.9
Georgia	0.0	1.6
Louisiana	6.9	17.3
Mississippi	12.9	19.7
North Carolina	0.0	7.9
South Carolina	0.0	4.7
Virginia	4.3	7.9
Texas	5.2	0.0
Kentucky	16.4	9.4
Missouri	1.7	0.8
Oklahoma	0.9	0.0
Tennessee	50.0	20.5
Wisconsin	0.9	0.0
Not known	0.0	1.6
Total	100.1	100.1

H. *Occupations*

	Sample (%)	Barracks (%)
Professional	0.0	1.6
Service entrepreneurial	1.7	0.0
Skilled	1.7	2.4
Semiskilled	2.6	3.9
Unskilled	19.0	8.7
Agricultural	1.7	1.6
Other	73.3	81.9
Total	100.0	100.1

Table 13   (cont.)

I. Literacy

	Sample (%)	Barracks (%)
Literate	30.2	16.5
Reads only	5.2	9.4
Writes only	4.3	0.8
Illiterate	21.6	40.9
Not applicable	38.8	32.3
Total	100.1	99.9

NOTE: Not applicable = individuals here are children.

J. School Attendance

	Sample		
	Children (%)	Adults (%)	Total (%)
Yes	14.6	3.4	18.0
No	41.4	40.5	81.9
Total			99.9
	Barracks		
Yes	9.4	3.1	12.5
No	39.4	48.0	87.4
Total			99.9

NOTE: Children were fourteen years of age or younger.

Table 14   Effective Wage Rates in Topeka, 1885, 1895

	1885 ($)	1895 ($)	Time Unit
Laborers	1.25	1.50	Day
Carpenters[1]	2.25	2.30	Day
Bricklayers[1]	2.54	4.00	Day
Masons[1]	2.54	3.50	Day
Painters	2.50	2.35	Day
Wagonmakers	2.00	2.25	Day
Blacksmiths	2.00	2.65	Day
Shoemakers	2.00	2.00	Day
Harness makers	2.00	2.00	Day
Tailors	2.25	2.25	Day
Printers	0.30	0.30	per 1,000 imps
Clerks	50.00	—	Month
Tinners	2.50	2.42	Day
Millers	3.00	3.00	Day
Milliners	1.25	1.75	Day
Seamstresses	1.00	1.00	Day
Washwomen	1.00	1.00	Day
Domestics[1]	2.00	3.00	Week
Servants[1]	2.00	—	Week
Boilermakers	—	2.70	Day
Machinists	—	2.65	Day

SOURCES: Kansas 1885, 1895 MS census.
[1] The wage rates in 1885 for the Third Ward were slightly higher than those throughout the city, usually fifty cents to a dollar.

Map 1.   Negro Institutions in Topeka, 1885

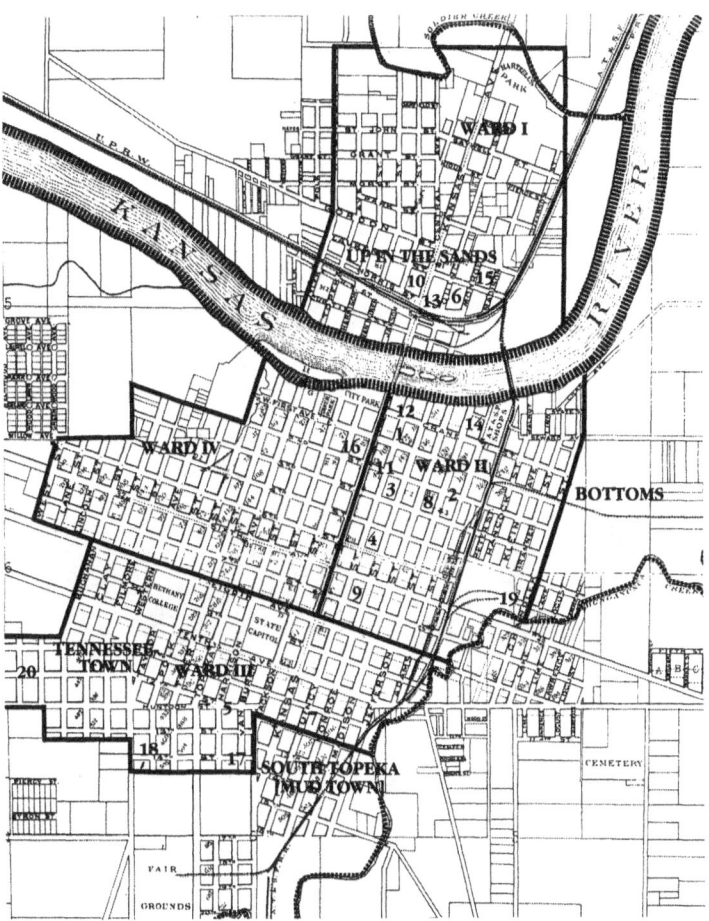

Ward boundaries from *Radges' Topeka Directory*, 1875–1880, and revised ordinances of Topeka, 1868, 1878, have been drawn on H. A. Needham's *Pocket Map of the City of Topeka*, 1882, KSHS. South Topeka became part of the Fifth Ward after 1881. Churches are (1) St. John A.M.E.; (2) Second Baptist; (3) Fourth Street Baptist; (7) Wesleyan A.M.E.; (8) First Cumberland Presbyterian; (9) Second Congregational; (10) Asbury A.M.E.; (13) St. Mark A.M.E.; (15) North Topeka Baptist; (16) St. Simon's; (17) Lane Chapel C.M.E.; (18) Primitive Baptist; (20) Shiloh Baptist; (21) Second Christian. Negro schools (4, 5), fraternal halls (11, 12), and the Santa Fe Shops (14) are also indicated.

Map 2.   Topeka , 1916

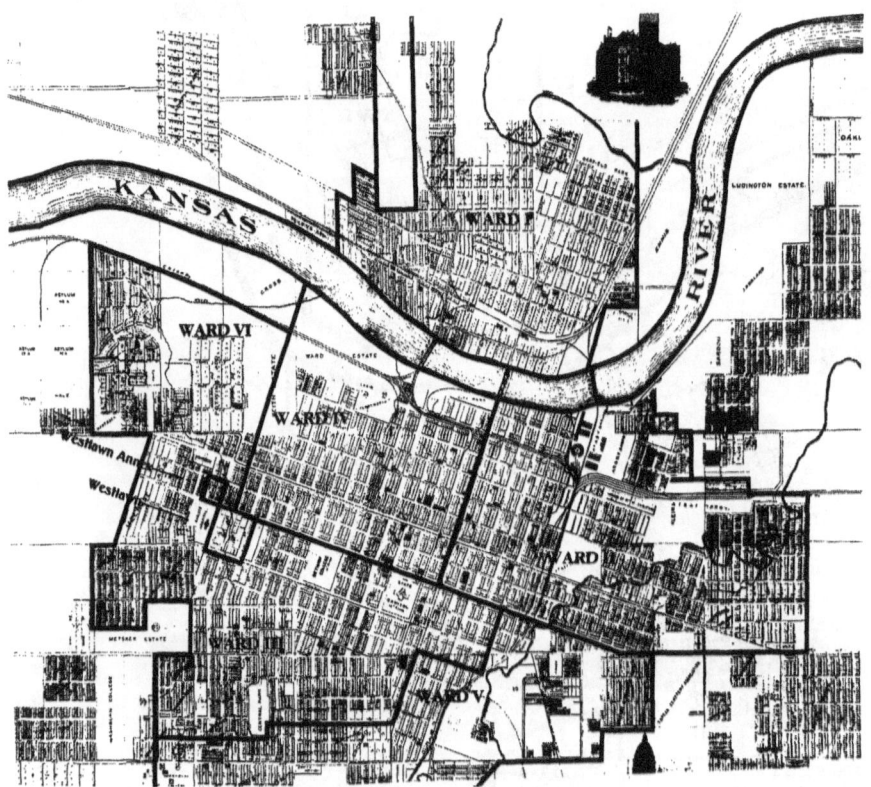

Ward divisions from *Polk-Radges' Directory*, 1916 are drawn on James F. McCabe's *Official Map of the City of Topeka*, 1906, KSHS.

Bibliography

Primary Sources

Manuscript Collections

Halbert, Leroy A., and M. L. Sherman, comps. "Tennesseetown Census, 1898." MS in Kansas State Historical Society Archives, Topeka.
Index, Topeka City Jail, 1875–1885. MS in KSHS.
Index of Inmates, Shawnee County Boys' Industrial School, 1883–1918. MS in KSHS.
Kansas Freedmen's Relief Association. Records. KSHS.
Kansas State Decennial Census Manuscripts. Shawnee County, 1865, 1875, 1885, 1895, 1905. Microfilm Division, KSHS Archives.
Topeka Board of Education. "The Colored Schools" [1922]. MS in KSHS.
U.S. Department of Commerce. Bureau of Census. Eighth Census, 1860. National Archives, Washington, D.C.
———. Ninth Census, 1870. National Archives.
———. Tenth Census, 1880. National Archives.

City, State, and Federal Documents

Agricultural and Industrial Institute Financial Statement. Topeka: Times, 1881.
Betton, Frank H. *First Annual Report of the Kansas Bureau of Labor and Industrial Statistics, 1886.* Topeka: State Printing Office, 1887.
Biennial Reports. Kansas State Board of Health, 1899–1900. Topeka: State Printing Office, 1900.
Biennial Reports of the Board of Trustees of the State Charitable Institutions of the State of Kansas, 1881–1912. Topeka: Kansas Publishing House, 1912.
First Annual and Biennial Reports of the Kansas State Board of Control, 1906–1916. Topeka: State Printing Office, 1916.

First Annual Report of the Freedmen's Educational Society. Topeka: Daily Capital-Journal Publishing Co., 1881.
First through Ninth *Biennial Reports.* Kansas Superintendent of Public Instruction, 1877–1893. Topeka: Morgan State Printer, 1895.
Fourteenth and Sixteenth Biennial Reports of the Board of Trustees of State Charitable Institutions of the State of Kansas. Topeka: State Printing Office, 1916.
In the Supreme Court of the State of Kansas—1890. Topeka: Crane and Co., 1890.
Kaimas, C. W. *A Statement to the Senate and the House of Representatives Against the "Full Crew Bill."* Topeka: State Printer, 1913.
Kansas Adjutant General. *Official Military History of Kansas Regiments During the War for the Suppression of the Great Rebellion.* Leavenworth: W. S. Burke, 1870.
Kansas Constitutional Convention: A Reprint of the Proceedings and Debates of the Convention Which Framed the Constitution of Kansas at Wyandotte in July, 1859 [and] *The Constitution Annotated to Date, Historical Sketches, Etc.*, by the Authority of the State Legislature. Topeka: State Printer, 1920.
Kansas General Laws, 1862. Topeka: State Printer, 1863.
Kansas Industrial Development Commission Report. Topeka: State Printer, 1901.
Kansas Legislative Documents, 1862–1899. Topeka: State Printer, 1901.
Kansas Legislative Handbook and Record of the 1913 Session. Topeka: State Printer, 1914.
Kansas Session Laws, 1861. Topeka: State Printer, 1862.
Kansas Session Laws, 1908. Topeka: State Printer, 1908.
Kansas Session Laws, 1919. Topeka: State Printing Office, 1919.
Kansas Special Session Laws, 1874. Topeka: State Printer, 1874.
Kansas State Bureau of Industrial Statistics, 1895–1915. Topeka: State Printer, 1916.
Nineteenth Biennial Report. Kansas Superintendent of Public Instruction. Topeka: State Printer, 1914.
Statutes of Kansas. Topeka: State Printing Office, 1889.
U.S. Congress. House of Representatives. *Report of the Special Committee Appointed to Investigate the Troubles in Kansas*, 34th Cong., 1st Sess., No. 200. Washington, D.C.: Government Printing Office, 1880.
———. Senate. *Report and Testimony of the Select Committee of the United States Senate to Investigate the Causes for the Removal of the Negroes from the Southern States to the Northern States*, 46th Cong., 2nd Sess. Washington, D.C.: Government Printing Office, 1880.
U.S. Department of Commerce. Bureau of Census. *Tenth Census of the United States, 1880.* Vol. I. Washington, D.C.: Government Printing Office, 1883.
———. *Eleventh Census of the United States, 1890.* Vol. I, Part 1. Washington, D.C.: Government Printing Office, 1893.
———. *Twelfth Census of the United States, 1900.* Part 1. Washington, D.C.: Government Printing Office, 1901.

Bibliography

———. *Thirteenth Census of the United States, 1910.* Washington, D.C.: Government Printing Office, 1912.
———. *Negro Population, 1790–1915.* Washington, D.C.: Government Printing Office, 1918.

Topeka Newspapers

American Citizen (black), 1888–89.
Baptist Headlight (black), 1893–94.
Benevolent Banner (black), 1887.
Blackman (black, North Topeka), 1894.
Capital-Commonwealth (white), February 2, March 10, 1889.
Colored Citizen (black), 1878–79, 1897–1903.
Colored Patriot (black), 1882.
Commonwealth (white), 1869–88.
Daily Capital (white), 1879—.
Daily Capital-Journal (white), March 3, 1883, June 19, 1915.
Daily Herald (white), November 1, 1901.
Evening Call (black), 1893.
Kansas Herald (black), 1879–80.
Kansas State Ledger (black), 1892–1906.
Mail and Breeze (white, North Topeka), 1895–1903.
People's Friend (black), July 7, 1893, December 11, 1896.
Plaindealer (black), 1899–1921.
State Journal (white), 1897–1932.
Times (white, North Topeka), June 30, 1879.
Times-Observer (black), 1891–92.
Tribune (black), 1878–80.
Tribune (white), August 17, 1866.
Weekly Times (white), March 11, 25, 1881.

Clippings (KSHS)

Baptist Church Clippings. Vol. I, 1879–1938.
Benjamin Singleton Scrapbook.
Exodus Matters.
Kansas Legislative Clippings. Vols. XIV–XV, 1917.
Methodist Church Clippings. Vols. I–III, 1879–1937.
Negro Clippings. Vols. I–VII, 1856–1956.
Population Clippings.
Protestant Episcopal Church Clippings. Vol. I, 1878–1933.
Public Schools—General Clippings. Vol. I, 1876–1916.
Republican Party Clippings. Vol. VI, 1906–1909.
Shawnee County Clippings. Vols. I–IX, XIX, 1861–1886, 1895–1900.

Pamphlets and Bulletins

The Afro-American State League. Topeka: n.p., 1912.
An Appeal for Justice to the Colored People. Topeka: n.p., 1914.
Brochure of Parents' Meeting at Sheldon Kindergarten. Topeka: n.p., 1906.
Colored Men's Independent State League. Topeka: n.p., n.d.
Comstock, Elizabeth. *Announcement.* Columbus: n.p., 1881.
———. *Broadside* [4]. Topeka: Kansas Freedmen's Relief Association, 1880–1881.
———. *Statement.* Topeka: Commonwealth, 1880.
Dorsey, John M. *Thoughts for Careful Consideration.* Topeka: n.p., 1906.
Eighth Annual Session of the NNBL. Topeka: n.p., 1907.
Halbert, Leroy A. *Across the Way.* Topeka: Central Congregational Church, 1900.
———. *A History of the Work of Central Church for the Redemption of Tennesseetown.* Topeka: Central Congregational Church, 1892.
Harrison, Shelby M. *Topeka Improvement Survey.* Topeka: Russell Sage Foundation, 1914.
Haviland, Laura. *Circular—1880.* Topeka: n.p., 1880.
Industrial Institute for People of Color. Columbus: n.p., 1881.
Kansas Freedmen's Relief Association. *Instructions to Visitors.* Topeka: n.p., 1880.
———. *Minutes of the Board of Directors Meeting, April 14, 1881.* Topeka: n.p., 1881.
———. *Second Semi-Annual Report.* Topeka: Daily Capital, 1880.
Kansas Hospital Aid Association. Topeka: Industrial Institute Press, 1919.
Kansas Industrial and Educational Institute. f18Annual Catalogue. Topeka: Industrial Institute Press, 1919.
Ninth Annual Message of Governor James M. Harvey: Delivered to the Kansas Legislature, January, 1869. Topeka: State Printer, 1869.
Paine, A. B. *A Kansas Almshouse.* Topeka: Crane and Co., 1894.
Perry, Susan T. *A Peep at the Warehouse of the K.F.R.A.* Topeka: n.p., n.d.
Proceedings of a Convention of Colored Citizens Held in the City of Lawrence, October 17, 1866. Leavenworth: Evening Bulletin, 1866.
Radges, Samuel. *Radges' Directory of Topeka and Shawnee County and Gazetteer of General Information.* Topeka: n.p., 1870–1917.
Seventh Annual Message of Governor Samuel J. Crawford: Delivered to the Legislative Assembly of the State. Reprint. Leavenworth: State Printer, 1967.
Sheldon, Charles M. *Some Facts Regarding City Government Together with a Catechism on Good Citizenship.* Topeka: Crane and Co., 1902.
A Sketch of the Garden of the West. Boston: Atchison, Topeka and Santa Fe Printing Office, 1876.
Thirteenth Annual Message of Governor Thomas A. Osborn: Delivered to the Kansas Legislature, 1873. Topeka: State Printer, 1873.
Thomas, P. C. *A Few Facts for Your Careful Consideration.* Topeka: n.p., 1908.
To the Colored Voters of Kansas. Topeka: n.p., 1898.

Articles

Godkin, E. L. "The Flight of the Negroes." *Nation* (April, 1879), 242.
Gross, George Wellington. "The Negro as a Factor in Kansas Politics." *Agora*, II (1893), 166–70.
Hartzell, J. C. "The Negro Exodus." *Methodist Quarterly Review*, XXXIX (1879), 722–47.
King, Henry. "A Year of the Exodus in Kansas." *Scribner's Monthly* (May–October, 1880), 211–18.
"Negro Migration." *New West*, II (1878), 24–27.
Sheldon, Charles M. "A Local Negro Problem." *The Kingdom*, Vol. VIII, No. 52 (April, 1896), 28.

Books

Barrows, Isabel C., ed. *Proceedings of the National Conference of Charities and Corrections*. Boston: George H. Ellis, 1901.
Cordley, Richard. *Pioneer Days*. New York: Pilgrim Press, 1903.
Dassler, C. F. W. *Compiled Laws of the State of Kansas*. St. Louis: W. J. Gilbert, 1879.
Giles, Frye W. *Thirty Years in Topeka: A Historical Sketch*. Topeka: Crane and Co., 1886.
Hale, Edward Everett. *Kansas and Nebraska: The History, Geographical and Physical Characteristics, and Political Position of Those Territories; an Account of the Emigrant Aid Companies, and Directions to Emigrants*. Boston: Phillips, Sampson and Co., 1854.
Haviland, Laura. *A Woman's Life Work: Labors and Experiences of Laura S. Haviland*. Cincinnati: Walden and Stowe, 1881.
Prentis, Noble. *Kansas Miscellanies*. Topeka: Kansas Publishing House, 1889.
Riis, Jacob. *The Poor in Great Cities: Their Problems and What Is Done to Solve Them*. Edited by Robert A. Woods and W. T. Elsing. London: Paul, Trench, Trubner, 1896.
Robinson, Charles. *The Kansas Conflict*. Lawrence: Journal Publishing Co., 1898.
Sheldon, Charles M. *In His Steps*. Originally published in 1897. New York: Grosset and Dunlap, 1972.
Sumner, Charles. *Speech of Hon. Charles Sumner in the Senate of the United States, May 19–20, 1856*. Boston: John P. Jewett and Co., 1856.
Thayer, Eli. *The Kansas Crusade*. New York: Harper, 1889.

Secondary Sources

Blake, Ella Lee. "The Great Exodus, 1879–1880, to Kansas." M.A. thesis, Kansas State College, 1942.
Caldwell, Martha Belle. "The Attitude of Kansas Toward the Reconstruction of the South." Ph.D. dissertation, University of Kansas, 1938.

McDaniel, Orval. "A History of Nicodemus, Graham County, Kansas." M.A. thesis, Fort Hays State College, 1950.
St. Clair, Sadie D. "The National Career of Senator Blanche K. Bruce." Ph.D. dissertation, New York University, 1947.
Schwendemann, Glen. "The Negro Exodus to Kansas: The First Phase, March–July 1879." M.A. thesis, University of Oklahoma, 1958.
Waldron, Nell B. "Colonization in Kansas." Ph.D. dissertation, Northwestern University, 1932.

Articles

Antovsky, Aaron. "Aspirations, Class, and Racial-Ethnic Membership." *Journal of Negro Education*, XXXVI (1967), 385–93.
Athearn, Robert G. "Black Exodus: The Migration of 1879." *Prairie Scout*, III (1975), 86–99.
Blumenthal, Henry. "Woodrow Wilson and the Race Question." *Journal of Negro History*, XLVIII (1963), 1–21.
Castel, Albert. "Civil War Kansas and the Negro." *Journal of Negro History*, XXI (1936), 125–38.
Cornish, Dudley T. "Kansas Negro Regiments in the Civil War." *Kansas Historical Quarterly*, XX (1952), 417–29.
"Events of Fifty-Six." *Kansas Historical Collections*, VII (1901–1902), 52–55.
"Everett Papers." *Kansas Historical Quarterly*, VIII (1939), 143–47.
Garvin, Roy. "Benjamin, or 'Pap,' Singleton and His Followers." *Journal of Negro History*, XXXIII (1948), 7–23.
Glick, G. W. "The Rehabilitation of the Santa Fe Railroad System." *Kansas Historical Collections*, XIII (1915), 141–46.
Hays, Samuel P. "Social Analysis of American Political History." *Political Science Quarterly*, LXXX (1965), 373–94.
Hickman, Russell K. "Founding a Pioneer Church." *Shawnee County Historical Society Bulletin*, No. 3 (March, 1905), 4–5.
Higgins, Billy D. "Negro Thought in the Exodus." *Phylon*, XXII (1971), 39–52.
Hill, Mozell C. "The All Negro Communities of Oklahoma: The Natural History of a Social Movement." *Journal of Negro History*, XXXI (1946), 254–68.
Hovey, George R. "How the Negroes Were Duped." *Journal of Negro History*, IV (1919), 55.
Katzman, Martin. "Opportunity, Subculture, and the Economic Performance of Urban Ethnic Groups." *American Journal of Economics and Sociology*, XXVIII (1969), 351–66.
Kessler, Sidney. "The Organization of Negroes in the Knights of Labor." *Journal of Negro History*, XXXVII (1952), 248–76.
Liberson, Stanley. "Stratification and Ethnic Groups." *Sociological Inquiry*, XL (1970), 172–87.
Link, Arthur S. "The Negro as a Factor in the Campaign of 1912." *Journal of*

Negro History, XXXII (1947), 84–99.
McCord, Theodore E. "The KIEL of Topeka." *Paul Jones Magazine* (October, 1919), 20–21.
Mandell, Bernard. "Samuel Gompers and the Negro Workers, 1886–1914." *Journal of Negro History*, XL (1955), 34–60.
Meier, August. "The Negro and the Democratic Party, 1875–1915." *Phylon*, XVII (1956), 173–91.
———, and David Lewis. "History of the Negro Upper Class in Atlanta, Georgia, 1890–1958." *Journal of Negro Education*, XXVIII (1959), 128–39.
Nichols, Roy F. "The Kansas-Nebraska Act: A Century of Historiography." *Mississippi Valley Historical Review*, XLVIII (1956), 187–212.
Noel, Donald. "Theory of the Origins of Ethnic Stratification." *Social Problems*, XVI (1968–69), 151–71.
Painter, Nell Irvin. "Millenarian Aspects of the Exodus to Kansas." *Journal of Social History*, IX (1976), 331–39.
Pickering, Loren O. "The Administration of John P. St. John." *Transactions of the Kansas State Historical Society*, IX (1905–1906), 378–94.
Prentis, Noble. "Aunt Ann's Story." Topeka *Commonwealth*, May 12, 1878. Reprinted in *Kansas Historical Quarterly*, XXXV (1969), 89–92.
Schwendemann, Glen. "The Exodusters on the Missouri." *Kansas Historical Quarterly*, XXIX (1963), 25–40.
———. "Nicodemus: Negro Haven on the Solomon." *Kansas Historical Quarterly*, XXXIV (1968), 10–31.
———. "Wyandotte and the First Exodusters of 1879." *Kansas Historical Quarterly*, XXVI (1960), 223–49.
"The Topeka Movement." *Kansas Historical Collections*, XIII (1915), 125–249.
Tuttle, William M., and Surendra Banaha. "Black Newspapers in Kansas." *American Studies*, XIII (1972), 117–24.
Wilson, Paul E. "Brown v. Board of Education Revisited." Reprinted from *Kansas Law Review*, XII (1964), 511.

Pamphlets and Magazines

Barker, John D. *Sixty-eighth Session of Kansas Annual Conference of the A.M.E. Church and the Seventy-fifth Anniversary of St. John A.M.E. Church.* Topeka: n.p., 1943.
———. *Souvenir Program of the Seventieth Anniversary of Shiloh Baptist Church, 1949.* Topeka: n.p., 1949.
Graduate Magazine of the University of Kansas, VII (May, 1909), 294–303.

Books

Abell, Aaron. *The Urban Impact on American Protestantism, 1865–1900.* Cambridge: Harvard University Press, 1943.
Anderson, George L. *Four Essays on Railroads in Kansas and Colorado.* Lawrence:

Coronado Press, 1971.
Andreas, Arthur T. *History of the State of Kansas*. Chicago: R. R. Donnelley and Sons, 1883.
Athearn, Robert G. *In Search of Canaan: Black Migration to Kansas, 1879–1880*. Lawrence: Regents Press of Kansas, 1978.
Bell, Howard. *The Negro Convention Movement, 1830–1861*. New York: Arno Press, 1969.
Bendix, Reinhard, and Seymour Lipset. *Class, Status, and Power: Social Stratification in Comparative Perspective*. New York: Free Press, 1966.
Berlin, Ira. *Slaves Without Masters: The Free Negro in the Antebellum South*. New York: Vintage Press, 1976.
Bernstein, Barton J., and Allen Matusow, eds. *Twentieth-Century America: Recent Interpretations*. New York: Harcourt Brace Jovanovich, 1972.
Berret, Howard. *Who's Who in Topeka*. Topeka: Adams Brothers, 1905.
Berwanger, Eugene. *The Frontier Against Slavery: Western Anti-Negro Prejudice and the Slavery Extension Controversy*. Urbana: University of Illinois Press, 1971.
Billington, Ray Allen. *America's Frontier Heritage*. New York: Holt, Rinehart and Winston, 1966.
Blackmar, Frank W. *Kansas: A Cyclopedia of State History, Embracing Events, Institutions, Counties, Cities, Towns, Prominent Persons, Etc.* 2 vols. Topeka: Standard Publication Co., 1912.
Bottomore, T. B. *Elites and Society*. London: Penguin Books, 1964.
Bremner, Robert. *From the Depths: The Discovery of Poverty in the United States*. New York: New York University Press, 1956.
Bright, John D., ed. *Kansas: The First Century*. 4 vols. New York: Lewis Historical Publishing Co., 1956.
Browning, Grace. *The Development of Poor Relief Legislation in Kansas*. Chicago: University of Chicago Press, 1935.
Bruno, Frank J. *Trends in Social Work, 1874–1956: A History Based on the Proceedings of the National Conference of Social Work*. New York: Columbia University Press, 1957.
Callow, Alexander B., ed. *American Urban History*. New York: Columbia University Press, 1964.
Clanton, O. Gene. *Kansas Populism: Ideas and Men*. Lawrence: University of Kansas Press, 1969.
Clark, Carroll D., and Roy L. Roberts. *People of Kansas: A Demographic and Social Study*. Topeka: State Planning Board, 1936.
Cohen, Nathan. *Social Work in the American Tradition*. New York: Holt, Rinehart and Winston, 1958.
Conference on Research in Income and Wealth. *Trends in the American Economy in the Nineteenth Century*. Vol. XXIV. Princeton: Princeton University Press, 1960. In *Studies in Income and Wealth*. 44 vols. Princeton: Princeton University Press, 1937—.

Connelley, William E. *History of Kansas, State and People.* 5 vols. Chicago: American Publication Co., 1928.
———. *History of Kansas Newspapers.* Topeka: State Printing Office, 1916.
Cornish, Dudley T. *The Sable Arm: Negro Troops in the Union Army, 1861–1865.* New York: Norton, 1966.
Craven, Avery. *The Coming of the Civil War.* Chicago: University of Chicago Press, 1957.
Cruden, Robert. *The Negro in Reconstruction.* Englewood Cliffs: Prentice-Hall, 1969.
Danforth, Mildred. *A Quaker Pioneer: Laura Haviland, Superintendent of the Underground Railroad.* New York: Exposition Press, 1906.
Davis, Allen. *Spearheads for Reform: The Social Settlement and the Progressive Movement, 1890–1914.* New York: Oxford University Press, 1967.
Donald, David. *Charles Sumner and the Coming of the Civil War.* New York: Knopf, 1960.
Drake, St. Clair, and Horace Cayton. *Black Metropolis: A Study of Negro Life in a Northern City.* 2 vols. New York: Harper Torchbooks, 1945, 1962.
Duberman, Martin, ed. *The Antislavery Vanguard: New Essays on the Abolitionists.* Princeton: Princeton University Press, 1965.
Du Bois, W. E. B. *The Souls of Black Folk.* Chicago: A. C. McClurg, 1903.
Dykstra, Robert. *The Cattle Towns.* New York: Atheneum, 1972.
Edwards, Edgar O., ed. *The Nation's Economic Objectives.* Chicago: University of Chicago Press, 1964.
Feder, Leah. *Unemployment Relief in Periods of Depression.* New York: Russell Sage Foundation, 1936.
Foner, Eric. *Free Soil, Free Labor, Free Men.* New York: Oxford University Press, 1970.
Foner, Philip. *The Life and Writings of Frederick Douglass.* 4 vols. New York: International Publishers, 1950–55.
———. *Organized Labor and the Black Worker, 1619–1973.* New York: Praeger, 1974.
Franklin, John Hope. *Reconstruction After the Civil War.* Chicago: University of Chicago Press, 1970.
Gaeddert, Raymond G. *The Birth of Kansas.* Social Science Studies. Lawrence: University of Kansas Publications, 1940.
Gates, Paul Wallace. *Fifty Million Acres.* Ithaca: Cornell University Press, 1954.
———. *Landlords and Tenants on the Prairie Frontier.* Ithaca: Cornell University Press, 1973.
Gerber, David. *Black Ohio and the Color Line, 1860–1915.* Urbana: University of Illinois Press, 1976.
Glad, Paul. *McKinley, Bryan, and the People.* Philadelphia: Lippincott, 1964.
Gordon, Milton. *Assimilation in American Life.* New York: Oxford University Press, 1964.

———. *Social Class in American Sociology*. New York: McGraw-Hill, 1963.
Greer, Scott. *The Emerging City: Myth and Reality*. New York: Free Press of Glencoe, 1962.
Griffin, Clifford S. *History of the University of Kansas*. Lawrence: Regents Press of Kansas, 1973.
———. *Their Brothers' Keepers: Moral Stewardship in America*. New Brunswick: Rutgers University Press, 1958.
Gross, Robert. *The Minutemen and Their World*. New York: Hill and Wang, 1976.
Handlin, Oscar. *Boston's Immigrants, 1790–1880: A Study of Acculturation*. Cambridge: Harvard University Press, 1959.
Harlan, Louis. *Booker T. Washington: The Making of a Black Leader, 1856–1901*. New York: Oxford University Press, 1972.
Harmon, J. H., Arnett G. Lindsay, and Carter G. Woodson. *The Negro as a Businessman*. College Park, Md.: McGrath Publishing Co., 1929.
Hays, Samuel P. *The Response to Industrialism, 1885–1914*. Chicago: University of Chicago Press, 1957.
Heller, Celia, ed. *Structured Social Inequality*. New York: Macmillan, 1969.
Hicks, John D. *The Populist Revolt*. Lincoln: University of Nebraska Press, 1961.
Hofstadter, Richard. *The Age of Reform: From Bryan to F.D.R.* New York: Knopf, 1955.
———. *America at 1750: A Social Portrait*. New York: Knopf, 1971.
———, and Seymour M. Lipset, eds. *Turner and the Sociology of the Frontier*. New York: Basic Books, 1968.
Hopkins, Charles. *The Rise of the Social Gospel in American Protestantism*. New Haven: Yale University Press, 1940.
Hyman, Harold M., ed. *New Frontiers of American Reconstruction*. Chicago: University of Illinois Press, 1966.
Jackson, Kenneth T., and Stanley K. Shultz, eds. *Cities in American History*. New York: Knopf, 1972.
Johnson, Samuel A. *The Battle Cry of Freedom*. Lawrence: University of Kansas Press, 1954.
Jorns, Auguste. *The Quaker as Pioneer in Social Work*. Translated by T. K. Brown. New York: Macmillan, 1931.
Kahl, Joseph. *The American Class Structure*. New York: Rinehart and Co., 1956.
Kansas State Historical Society. *Annals of Kansas, 1886–1925*. 2 vols. Topeka: Kansas State Historical Society, 1911, 1926.
Katzman, David. *Before the Ghetto: Black Detroit in the Nineteenth Century*. Urbana: University of Illinois Press, 1973.
Keller, Suzanne. *The Urban Neighborhood: A Sociological Perspective*. New York: Random House, 1968.
King, James L., ed. *History of Shawnee County, Kansas, and Representative Citizens*. Chicago: Richmond and Arnold, 1905.
Kluger, Richard. *Simple Justice*. New York: Knopf, 1976.

Kusmer, Kenneth L. *A Ghetto Takes Shape: Black Cleveland, 1870–1930*. Urbana: University of Illinois Press, 1976.
Kuznets, Simon, ed. *Economic Growth and Structure: Selected Essays*. New York: Norton, 1965.
Landes, Benson Y., ed. *Rauschenbusch Reader*. New York: Harper and Brothers, 1957.
Link, Arthur S. *Wilson: The New Freedom*. Princeton: Princeton University Press, 1956.
———, and William B. Catton. *American Epoch: A History of the United States Since the 1890s*. New York: Knopf, 1967.
Litwack, Leon. *North of Slavery: The Negro in the Free States, 1790–1860*. Chicago: University of Chicago Press, 1961.
Lubove, Roy. *The Professional Altruist: The Emergence of Social Work as a Career, 1880–1930*. Cambridge: Harvard University Press, 1965.
McPherson, James M. *The Abolitionist Legacy: From Reconstruction to the NAACP*. Princeton: Princeton University Press, 1976.
———. *The Negro's Civil War: How American Negroes Felt and Acted During the War for the Union*. New York: Vintage Press, 1965.
———. *The Struggle for Equality: Abolitionists and the Negro in the Civil War and Reconstruction*. Princeton: Princeton University Press, 1964.
Malin, James C. *Grasslands: Prolegomena*. Ann Arbor: University of Michigan Press, 1948.
———. *John Brown and the Legend of Fifty-Six*. Philadelphia: American Philosophical Society, 1942.
———. *The Nebraska Question, 1852–1854*. Lawrence: University of Kansas Press, 1953.
May, Henry. *Protestant Churches in Industrial America*. New York: Harper and Brothers, 1949.
Meier, August. *Negro Thought in America, 1880–1915*. Ann Arbor: University of Michigan Press, 1963.
———, and Elliott Rudwick. *From Plantation to Ghetto*. New York: Hill and Wang, 1970.
Merk, Frederick. *Manifest Destiny and Mission in American History: A Reinterpretation*. New York: Knopf, 1963.
Miller, Wallace E. *The Peopling of Kansas*. Columbus: Fred J. Herr Press, 1939.
Morgan, Edmund. *American Slavery, American Freedom: The Ordeal of Colonial Virginia*. New York: Norton, 1975.
Mowry, George. *The Era of Theodore Roosevelt and the Birth of Modern America, 1900–1912*. New York: Harper Torchbooks, 1958.
Nevins, Allan. *Ordeal of the Union*. 8 vols. New York: Scribner, 1947.
Nichols, J. L., and William H. Crogman. *Progress of a Race or the Remarkable Advancement of the American Negro*. Chicago: Wilmore Book and Bible Co., 1920.

Niebuhr, H. Richard. *Social Sources of Denominationalism*. Hamden, Conn.: Shoe String Press, 1954.
Oates, Stephen. *To Purge This Land with Blood: A Biography of John Brown*. New York: Harper and Row, 1970.
Osofsky, Gilbert. *Harlem: The Making of a Ghetto*. New York: Harper Torchbooks, 1966.
Ovington, Mary White. *Half a Man: The Status of the Negro in New York*. New York: Negro University Press, 1911.
Painter, Nell Irvin. *Exodusters: Black Migration to Kansas After Reconstruction*. New York: Knopf, 1977.
Pierce, Joseph A. *Negro Business and Business Education: Their Present and Prospective Development*. New York: Harper and Brothers, 1947.
Potter, David. *People of Plenty*. Chicago: University of Chicago Press, 1954.
Pumphrey, Ralph, and Muriel Pumphrey. *The Heritage of American Social Work*. New York: Columbia University Press, 1961.
Quarles, Benjamin. *Allies for Freedom: Blacks and John Brown*. New York: Oxford University Press, 1974.
———, ed. *Blacks on John Brown*. Urbana: University of Illinois Press, 1972.
Rawley, James A. *Race and Politics: Bleeding Kansas and the Coming of the Civil War*. Philadelphia: Lippincott, 1969.
Reams, B. D., and Paul E. Wilson. *Segregation and the Fourteenth Amendment in the States: A Survey of State Segregation Laws, 1865–1953*. Buffalo: William S. Hein, 1975.
Rich, Everett, ed. *The Heritage of Kansas: Selected Commentaries on Past Times*. Lawrence: University of Kansas Press, 1960.
Rischin, Moses. *The Promised City*. Cambridge: Harvard University Press, 1962.
Rose, Willie Lee. *Rehearsal for Reconstruction: The Port Royal Experiment*. New York: Vintage Press, 1964.
Smith, Henry Nash. *Virgin Land: The American West as Symbol and Myth*. Cambridge: Harvard University Press, 1950.
Spear, Allan H. *Black Chicago: The Making of a Negro Ghetto*. Chicago: University of Chicago Press, 1969.
Speer, John. *Life of General James H. Lane*. Garden City, Kans.: John Speer, Printer, 1896.
Stampp, Kenneth. *The Era of Reconstruction, 1865–1877*. New York: Vintage Press, 1967.
———, ed. *The Causes of the Civil War*. Englewood Cliffs: Prentice-Hall, 1965.
———, and Leon Litwack, eds. *Reconstruction: An Anthology of Revisionist Writings*. Baton Rouge: Louisiana State University Press, 1969.
Swan, Robert. *The Ethnic Heritage of Topeka, Kansas: Immigrant Beginnings*. Topeka: Kansas State Historical Society, 1974.
Territorial Kansas: Studies Commemorating the Centennial. Social Science Studies. Lawrence: University of Kansas Publications, 1954.

Thernstrom, Stephan. *Poverty and Progress: Social Mobility in a Nineteenth Century City*. Cambridge: Harvard University Press, 1964.
Vidich, Arthur, and Joseph Bensman. *Small Town in Mass Society*. Princeton: Princeton University Press, 1968.
Warren, Roland L. *The Community in America*. Chicago: Rand McNally, 1963.
Washington, Booker T. *The Negro in Business*. Originally published in 1907. Chicago: Afro-American Press, 1969.
Webb, Walter Prescott. *The Great Plains*. Boston: Ginn, 1931.
Weber, Max. *Essays from Max Weber*. Translated and edited by H. H. Gerth and C. Wright Mills. New York: Oxford University Press, 1946.
Wiebe, Robert H. *The Search for Order, 1877–1920*. New York: Hill and Wang, 1967.
Wilder, Daniel W. *Annals of Kansas*. Topeka: George W. Martin Publishing House, 1885.
Williams, Robin. *American Society: A Sociological Interpretation*. New York: Knopf, 1965.
Williamson, Joel. *After Slavery: The Negro in South Carolina During Reconstruction, 1861–1877*. Chapel Hill: University of North Carolina Press, 1965.
Woodson, Carter G. *A Century of Negro Migration*. Lancaster, Pa.: New Era Printing Co., 1918.
Woodward, C. Vann. *The Origins of the New South: 1877–1913*. Baton Rouge: Louisiana State University Press, 1971.
―――. *The Strange Career of Jim Crow*. New York: Oxford University Press, 1966.
Zornow, William Frank. *Kansas: A History of the Jayhawk State*. Norman: University of Oklahoma Press, 1957.

Index

Adams, Henry, 37–39
Addams, Jane, 141
Afro-American League, 134, 187
Agricultural and Industrial Institute, 68–69
Alpha Assisi Charity Club, 142, 143, 163, 182
Anthony, Charles, 73
Anti-Taft League, 82
Armstrong, Samuel Chapman, 69 n
Atchison, David R., 8
Atchison, Topeka, and Santa Fe Railroad: proximity to black neighborhood, 19, 33; promotes migration, 36; and discrimination, 30, 59, 116; hiring policy of, 94; largest private employer, 115–16; and full crew bill, 170

Baily, Joshua, 70
Barber, John W., 133
Barnett, Ida Wells, 97, 141
Barracks: location of, 59; demography of, 61; description of, 61–62; as employment bureau, 64–65; educational facilities, 68
Barrett, J., 59
Big Springs Convention, 9–10
Birth of a Nation, 169
Blatchley, Eben, 158–59
Bleeding Kansas, 3
Board of Trustees of State Charitable Institutions, 138, 139
Boyd, James, 191
Boyd, Tolliver, 86, 90
Brashears, J. H., 123
Bray, Etta, 107
Bridgeforth, George, 143, 154. *See also* Kansas Industrial and Educational Institute
Brooks, William, 30, 173
Brown, John M.: KFRA activity of, 57, 60; and Colored State Emigration Board, 76; political preferences of, 130, 131, 133; and Sunflower State Agricultural Association, 157
Brownsville Riot, 194, 195
Brown v. Board of Education of Topeka, 112
Bruce, Blanche K., 39 n, 39–40
Bryan, William Jennings, 192
Bryan Club, 187
Buckner, Robert, 98–99, 101, 161, 179, 184
Business development, 82–83, 90–91
Businessmen, 97, 163, 171

Capper, Arthur, 154, 182
Carbondale, Kansas, 118
Carey, George W., 73
Carnegie, Andrew, 155
Carter, John, 30, 123
Carter, William, 153–54, 156
Case, Michael C., 49, 54

Central Congregational Church, 144–52. *See also* Sheldon, Charles M.
Chiles, Nick, 101, 106–107, 158, 190
Civil Rights Act of 1875, 117
Civil War, 17–19
Cleveland, Grover, 131
Colored Alliance, 126–27
Colored Citizen, 83–84
Colored Civil War Veterans Club, 98
Colored Free Silver League, 132, 187
Colored League, 134
Colored Men's State Convention, 120
Colored Republican Club, 188
Colored State Emigration Board, 76–77, 89
Colored Women's Suffrage Association, 107–108
Commercial Club, 171, 174
Committee of Twelve, 55. *See also* State Central Relief Committee
Compromise of 1877, 34
Comstock, Elizabeth, 57, 58, 66, 67, 68, 72–73, 76
Cooper, William Damascus, 158
Coterie, 97
Crawford, Samuel T., 25–26
Currin, G. I., 125

DeFrantz, Alonzo D., 37, 74, 88–89
Democratic party, 130–32
De Randamie, C. L., 88, 173
Discrimination: in the military, 17, 18, 192–93; in education, 27, 112–15, 123, 167–68, 170; in social services, 48–50, 105, 139; in employment, 115, 171; general, 117, 119–20; politics, 118–23, 189, 194–96; and Spanish-American War, 193
Dorsey, John M., 189
Douglass, Frederick, 40, 69
Douglass School, 182
Dred Scott case, 8, 15
Du Bois, W. E. B., 140, 141, 152, 166, 180
Duke, B. C., 147

Eagleson, William L.: and Colored State Emigration Board, 76; as editor of *Colored Citizen*, 83–84; social life of, 89–90; on Oklahoma, 104; on temperance, 106; on juvenile deliquency, 108; on reform, 110; and politics of, 123, 128–33 *passim*; independent journalism of, 189; on Spanish-American War, 193

Education, 96, 111–15, 204
Emporia State Teachers College, 160
Euclid Lodge, 32
Everett, John, 5
Exodus, 31, 41, 42–44, 46–48. *See also* Kansas Freedmen's Relief Association
Exodusters, 43, 62, 63–67, 79–81, 163, 209–12
Ex-Slaves Pension Association, 98

Fairfax, Alfred, 123
Farmers' Alliance, 126, 130
First African Baptist Church, 31. *See also* Second Baptist Church
First Congregational Church, 19
First Voters Club, 88
Fishback, C. G., 180
Fisk University Jubilee Singers, 151, 152
Florence Crittendon Home for Unwed Mothers, 140
Fortune, T. Thomas, 103, 134. *See also* Afro-American League
Foster, Blanche, 127, 128
Freedmen's Congregational Church, 19, 148
Freedmen's Educational Society, 68
Free-State movement, 2, 4–10, 14–15
Frontier, 35–37, 41–42
Fugitive Slave Law, 3
Full crew bill, 170, 181
Funston, "Hook Jim," 105

Garfield, James A., 51
Garfield Club, 121
Garrison, William Lloyd, 69, 180
Gilbert, James E., 53
Giles, Frye W., 5, 62, 63, 64
Good Samaritan Lodge, 32
Gould, Jay, 36
Grace Cathedral, 102
Grant, William L.: and Shiloh Baptist Church, 101, 144; and populism, 130; on Tennesseetown 144–45; and Village Improvement Society, 149; politics of, 160
Grasshopper Plague of 1874, 50–51
Great Western Lodge, 32, 85
Greeley, Horace, 5, 35
Greenbackers, 121
Gross, George Wellington, 133
Guy, Ira, 175
Guy, James: social and religious activity of, 98, 101, 102; on segregated education,

Index

114; as KIEI supporter, 153, 154, 157; prominence of wife, 161; and NNBL, 174; and NAACP, 183; politics of, 189
Guy, John L., 124

Hagan, George, 183
Halbert, Leroy A., 150. *See also* Tennesseetown census
Harris, Lulu, 162
Harvey, James M., 26–27
Haskell, D. C., 52
Haviland, Laura, 57, 64, 65–66, 69, 71, 73, 76
Hawkins, Spencer, 178
Henderson, Thomas W.: and State Central Relief Committee, 54; on Exodus, 74; and National Convention of Colored Men, 78, 79; and *Colored Citizen*, 83–84; on political office, 122
Hiawatha, Kansas, 117
Hibben, John B., 67–68
Hodges, George, 143, 154, 187
Homestead Act, 41–42
House Resolution 523, 51
Hughes, Charles Evans, 196
Hutchinson, William, 112

Independent Voting League, 133
Indigency statutes, 49–50. *See also* Exodus
Ingalls, John J., 51, 118
Ingersoll, Robert, 70
International Industrial Association, 91
Interstate Literary Association, 98, 161
Ivy Club, 161

Jackson, George W., 98
Jamison, J. M., 94, 161
Jamison, Wesley I., 124–25, 139–40, 179, 190–91
Jane C. Stormont Hospital and Training School for Nurses, 143
Jeltz, Fred, 107
Jennings, John J., 88
Johns, Nellie, 144
Johnson, Columbus M., 37, 74, 76, 88–89
Johnson, W. J., 109, 114
Jones, Paul, 52
Jordan, Benjamin (Andrew), 107, 147

Kansas Alliance, 126. *See also* Farmers' Alliance
Kansas A.M.E. Conference, 156, 159
Kansas Bureau of Labor and Industrial Statistics, 150–51
Kansas Conference, Methodist Episcopal Church, 52
Kansas Freedmen's Relief Association, 42, 45, 55, 56, 70–71, 72–75, 76–78
Kansas Home for the Friendless, 138
Kansas Hospital Aid Association, 142-3, 154
Kansas Industrial and Educational Institute, 142, 143, 152–58, 181
Kansas-Nebraska Act, 3, 4
Kansas Pacific Railroad, 59, 60, 116
Kansas River flood, 137–38
Kansas State Board of Health, 138, 143
Kansas State Ledger, 84. *See also* Jeltz, Fred
Kansas Supreme Court, 117
Kansas Vocational Institute, 155. *See also* Kansas Industrial and Educational Association
KFRA. *See* Kansas Freedmen's Relief Association
KIEI. *See* Kansas Industrial and Educational Association
King, Henry, 48, 50
King Bridge Company, 30, 173
Knights of Labor, 127, 130. *See also* Populism
Ku Klux Klan, 131
Kuykendall, A., 123, 124

Laborers, 64, 92–94, 163, 169–71. *See also* Discrimination; Social stratification
Ladies Free Silver Club, 132
Ladies Relief Committee, 193. *See also* Spanish-American War
Lane, James H., 17, 24
Lane School, 124
Langston, Charles H., 26, 29, 77, 117
Lawrence, Amos, 6. *See also* New England Emigrant Aid Company
Leedy, John W., 131, 188
Lewis, R. L., 124
Literacy rates, 165, 204
Lodge federal elections bill, 127
Lowman-Hill School, 113
Lynch, John R., 39–40, 78
Lynch, William O., 57, 58, 73–74, 115
Lytle, John, 127, 130
Lytle, Lutie, 94–95, 129

McCabe, Edwin P.: and National Refugee Relief Board, 52; goes to Oklahoma, 104; as state auditor, 122, 123, 191
McCrary, George W., 51

McDowell, William, 11–12
McKinley, William, 192, 193, 194
McKinley Club, 187
McKnight, William, 183
McNeal, Pearle, 95
Malone, Sarah, 140. See also Florence Chrittendon Home for Unwed Mothers
Marlow, George, 36, 37. See also State Labor Union
Metsher, David, 124, 125
Migration, 4–6, 17, 19, 34, 36–42, 37 n, 89, 103–104, 136, 205
Missourians, 1, 4, 5
Monroe School, 112
Morrill, Edmund, 132–33
Mount Auburn Cemetery, 91. See also Ritchie, John
Municipal employment, 125, 163, 189–90, 191

NAACP. See National Association for the Advancement of Colored People
National Association for the Advancement of Colored People, 172–73, 180–83
National Conference of Charities and Corrections, 139
National Convention of Colored Men, 78–79
National Federation of Colored Women, 161–62
National Negro Business League, 171–80
National Negro Democratic League, 132
National Refugee Relief Board, 52
National Unionists, 25
Negro Convention movement, 119
Negro population statistics (social and demographic analyses), 6–7, 14–20 *passim*, 33–35, 41–45, 82–83, 136
Negro teachers, 113
New England Emigrant Aid Company, 5–6
New Men, 87–90. See also Social stratification
New Military Band, 98
Nichodemus, Kansas, 41, 63 n
NNBL. See National Negro Business League
North Topeka Baptist Church, 133

Oakleaf Club, 161
Occupation profile, 203
Occidental Lodge, 32
Odd Fellows, 99

Oglesvie, Martin, 177–78
Oklahoma, 103–104
Oklahoma Immigration Association, 104. See also Rolfe, Henry
Olden, George, 101
Old Guard, 85, 87. See also Social stratification
Oliphant, Nat, 116
Oriental Club, 161
Osborn, Thomas A., 27, 50

Page, James, 125
Paul Jones Magazine, 142
People's Party Club, 129. See also Populism
Pinchback, P. B. S., 78
Pleasant Hour Literary Circle, 97
Plessy v. Ferguson, 111, 117
Polk, Leonidas, 126–27
Pomeroy, Samuel, 24
Populism, 127–30
Populist Flambeau Club, 129
Press, black, 83–84
Primitive Baptist Church, 102
Professionals, 97, 101, 171–72. See also Discrimination; Social stratification
Progressive League, 188–89
Progressivism, 186–87, 193–96. See also Roosevelt, Theodore; Wilson, Woodrow
Prostitution, 107

Quakers. See Society of Friends
Quincy School, 84

Race violence, 116
Radical Republicans, 24, 25
Ramsey, E. B., 67, 68
Reconstruction, 24, 25
Reddick, Lizzie, 152
Reform: social welfare and philanthropy, 61–63, 67–71; juvenile deliquency, 80, 108–109; temperance, 105–106; adult crime, 105–106; women's activism in, 141–44, 166
Republican party: free soil, free labor, antebellum politics of, 7–8; and discrimination, 118; black disaffection from 120–21; and black officials, 121–22, 126; after McKinley, 186–88, 189; after Roosevelt and progressivism, 193–95
Reynolds, William, 113
Ritchie, John, 15, 91
Robinson, Charles, 72
Rolfe, Henry, 104

Index

Roosevelt, Theodore, 160, 187–88, 193–95
Ross, Edmund, 25
Roundtree, Fred, 124, 176
Roundtree, Julia D., 180, 182–83
Russell Sage Foundation, 138
Rust, Horatio N., 69–70, 73
Ryan, Thomas, 71

Safety valve thesis, 36
St. John, John P., 51, 53, 55, 73
St. John A.M.E. Church: 1873 protest meeting, 30; founding, 31; new location, 80; charity work, 144; cooperation with KIEI, 157; and social class, 102, 104, 142; mentioned, 83, 86, 87
St. Louis, Missouri, 77–78, 78 n
St. Mark's Christian Church, 147
St. Simon's Episcopal Church, 102, 142
San Jaun Hill, 194, 195. *See also* Spanish-American War
Sawyer, Nathaniel, 183
Schroud, William, 95
Second Baptist Church: and 1872 bond issue, 30; founding, 31; sponsors Colored State Emigration Board, 76; new location, 80; charity work, 144; mentioned 83, 87, 102. *See also* First African Baptist Church
Second Christian Church, 147
Seward, William, 5
Shaffer, George, 153, 168
Sharp, William, 191
Shattio, Ann Davis, 1–2, 21
Shattio, Clement, 1–2, 21; mentioned, 16
Shawnee Cornet Band, 90
Shawnee County Colored Horse Fair Association, 84, 85
Shawnee County Commissioner for the Poor, 49–50, 105
Shawnee Mission Lodge, 19
Sheldon, Charles M., 144–51, 167. *See also* Central Congregational Church; Tennesseetown; Social Gospel
Shelley, George W., 51
Shiloh Baptist Church: founding, 131; and social class, 101, 102; proximity to Tennesseetown, 144; mentioned, 83, 86, 87. *See also* Grant, William L.
Singleton, Benjamin "Pap," 37, 38, 40, 98. *See also* Tennessee Real Estate and Homstead Association; United Colored Links
Skilled laborers, 94, 161, 170–71. *See also*

Discrimination; Social stratification
Snoddy, James D., 105
Social Gospel, 144, 146
Social stratification: definition of, 33, 34, 95–96; methodology, 33 n, 34 n, 96 n; pre-Exodus, 37–40; Exodus, 84–90; of working class, 99; consumption and interraction, 100–104; leaders and elites, 151, 153, 162–65, 206–208
Society of Friends, 69–70
Southern Kansas Colonization Society, 89
Southern Refugee Relief Society, 70. *See also* Kansas Freedmen's Relief Association
Spanish-American War, 193–95. *See also* Roosevelt, Theodore
Stanley, William, 130
Stanton, H. H., 59
State Central Relief Committee, 53–55, 58, 70. *See also* Exodus; St. John, John P.
State Labor Union, 36, 37
State Teachers Association, 27
Status anxiety thesis, 141
Stephens, Edward, 152–53, 174
Stern's restaurant, 116–17. *See also* Discrimination
Stewart, James H., 87–88, 90
Stockton, J. S., 51, 78 n
Stonestreet, Fred, 124
Sulu Treaty, 193. *See also* Spanish-American War; Discrimination
Sunflower State Agricultural Association, 157–58

Taft, William H., 187, 194–95
Tandy, Charles, 78 n. *See also* St. Louis, Missouri
Taylor, Oliver A., 180, 183
Temperance, 105–106. *See also* Reform
Tennessee Real Estate and Homstead Association, 37, 40, 63 n, 74. *See also* Singleton, Benjamin
Tennesseetown: early site of black settlement, 31; Exoduster settlement, 62, 63; locale of crime 80, 107; social, demographic character of, 145, 150–51; physical environment of, 149; Sheldon's program for, 145, 151
Tennesseetown census, 150–51. *See also* Halbert, Leroy
Territorial Census of 1855, 6
Thatcher, Solomon, 13
Thayer, Eli, 5. *See also* New England Emi-

grant Aid Company
Thompson, Lena, 95
Tillman, "Pitchfork Ben," 194
Topeka, Kansas, 5, 6
Topeka Association for the Prevention and Cure of Tuberculosis, 138
Topeka Board of Education, 112, 113, 170. *See also* Discrimination
Topeka City Council, 93–94
Topeka Convention, 9–10. *See also* Free-State movement
Topeka Fairgrounds, 58–59
Topeka High School, 114
Topeka Ministerial Union, 155–56
Topeka Railway Company, 115
Topeka *Tribune*, 84
Townsend, Willliam B., 191
Trotter, William Monroe, 181
Twenty-third Kansas Colored Regiment, 193. *See also* Spanish-American War
Twenty-third Kansas Colored Volunteers, 193
Twyman, Anne, 115
Tyler, Ralph, 177

Union Pacific Railroad, 36
United Colored Links, 89, 98
United States Supreme Court, 8, 118

Vernella, Seth: origins, 68; and Colored State Emigration Board, 76, social activity of, 89–90; affluence of, 95, 98–99, 101; residence of, 97, runs for county coroner, 124; and KIEI, 157. *See also* Social stratification
Vernon, William Tecumseh, 159–60, 194
Villard, Oswald Garrison, 180

Walker, Mack, 95
Ward politics, 189–90
Ware, David, 85–86, 89–90

Washburn, Avery, 15
Washburn College, 160
Washington, Booker T., 152–60 *passim*, 173–77 *passim*, 194
Watkins, Solomon: biography, 86; and St. Simon's, 102; on discrimination, 117, runs for city clerk, 124; and NAACP, 182; politics of, 189
Watson, John M., 57
Wesleyan A.M.E. Church, 31
Western University, 158–60, 181
White, E. H., 84, 112
Wilson, Henry Clay, 21–23, 86–87
Wilson, Laura Shattio, 21–22
Wilson, Woodrow, 181, 195–96
Windom, William, 52
Windom Resolution, 52
Winn, L. W., 122
Winn, W. T., 115
Winter, Jacob, 28
Women, 95, 141–44
Women's Benevolent Society, 108
Women's Equal Suffrage League, 107
Women's rights, 26, 108–109
Wood, Samuel, 26, 71
Wright, John R.: as deputy county clerk, 95; religious activity of, 102; politics of, 128; and KIEI, 154, 157; prominence of wife, 161; and NNBL, 176, 177; biography, 178; as city treasurer and county clerk, 190–91
Wyandotte Constitution, 2, 10–14
Wyandotte, Kansas, 48, 51

YMCA. *See* Young Men's Christian Association
Young Ladies Charitable Union, 108
Young Men's Christian Association, 106, 167, 181
Young Men's Educational Association, 181, 184
Young Men's Independent Club, 90

www.ingramcontent.com/pod-product-compliance
Lightning Source LLC
Chambersburg PA
CBHW022056160426
43198CB00008B/251